GRANADA, CITY OF MY DREAMS

*Wanderings through the city of Granada
and its Moorish palace, the Alhambra*

written and illustrated by
Lawrence Bohme

To the curious traveller

I first came to this part of Spain almost four decades ago, but I never thought that one day I would be unravelling its mysteries for other curious travellers – I prefer this term to "tourists" – like myself.

Not, that is, until some years ago, when a Spanish lady who often hires me as an interpreter proposed a quite different kind of job for which she felt I was ideally suited. A group of economists and their wives had been invited to spend several days here by a Japanese bank, and the lady's company had been asked to call in an expert from the university to give an informal talk on the history and culture of Granada. María del Pilar, an outspoken woman, told the man from the Bank of Tokyo that professors are academically-minded people by nature (I confess that the word she really used in Spanish means "boring"), and quick-wittedly proposed instead the services of an uprooted Englishman who had lived here for many years and had a keen, unpedantic interest in precisely the things they wanted to hear about.

It is true that I had always been fascinated by Spain's, and Granada's dramatic history, although I felt a bit uneasy about holding forth for half an hour to several dozen well-travelled people who, my patroness said, included, among the wives, two museum curators. But Doña Pilar does not easily take no for an answer, and a few hours later I was poring over the learned book on the subject which she sent up to my farm.

The next evening – a silky-smooth September evening – attired in a light summer jacket and white shirt open at the throat, I headed rather nervously to the Alhambra, in the company of my father, also an old Spain-hand, who was staying with me at the time. The gathering of Germans, British, Americans and one Japanese were in dinner dress, standing in the intimately lit patio of the Parador de San Francisco, which before becoming one of Spain's finest hotels was successively a Moorish palace and a Franciscan monastery. Pilar could not have chosen a finer setting for my first solo performance as "explainer" of Spain.

I arranged my clients on rattan chairs in a corner of the patio (which was once the cloister of the monastery) and, champagne glass in hand, began to talk about Granada, the Alhambra, the place we were in with its fabulous history, the Reconquest, the gypsies, flamenco singers, my village in the hills… I talked without glancing at my page for almost one hour. By the time my father and I had reached Montefrio, it had become clear to me that I had what is called an "affinity with the subject".

Granada has a special place in everyone's imagination, whether one has been here or not. The very song which has become the city's unofficial anthem, "Granada", was written by a Mexican, an alcoholic composer of boleros who himself had never even set foot in Andalucia. The operatic opening line even says this, indirectly: *Granada, tierra soñada por mí*, which I have translated to use as my title, for the good reason that Granada has always been the stuff of dreams for me, just as it was for Agustín Lara.

This picture of his haunted face, with the famous scar left on it by a jilted chorus girl, seems, I think, to represent the kind of eccentric who has always been attracted to the city of the Alhambra.

Agustín Lara

In these pages you will not find many of the monuments usually covered by guide books, particularly the ones from the baroque period. I have left them out because I feel certain that the curious traveller wants to spend his or her time discovering the places which, when mixed together in the alchemist's mortar of our minds, produce the bewitching concoction of images and stories which we all think of as uniquely Granada.

What fascinates us is the encounter between Moor and Christian, gypsy and Jew, medieval and Renaissance, mountain and plain, glistening snow and Mediterranean sun, in this lush balcony of Europe overlooking the naked shores of Africa. This was the adventurous chapter of our history, stretching from to the end of the 16th century.

But after the fusion of cultures ended with the irresistible predomination of European civilization, Granada returned to its provincial mediocrity and became a minor element in the Spanish mainstream. The wealth brought back from the discoveries in America was squandered, here as in Toledo and Seville, to build ostentatious churches and palaces decorated with gold and mahogany, but which do not express the lightness and joy of baroque architecture as it was conceived in other lands. This is why these monuments are only mentioned here in their relation to the rest.

The curious traveller seeks that which is distinctive, and this was precisely what my fairy god-mother, Pilar Lopez Moreno, had in mind when she unwittingly launched me on yet another life project, the latest manifestation of which is the volume you hold in your hands. May it help you to dream of – and discover – Granada in turn.

A history of Granada, as small and weet as a pomegranate seed

Before history was written down, there was a village called Ilbyr. A wandering tribe, whose name we shall never know, settled atop the steep hill on the right bank of the river, overlooking the great plain, its huts of stone and branches huddled inside a circle of rough walls. When the Romans came, they established their military outpost and civic buildings on the hilltop, and called it Iliberis.

But even before the arrival of the Romans, a group of Jews, roaming the Western Mediterranean in search of a home, settled on the hill on the left bank of the river. They also protected their town with a fort and gave it a mysterious name which has come down to us as Granada.

When the Arabs swept across the ruins of the imperial colony of Hispania in the early 8th century, they took over the old Roman fort from the barbarians who then ruled most of the peninsula, and its name became arabized as Elvira. The town on the east bank they called *Garnata-al-Yahud*, Granada of the

Jews, and it was this name which predominated when the two cities were merged into one.

For over five centuries, the Arab city was centered around the fortress, or *alcazaba*. But as the displaced Christians continued in their drive to win back Spain from the Moors, the circle began to close around the Islamic rulers of *al-Andalus*, as they called the Iberian Peninsula. When their greatest city, Cordoba, fell, in 1236, its people fled to Granada. Seville soon followed.

This influx of wealth made it necessary to build a much larger and stronger fortress, and the best place was the long ridge on the other side of the river, on the lowest and southernmost part of which stood the fortress of the Jews, which was now rebuilt and enclosed in the walls of the new *alcazaba*.

A century later, a new series of attacks by the Christians pushed the frontier even further south, and more refugees, many of whom were wealthy, fled to Granada, which had the effect of making it the richest city in Moorish Spain. This was when the kings of the Nasrid dynasty began building a magnificent palace to the north of the Alhambra's great towers, with halls and gardens of unequalled elegance and luxury where the sultan and his harem could enjoy the final years of their dominion.

By the end of the 15th century, the monarchs of Spain, Isabel and Fernando, who had by marrying united the often quarrelsome Christian kingdoms, set out to rid the South of the Mohammedans. After long and often bloody sieges and battles, in 1492, Granada and its great palace the Alhambra fell, ending Islamic rule in Spain forever.

Much of what the Moors had built in the city disappeared with them. The short-lived flow of gold from America first made Spain rich – making it possible to replace of many of Granada's Moorish and Renaissance temples and palaces with baroque constructions. The flow of gold dwindled, leaving the country ruined and vulnerable to foreign invasion, which came at the beginning of the 19th century in the form of Napoleon.

When the French troops were forced to withdraw, they bitterly sacked and in some cases destroyed Granada's treasures, even attempting to blow up the Alhambra. And just a few decades after they had been driven out, the Spanish government, influenced by the anti-clerical ideas which the French had sown throughout Europe, confiscated most of the Catholic Church's enormous landholdings. The result was the mutilation and abandonment of churches and monasteries everywhere.

At about the same time, the river which flows through the old city, the Darro, began to be covered to create an avenue, from the foot of the Alhambra, at Plaza Nueva, all the way to its meeting with the River Genil on the plain in the south of the city, doing away with all of the city's arched stone bridges, except the two which still survive.

The universal fascination with Granada was born with the 19th century "romantic" passion for ruined medieval castles, towering pinnacles and mysterious legends –the "flight into the past" of the discontents of the Industrial Revolution. This posture was, and still is so popular that the journals, tales and etchings which the travellers of the period produced did much to create the poetic image we cherish of the city today. In the 1920's Granada became the center of a dynamic artistic movement, the best known leaders of which were the poet Federico García Lorca and composer Manuel de Falla. In their words and music they paid eloquent homage to their Andalucian roots, and added considerably to Granada's fame and magnetic appeal around the world.

San Miguel Alto

When I take my guests for a visit to Granada, I usually end our afternoon of exploring tortuous alleyways by driving them up to the Hermitage of *San Miguel Alto* (not to be confused with San Miguel Bajo, which is in the Albaicín). There, we sit on the balustrade in the cool evening breeze, while the sun disappears behind the Sierra de Parapanda and I point out the various places we have visited during our expedition.

Whether you see it at sundown or the height of noon, it is an extraordinary spectacle. In this same place on the hill called *El Cerro del Aceituno* or "Mount Olive", once stood a mosque - at the highest point of the great wall which stretches to either side, built by the Arabs in the 14th century to protect the new palace of the Alhambra,. The Christians replaced this mosque with a shrine, installing in it a lifelike baroque statue of Saint Michael which is the subject of one of Lorca's most charming poems.

Unfortunately for us, the church is almost always closed, except for Saint Michael's feast day which is celebrated on the last Sunday of September, when the locals come up to enjoy drinks and *tapas* in a jolly little fair which is set up behind the church, before taking out the statue for a procession through the Albaicín. Saint Michael has since the Reconquest been revered as a *santo guerrero*, a "warrior saint" who helped to rid the land of heresy, which is why the statue of the devil which we can see dying under his right foot is crudely meant to look like one of the Moorish invaders. Know thine enemy!

From here, we have it all before us: on the far left, the snowy peaks of the Sierra Nevada, on the far right the long hump of the Sierra de Parapanda with the round knoll on top, beyond which lies my dear Montefrio, the town where I spent so many years... To the south, the great plain of Granada and the hill on which the defeated Moorish King Boabdil stopped to cast a last sad glance at the paradise he had lost, and which has ever since been called *El Suspiro del Moro* - the Sigh of the Moor. We see how the River Darro cleaves a deep gorge between the two hills, the Alhambra, on the left, and the Albaicín, on the right, with the cathedral quarter and the modern city spread at their feet. Immediately below the belvedere we can see some of Granada's cave dwellings with their cactus trees and whitewashed fronts, several of which are still inhabited.

A fascinating detail: the massive church which we see immediately below us in the Albaicín is the *Colegiata del Salvador*, and from here we can look down into its "cloister", which is nothing less than the *Patio de los Limoneros*, the courtyard of ablutions, which before the conquest by the Christians was part of the Great Mosque of the Albaicín.

Mirador de San Cristóbal

If you drive there, this magnificent viewpoint is on the way up to San Miguel - you'll see a column with an iron cross on top and San Cristobal written vertically on the side facing the road, and a balcony for enjoying the panorama. If you are on foot, you can get there easily from the Puerta de Elvira: walk up the Cuesta de la Alhacaba and turn left at the picturesque steps called the *Cuesta de San Cristobal*. The squat ochre-coloured church towers above you as you climb, like the Sacré Coeur in Montmartre when seen from below.

The interesting perspective from the *mirador* is composed of three overlapping layers, like the cardboard cut-outs in children's books which unfold to create a multi-tiered landscape. Immediately in front of us, we see the Albaicín, with the fortified wall and towers of the original castle, or *Alcazaba Kadima* - "old fortress"- enclosing the Albaicín quarter with its church towers and walled gardens. Just beyond and slightly above it in our line of vision is the Alhambra (what we don't see is the deep river valley separating them, and this confuses the eye, creating the illusion that the two hills are a single mass), built much later than the old fortress, which it eventually replaced. The snowy peaks of the Sierra Nevada form the third layer of this unique vista.

Let us explore the spectacle in detail. On the hill immediately in front of us, called *El Albaicín*, we have, on the far right, the steeple of the Church of San Miguel and, to the left, the steeple of the Convent of Santa Isabel la Real, jutting up behind the walls of the convent grounds. In the foreground, behind the city wall, is the Palace of Dar-al-Horra, the home of the rejected wife of Sultan Muley Hasan. To the far left of the hill stands the broad steeple of the *Colegiata del Salvador*, the mission built on the site of the Great Mosque of the Albaicín for the purpose of converting the recently conquered people of Granada to Christianity.

On the highest point of the hill it is impossible not to see the rather gaudy pseudo-Moorish villa - or *carmen* - set among lush gardens and white walls, perhaps the finest spot for a house in the whole city. It is connected to a curious story, which took place in the 18th century, when the new science of archaeology had created a rush to find anything built by the ancient Greeks and Romans so revered by the artists and architects of the day. Extensive Roman remains were discovered on this site, including a fortress, theater and forum, as result of which the Moorish streets were torn away and a wide hole was dug in the ground. This hole was known as the "mine", giving rise to the current name of the street which runs along the fortified wall, *Calle de la Mina.*

The Church eventually stepped in and called the whole thing to a stop because, for the priests, anything that existed before Christ smelled of paganism. After the digging ceased, a huge vacant lot remained which was bought up by a nobleman, and eventually became the site of the villa which we see before us. It's easy to imagine a Roman temple standing in its place, isn't it?

THE CATHEDRAL QUARTER

Plaza Bibarrambla

It was in the Plaza Bibarrambla that I first saw you, goes the flamenco verse in the *granaínas* mode – the chant of Granada - which my old friend Manolo Avila used to sing to me, stretching out the long arabesques of reedy sound as if to ring from them every last drop of tragedy and nostalgia...

No place is more emblematic of the "Christian" part of the city. Surrounded by 19th century town houses, shaded by leafy lime trees - and in the midst of a large pedestrian zone - the Plaza Bibarrambla is the real heart of the city's social life. Much of the square is in the warm months filled with sidewalk cafés, where you can enjoy hot chocolate and *churros*, and, on summer afternoons, freshly made *horchata de chufas*, a refreshing milkshake made of a root called an "earth almond".

The market district further west sprawls over the lively Plaza de la Pescadería (the fishmonger's square) and the narrow streets which lead off to the right, near the Cathedral.

Chumbos, snails and chirimoyas

There may be a lady there selling *chumbos*, or cactus pears, which she peels with gloved hands and holds out for you to eat between your fingers. They're nice, but gritty - but if you haven't tried at least one, you'll never be a *granaíno!*

To get to the Mercado de San Agustín, where mainly fish and meat are sold, walk up the esplanade with the palm trees. It is interesting to see the great variety of fresh fish of which Spaniards are so fond - the small signs chalked with the word *Motril* stuck into heaps of fresh anchovies and sardines mean that they have just been hauled out of the Mediterranean on the south coast (where Motril is) and not trucked in from the big fish-producing regions of northwestern Spain.

In the streets around the market you will see squaw-like, aproned gypsy women - just like the ones in the 19th century etchings - seated on wicker chairs behind baskets crawling with live rock snails, the *caracoles* which the taverns of the Albaicín serve as tapas in a pungent sauce. The coastal valleys of the region are a veritable horn of plenty, and here you will see delicious tropical fruits such as the *chirimoya* (custard apple) which you cut in half and eat with a spoon like a cup of ice cream (don't forget to spit out the shiny black seeds). Like all Mediterranean people, the Andalucians are mad about mushrooms, and here you will see both the standard white "Paris" variety, and the delicious *setas* or oyster mushrooms, which grow in the roots of trees. They are usually used to stuff omelettes, but I prefer to grill them over an open fire, after spending a few hours in a marinade of olive oil and garlic. When they get crisp they make an excellent substitute for bacon, if your faith doesn't allow you to eat pork...

Returning to the Plaza Bibarrambla, we see the cathedral's single bell tower jutting up over the façades of the north side of the square, on the north side of which is the tiny arched entrance to the old Moorish market, the Alcaicería.

The center of this handsome plaza is decorated with a baroque fountain, consisting of a circle of grotesque figures spurting water - known as the *gigantones* - bearing on their hunched shoulders a rather undersized white statue of Neptune.

History of a plaza

Like so many oblong spaces in medieval cities, Bibarrambla was originally a field just outside the city walls used for tournaments, so let us for a moment fancifully imagine the Moorish nobles jousting here on their Arabian steeds... The many English, German and French travellers who visited the city after the Christian conquest have described the bullfights which were held in the square, with the noble families sitting in the balconies behind richly embroidered mantles and banners.

But the bullfights of yesteryear were not the two-hour affairs for connoisseurs that we have today - rather, they were day-long marathons which were attended by the entire city. In one *corrida* which went down in history, held in August of 1609, 20 bulls were fought which before dying succeeded in killing 36 men and wounding 60 others, except for the last bull which no one had the courage to "grab" (bullfighting then was basically a question of laying one's bare hands on the animal's horns and throwing it to the ground) so that it had to be shot dead with a blunderbuss.

As the largest square in the city, Bibarrambla was also the scenario for the *autos-da-fe* which were held frequently after the conquest, in which the Holy Inquisition condemned "heretics", who were often rich Jews - that is, the ones who had property which the Princes of the Church wished to confiscate.

The *autos* were organized like great festivals aimed at impressing, and frightening, the people. Early in the morning two processions converged on the plaza, one coming from the prison with the accused, often a large crowd of them, and the other led by the authorities who had gathered in a nearby church. First, the judges solemnly swore to stamp out heresy wherever they found it, and then a Mass was sung, with a sermon designed to create the proper moral state in the minds of the onlookers. Next, the accusations were read in exhaustive detail, with a pause at noon for a banquet which the inquisitors enjoyed right there in the plaza, under the eyes of their victims. After lunch the sentences were read, the condemned being handed over to the jailers to mete out punishment which could be prison or death, and the others being absolved with a Te Deum. When all was done, the authorities returned to the church they had left in the morning in a torch-lit procession.

Corral del Carbón

The Arabic word *bib* means gate and *rambla* river bank. Until the end of the 19th century there stood, at the plaza's east end, a large Moorish gate which gave the place its name - literally, Gate of the Strand, because it stood on the sandy bank of the river which now flows unseen beneath the Calle de los Reyes Católicos. A bridge connected it to the merchants' inn or caravanserai on the other side, today known as the *Corral del Carbón* because, after the Moorish period, charcoal vendors brought their wares down from the forests to be sold in its patio. This is one of Granada's oldest and best preserved monuments, with the double-arched gate, inner flagstoned courtyard and central well typical of Moorish *fondaks*. I once stayed in a similar one in Fez, although it didn't have the magnificent façade.

The building's curious name "corral" was the generic term in the 17th century for theater which as a rule resembled large livestock pens. Few purpose-built auditoriums existed then, so the courtyards of palaces, convents and inns, with their surrounding balconies, were used instead. This sort of open-air theater was called a *corral de comedias*, hence the name for Granada's Corral del Carbón, which could be translated as the "Charcoal Market Theater".

Later, the former inn became a ramshackle tenement house, until it was restored for the performance of flamenco shows and musical concerts in the summer months... An interesting vestige from the time when it was still necessary to cross the river in order to get to the bazaar is the name of the street which leads from it to the Calle Reyes Católicos: *Calle del Puente del Carbón*, "Coal Bridge Street".

After the Christian conquest, the patio was used as a theater, and it is easy to imagine it, in the *Edad de Oro*, all decked out for a comedy of Lope de Vega (who was the Spanish counterpart of our Shakespeare), with its sunny and shady sections just like today's bull rings, and subdivided into separate areas for men and women, to prevent licentiousness...

Alcaicería, Madraza and mosque

Now we shall step into the small arched door in the northern side of the square, which leads into the alleyways of what was, in Moorish times, the great bazaar called the *Alcaicería*, now occupied by souvenir shops selling Granada craftwork, such as *taracea* – wooden inlay - and *fajalauza* pottery.

Caesar's market

There is a fascinating story behind the name of the bazaar. Long before the Moorish invasion of Spain, the Byzantine Emperor Justinian granted to the Arabs exclusive rights over the manufacture and sale of silk. They showed their gratitude by calling all silk markets, and with time all markets in general, "the place of Caesar" - *al-Caicería*. Granada's stretched all the way to the foot of the Alhambra and was famous throughout the known world, continuing to function for centuries after the Christian conquest.

But the current souvenir market is a fake - in 1834 the whole thing burned down, after a workshop which produced Granada's first cardboard matches caught fire in the night. The current, much smaller pastiche was built next to the plaza, with lacy plaster archways in the Moorish style, which are already much the worse for wear.

A telling trace of the old bazaar is the Arabic name of the smart shopping street - *Calle Zacatín* - which runs along the eastern side of the Alcaicería and was at first nothing more than a row of huts on the edge of the river, known for its filth and mud, as well as the old clothes and rags sold there: "The Street of Old Clothes Merchants"...

Leaving the Alcaicería we step out on the Cathedral square, at the southeast corner of the Sagrario church. Turn right and walk up the Calle de Oficios along the side of the Cathedral, past the ornate Royal Chapel until you come to the baroque palace, which is popularly known as *La Madraza* but officially called by its Christian name, *La Casa de Cabildos*. This was the Muslim university, receiving learned men from all parts of North Africa and the Middle East, until the Christians made it their town council or *ayuntamiento*, which moved to the current site on Plaza del Carmen at the end of the 19th century. The palace was entirely rebuilt in the baroque period, leaving only one small but precious vestige of the Islamic university: the mosque which stands on the far side of the entrance hall. This *mirhab*, or oratory, was built in the same period as the ornate Nasrid palaces, and is decorated with the same stalactite-like plaster encrustations called *mocárabes*.

Let us now consider the three separate churches which are generally lumped together as "the Cathedral", and try to visualize how each of them came to be where it is.

Metamorphosis and death of a mosque

The ensemble of Granada's Cathedral and Royal Chapel is unique because, among other things, the chapel is older than the church of which it would normally be an appendage. And this is because of the Moorish mosque which continued to stand on the site for two centuries after the Christian conquest, providing a graphic example of how the two cultures momentarily overlapped before the stronger obliterated the weaker.

When you emerge from the Alcaicería, you find yourself at the foot of what seems to be the southeast corner of the massive Cathedral. In fact, this is not really the Cathedral but *El Sagrario*, a parish church built next to the Cathedral in the 18th century. If you stand before the front of the church, you will see that it is an independent building of its own, even though it forms a solid block with the Cathedral to its left and the Royal Chapel behind it.

The Great Mosque of Granada stood here. Its minaret rose on the site of the Cathedral and its courtyard of ablutions occupied the plaza in front of the entrance to the Royal Chapel, where, next to the gate, we can still see the well which supplied the faithful with water for the ritual washing.

The well is the only thing that survives of the Muslim temple, even though the drum was rebuilt in the style of the chapel, with its own grating. Churches don't have wells, but no Spaniard in his right mind would plug one up just because it was once part of a mosque.

Soon after the conquest, Isabel and Fernando blessed the mosque as Granada's Cathedral. Some 15 years later, work began on the Royal Chapel, just behind the cathedral-mosque. Since there was still no thought of building a new cathedral adjacent to it, the main gate to the Chapel was placed in the western wall of the nave, opposite the current entrance. But when the Cathedral was built against this wall, the door was rendered useless, and a new door, imitating the original one, had to be cut into the eastern wall, which is the one used now.

Some 20 years later, it was decided to build a new cathedral running fully alongside the two existing churches. In order to clear the site the minaret was demolished, and when the new Cathedral was completed, the shell of the Muslim building was used as a cloister. Much later, at the beginning of the 18th century, the by now ruinous Muslim construction was demolished to make way for the current church, *El Sagrario*, thus eliminating the last trace of the Great Mosque.

I have reproduced a detail of the famous pictorial map of Granada drawn by Ambrosio de Vico, in which we see a simplified image of what the three churches looked like in the early 17th century: the Cathedral half-built; the Royal Chapel long since completed and with its façade still showing; and the old mosque which had by then been consecrated as the Sagrario church, although the huge building we know today, and which covered up the front of the Royal Chapel, wasn't made until much later. Ambrosio might have kindly said it was a former mosque, but respect for other people's religions was not in vogue then!

"A" is the Cathedral, with the dome and belltower (lower left) complete but the nave still unbuilt, except for the square foundations awaiting the great columns. "B" is the Royal Chapel, whose façade was later covered by the parish church called El Sagrario. "C" is shown in the map index as "Sagrario", then still housed in the old mosque, which is represented here by three rows of tiled roofs, similar to those of Cordoba's Mezquita (although in reality there must have been many more than three).

The Royal Chapel

As we approach the *Capilla Real*, we are filled with a feeling of excitement: this is a very special place, with something exotic and fairy-tale like about it. The bristling forest of crenulated spires on the low-lying roof, the pagoda-like turrets rising luxuriantly everywhere, have an almost Oriental magic. There is a sense of medieval pageantry, as if the figures petrified on either side of the gate are about to raise long horns and sound a *Salve Regina* for their conquering Queen, *Isabel la Católica*. But here I feel bound to confess that I am madly in love with the Spanish music of that adventurous period, and this might affect my way of seeing things!

This three-sided plaza always reminds me of the stage of a fantastic theatre, and this is partly due to another building which seems to belong to the chapel but was in fact designed quite separately and for clearly gainful purposes, the *Lonja de Mercaderes*, or "Merchants' Guildhall". It was built shortly after the chapel by a Genoese banker by the name of Stefano Centurione, and designed, in the florid Italian style, to house his offices, more like stalls, and those of other tradesmen and brokers of the city. The Genoese merchants had been an institution in Granada since Moorish times, when they formed a privileged community, enjoying the right to lead their independent Italian way of life, even during the darkest moments of their hosts' struggle with the Spanish Christians. The Sultans of the Alhambra, like all good rulers, were able to put their ideals to one side when economic interests were at stake, and when the Castilians arrived, the countrymen of Machiavelli hastened, *molto vivace*, to provide their financial services to the big-spending *hidalgos*, even helping them to import the marble and craftsmen they needed to build their grandiose palaces in the new *estilo romano* of the Renaissance.

However, after admiring the wreathed columns of the Lonja, which before the plate glass windows were put between them formed an open loggia in the Florentine style, we will turn our attention once more to the Royal Chapel, that touchstone in the history of Spain and supreme symbol of the conquest of Granada by the Catholic Monarchs, *los Reyes Católicos*. This was the title given to Queen Isabel and Fernando by the Pope (who not accidentally was Spanish himself) for their struggle against heresy, and by which they are commonly known to Spaniards today.

Even though the Royal Chapel is essentially a mausoleum, it is by far the brightest, most elegant and inviting of the three churches. Whenever I enter its light-filled nave of pale stone, delicately divided in two by the elaborately worked grill - which more than a piece of ironwork resembles a brocaded see-through curtain - it gives me a feeling both of exhilaration, because of the visual adventure which it is, and of satisfaction just at being inside it, which, as a self-taught architect, is what I think a house should do.

As we step down from the entrance door into the nave, if we look to our left before proceeding, we can glimpse, all alone in the shadows and quite forgotten, the beautifully carved gate in almost-white stone which was the chapel's "real" entrance gate, but had to be sealed when the huge Sagrario church was built in front of it...

We find ourselves in a not very large but very imposing Gothic church, the most distinctive features of which are the iron grill or chapel screen I have mentioned, an extraordinary work by a master blacksmith from Jaen (in the northern part of Andalucia, which had been Christian for centuries by the time Granada was taken) vivaciously, almost naively depicting scenes from the Gospels; and the recumbent figures of Isabel and Fernando superbly carved in Carrara marble and brought from Genoa, with those of their daughter Juana "the Mad "and her husband Felipe "the Handsome" beside them on the left. These two unfortunate people were so called because the German prince was handsome and unfaithful, and the Spanish queen so jealous that she became mentally unbalanced. She went completely mad when her gallant husband died suddenly, poisoned by the Castilians they say, who feared the Aragonese foreigner might, as Juana's husband, become their King.

It is the optical effect created by these natural-seeming figures through the ironwork filigree, as they gaze up at the gilded altarpiece before them, which makes everything seem to be suspended in light. This supremely vertical scene always reminds me that Isabel and her husband were real monarchs, in the sense that they believed God had given them a mission and made them different from other humans so they could perform it.

Just below these sculptures there is a narrow staircase leading down into the crypt, where you can see their battered and blackened caskets. The child's coffin, marked with the letters PM, belongs to Prince Miguel, the grandson of Isabel and Fernando, the one who, if he had lived, would have become king, and not the foreigner Carlos.

The enormous altar piece of carved and painted wood is one of the earliest examples of the Spanish Renaissance style known as *plateresco*. Its main interest for us are the scenes of the surrender of Granada to the Christians.

To the left and right of the altar, on the floor level, we see, in the panels reproduced below, the Monarchs implacably advancing on horseback toward the Alhambra, the Moors' forced conversion with priests sprinkling the heads of terrified men and women, and the vanquished Moors emerging from the Alhambra with their hands crossed in front of them in resignation, as their humbled King leads the way, the keys to the city and its palace in his hand.

A style imported from Castile

In the Middle Ages, the kings and queens of Spain had been buried in monasteries scattered throughout the north, but in Moorish Granada there were no Christian temples, except the temporary installations made in the city's mosques, which were obviously unsuitable, and Isabel and Fernando wanted to be buried in Granada. So for the first time a "dedicated" church had to be built just for the royal mausoleum - which, inversely, was to be one of the last churches built in the medieval style in Spain.

This required expensive labour imported from Castile. In the decades after the conquest, the work force was largely made up of Moorish tradesmen, and these were only skilled in covering buildings in house-like timber-and-tile roofs. But the Royal Chapel, in the extraordinary circumstances of the moment, had to be a blue-blooded ambassador of the "style of Toledo" to the newly conquered Kingdom of Granada, with masonry, sculpture and above all a vaulted roof of stone using the pointed arch and ribbing characteristic of the Gothic style.

Like the sailing ships, firearms and horses of the *conquistadores*, it had to impress - and even intimidate - the vanquished. The building's symbolic importance was so great that, in 1526, Carlos V chose to celebrate in it the famous *Junta* or assembly which tried to regulate the agonized relationship of the *moriscos*, the descendants of the old Arab inhabitants of Granada, and the dominant Castilian society. All this meant that the architects, craftsmen and masons had to be brought from other parts of Spain.

We step through the exquisite Gothic door at the back on the right, and into the Sacristy, in which the church treasure was installed half a century ago. Among the exhibits is Isabel's own mirror and the chest for the jewels which, legend has it, she sold to finance Columbus' journey of exploration, as well as the trappings used by the Monarchs when they ceremoniously took Granada in 1492: swords, banners, tunics, moth-eaten but majestic, and which were left to the Chapel so that they could be displayed in the yearly procession commemorating *la toma* or "the taking" of the city.

But the greatest artistic treasure is undoubtedly Isabel's own collection of Flemish paintings. The Queen was a great admirer of the Gothic masters of her time who painted in the peculiar style of Flanders, with their deep, subtle colours, elegant compositions and intensely mystical figures. Unfortunately, many of the works found their way into other hands over the centuries. Many are in France, of course, thanks to Napoleon, and there is even one - the third panel in the triptych by Van der Weyden - in the Metropolitan Museum in New York. I have always loved Memling above all the other artists of the Flemish School, and his Deposition from the Cross which we see here is a thing of perfection, with a psychological refinement in the portrayal of the faces, especially that of the world-weary middle-aged man on the right, which, in spirit if not in style, is uncannily contemporary.

It was indeed extraordinary that this couple, Isabel and Fernando, should have made of a handful of feudal, warring kingdoms the first Nation-State in history, founding the Spanish Empire in the process. But their immediate successors did not have the same historical hindsight, and ended up disobeying their solemn wish that Granada should become the definitive resting place for all of Spain's royal family. That is why, today, the mausoleum only contains their own graves and those of their daughter, son-in-law and grandson. And it is, in itself, fascinating to discover how this came about.

Rise and fall of the Royal Chapel

Isabel, a devout Franciscan, desired an austere mausoleum in the medieval style, appropriate for a woman who had confessed her sins and turned her back on the world. But she died before work on the chapel could even begin. King Fernando supervised the first years of the construction, taking a few liberties with her precise instructions because he himself, like most men of his time, was fascinated by all the exciting new things going on in Italy – the movement we call the Renaissance. And after Fernando died, the throne went to his grandson Charles, who wasn't even a Spaniard - he was born and raised in sophisticated Ghent and brought with him all those humanistic ideas which Isabel can only have dreaded.

For the men of the Renaissance, a mausoleum was meant to exalt the occupant's worldly achievements, his physical and mental attributes - and when the new King arrived on the scene, in 1517, he was dismayed to find that such a plain, old-fashioned and downright "small sepulchre" - *estrecho sepulcro* - was being built for his grandparents. Charles - *Carlos Quinto*, as he is universally known - made several major changes and additions, such as the iron screen and the altarpiece, which gave the whole thing a more contemporary dash.

Charles' next step was to build a cathedral alongside, to supplant the makeshift one in the old mosque which stood at the foot of the Royal Chapel. And this time he gave full rein to his

Italianate leanings. He ordered a massive temple in the classical or Hellenic style (what the apologists of the time curiously called the "Roman style" to draw attention away from its pagan origins). He even decided to jettison the Royal Chapel altogether and move its occupants to a new - and much grander - Pantheon of Kings in the middle of the new Cathedral, a project which, like many others he had, was never carried out, fortunately since this would have entirely stripped the Capilla Real of its *raison d'être*.

As it was, Charles had himself buried in the remote monastery of Yustes, near Portugal, where after abdicating the throne he spent the last years of his life, disillusioned by his failure to impose Catholicism on the peoples of the Netherlands, then under Spanish rule. And not only did he expressly desire to break with his grandmother's wish, but, in his final moments, he even staged a famous rehearsal of his own funeral, which he watched from the coffin to be sure that the monks had every detail right! It is indeed curious to imagine him lying there observing it all with his eyes half-open...

However his son, Philip II, was wont to doing things on an even grander style: he saw Spain, quite simply, as the God-ordained center of the world, and to provide this center with an appropriate inner sanctum he built El Escorial, the vast monastery-palace where he was to spend the rest of his life, overlooking a barren plain north of Madrid. Deep in its cellars his workers carved the circular Pantheon of Kings, lining it with green marble and gold. As soon as it was done he had the bodies in the Royal Chapel, with the exception of the original five, brought from Granada. Again, it is wonderful to imagine the convoy of mules, soldiers and priests wending its way through mountain passes and across arid plains with the cargo of... old bones! Philip also took away the chapel's precious books to add to the monastery's already incomparable library. The effect was to strip the old sepulcher of much of its prestige and financial support, and by the time Napoleon's troops broke open the coffins two centuries later, it had become a half-forgotten relic.

A touching episode in Philip's youth suggests that he had a very special reason for wanting his family's remains closer to home. When his mother, Isabel of Portugal died, her corpse had to be carried on a bier all the way from Toledo to Granada for burial, in the stifling heat. The bereaved Charles was so shattered that he withdrew into a monastery, and ordered his 12-year old son to take his place at the burial. The funeral procession took several weeks, although the smell of the poorly embalmed body had the effect of hastening the grievers on their way. According to tradition, the coffin had to be opened before burial, to ascertain that the Queen was really the one inside, and the experience of viewing his mother's decomposed remains was to mark Philip forever, especially since she was once renowned for her beauty... It seems to me likely that he swore then to put an end to his great-grandmother's dream and bring as many of his relatives back to Castile as he decently could.

The young Philip was accompanied on his journey by the personal escort of the Queen, the Duke of Gandía, and it was his official duty to confirm that the corpse about to be buried was "the right one". When the moment came, at the place near Granada thereafter known as "The White Cross", since in Spanish everything pertaining to ladies was chivalrously called white, the Duke was so horrified by what he saw that he immediately decided to devote the rest of his life to God and charity.

He touchingly expressed himself thus, before the mourners who held perfumed handkerchiefs to their noses, such as the man holding the coffin open in the painting below (The Conversion of the Duke of Gandía by José Moreno Carbonero, 1884, in which we see him sobbing on the shoulder of one of his knights), "I cannot swear that this is Her Majesty, but I swear that I put her body here", and after settling his worldly affairs turned his back on the world, with the solemn declaration, "No longer shall I serve Lords whom Death can take from me". It is believed that he was secretly, if platonically enamoured of the young woman, which only adds to the story's pathos. The Duke of Gandía became a Jesuit missionary, and a century later was canonized as Saint Francis Borgia. He went as a missionary to the New World, where one of Brazil's greatest rivers is named for him, the Río São Francisco.

The Cathedral and El Sagrario

I myself am very fond of the Cathedral of Granada, but for a reason which may seem out of place here, namely that its great backdrop of a façade and the marble-paved plaza or stage in front of it, enclosed by three walls of gaily coloured houses, reminds me of another "city of my dreams", Rome. I often sip a glass of something at a table in front of the Cathedral and imagine I am a student again sitting at a sidewalk café in some similarly theatrical piazza near the Fontana di Trevi... The Moors nostalgically compared their Granada to the ancient city of Damascus, but 500 years after their departure it can be better described as an amalgam of Damascus and Rome, crowded together into a much smaller city than either of them.

This said, for the traveller who is mainly curious about Granada's Moorish past and who is only staying for a few days, it is not essential to visit either the Cathedral or its semi-detached neighbour the Sagrario Church, whatever the locals may proudly tell you. Unlike the also adjacent Royal Chapel, both of them steadfastly turn their backs on our history's "adventurous period", namely the saga of the Moorish Kingdom and how the Christian one slowly pulled it down and swallowed it up. For this reason, I will only highlight those features which distinguish these two rather dour buildings from other ecclesiastical productions of the Classical and Neo-Classical periods that you can find almost anywhere in Europe.

To begin with the Cathedral's one great saving grace, from the standpoint of originality, the beauty of its façade - created by the 17th century *granadino* architect Alonso Cano - is owed less to the design of the façade itself than the three great arches within which it is recessed. The three-dimensional effect it creates always reminds me of some ancient Roman ruin in an engraving by Piranesi.

As you can see in my photo, the words AVE MARIA are engraved above the main gate, to signify that the Cathedral was dedicated, like most churches built after the expulsion of the Moors, to "La Encarnación", the incarnation of God in Man by means of the miraculous birth of Jesus to Mary. This point of the virgin birth was constantly used by Christians as proof of their religion's superiority, in the psychological battle with the followers of the Prophet Mohammed, who was a mortal human being...

Never had politics and faith been so shamelessly intertwined. The Castilians first installed a makeshift Cathedral in the mosque of the Alhambra, but Queen Isabel wanted it to be moved down to the lower city to take the place of Granada's Great Mosque, as a symbol of Christianity's victory.

Once again, this early Cathedral used the old mosque as a church, and also its minaret to serve as bell tower - for almost a century, just as the Cathedral of Seville still uses its much taller Moorish tower for the same purpose. Granada's minaret, equipped with bells, was on the right hand side of the façade when seen from the plaza, so the architects of the new Cathedral began by building the one on the left.

But a few years before this monolith was finished the old one showed signs of collapsing and had to be demolished. What with the general lack of funds at the time, the old minaret was never rebuilt, and the new tower was left as a very tall stump. Its octagonal and elegantly tapered baroque spire had to be removed when, not long after completion, it was observed that one of its corners was crumbling. So what we have today is the bottom two-thirds of the planned bell tower, square and massive, but still, with its remaining 57 meters, very impressive.

Here, the enormous base of the tower, on the alleyway appropriately named Calle Pie de la Torre - Street of the Foot of the Tower.

The second lateral gate of the one-sided Cathedral (the other being covered by the Sagrario Church) is the justly famous Puerta del Perdón - "Door of Pardon" - considered by some to be the masterpiece of the great *granadino* architect Diego de Siloé, whose artistry graces so many of the city's and region's churches. The gate is so called not, as some misinformed people say, because an outlaw sought refuge there and was pardoned for his crime, but simply due to the fact that many Spanish shrines receiving pilgrims had a special gate for them to request, after giving their alms, indulgences for their sins, or those of the people who, unable to make the journey, had entrusted them with the task.

Like all the work of this architect, who was half-Flemish (hence his unusual surname, Siloé), the gate is unpretentious but refreshingly refined, with its graceful design and spiritual lightness. Whenever I pass by on the narrow street which it overlooks - Calle de la Cárcel Baja, for the "lower prison" which once stood there - I pause to admire its exuberant and yet perfectly orchestrated detail. The optimism of Siloé's first half of the 16th century - which soured when the flow of American gold dwindled later on - is expressed by the two "banners" carved on the columns, shown in my photograph below, each with one word of the motto of the Empire, PLUS ULTRA. It was still believed that the lands of Spain and with it the Holy Faith would spread "ever further" until the sun would always be shining on some part of them...

The upper part of the monumental gate is the work of Ambrosio de Vico, most famous today for his pictorial map of the city, of which I have made extensive use in this book. Although the figures below are said by experts to be amateurish,

I love their lively depiction of God the Father joyously gesticulating down to us mortals, with David and Isaiah, both of them very human-looking, on His either side. The spirit of the ensemble is almost naïve, more late-Medieval than the prissily perfectionist Renaissance, which for my taste is just fine!

Just beneath the charming trio shown above is a disconcertingly bare rectangle of stone blocks, naked of any decoration whatsoever. A large relief representing, once more, the Incarnation was to be sculpted here, but for some reason the plan was shelved and never revived. This, as we will see below, was the fate of much of Granada's oversized, not to say ostentatious cathedral...

Inside the huge nave, the visitor is struck, not very pleasantly, by the fact that the soaring columns and Ionic capitals are greyish white. The builders were planning to coat it all with gold and silver, but only got as far as the white undercoat when they ran out of money. Since Spain's empire began to wane at the same time, that's the way it has remained ever since.

Even so, the Cathedral was greatly admired in its day, and depending on how you measure it, said to be second in size only to Saint Peter's of Rome. It took 180 years to build, which is three times as long as Notre Dame in Paris!

Curiously, and sadly, the construction of the Cathedral plunged into shadows the Royal Chapel's splendidly carved original gate - of which the current ceremonial entrance on the Calle de Oficios is only a simplified imitation. Since this gate is no longer in use, it has been unjustly forgotten in a dark corner of the huge nave.

If you want to see the chapel gate, and I can't imagine why any curious traveller wouldn't, you must seek it out, to your right when entering the Cathedral. I trust that very soon it will be given a cleaning with some tasteful lighting to make its merry pages and sensuous Renaissance mouldings seem less neglected and grubby.

Again, our incomparable sculptor Diego de Siloé carved the coats-of-arms of the Reyes Católicos as well as other parts of this artwork of petrified brocade. The fuzzy quality of my picture below is due to the grime which coats the gate - none of the other very few photos of it I could find were any better. Being especially fond of the lifelike heralds on either side I have added enlargements so that you can enjoy them as much as I do, until you can see the gate for yourself...

Here, the "new" gate to the Royal Chapel, which as you can see, is no comparison to the older, original one now forgotten between the two temples. It is opened for worshippers only, and then free of charge, whenever Mass is being held...

In the Royal Chapel itself we can see the "inner" side of this gate, boarded up for the official reason that the two churches function independently of one another. Apparently the rather un-Catholic reason for this "divorce" was a squabble over the right of processions leaving the Royal Chapel to ritually pass through the Gate of Pardon, which meant crossing the nave of the Cathedral, leading the priests in charge of the Cathedral to simply lock their side up, and so it has remained. But here too, as with the door between the Royal Chapel and the Sagrario, you can peek through the cracks between the boards and see into the Cathedral. Nowhere else, I believe, are three such great churches contiguous with one another and yet always divided.

Adjacent to the façade of the Cathedral, as I have said, is the much less striking one of the parish church which is known to all as El Sagrario, "The Tabernacle". At first glance, it's indistinguishable from its big brother because of the similar style. Once inside, however, the square-shaped church's unusual circular arrangement of arched columns, under a dome opened all around with windows from which daylight streams down, creates a fine effect of what can best be called celestial perspective.

In the far left-hand corner of the nave, half-hidden by the altar is buried a legendary hero whose story is, from the viewpoint of Granada's history, what gives the church its special interest.

The heroic deed of Hernando del Pulgar

During the siege of Granada, in the year 1490 - two years before the city was finally taken - a Christian knight carried out a daring feat calculated to undermine the obstinate enemy's morale. With a few brave companions, Hernán or Hernando del Pulgar (literally, Hernando of the Thumb), stealthily penetrated the city walls by creeping along the river bed and, under cover of darkness, making his way through the deserted bazaar. When he arrived at the door of the Great Mosque, he nailed on it a parchment with the words AVE MARIA written in red ink, and an announcement in Latin saying that he herewith took possession of the mosque for the Holy Virgin. He then nailed a flaming candle or torch to the door before beating a hasty retreat, in the course of which he and his companions set fire to the nearby silk market, known until today as the Alcaicería.

There was great consternation among the Moors when they found that some unearthly hand had scrawled such a fearful omen on their place of worship, which they rightly interpreted as a sign that the city would soon be conquered by the enemy. Pulgar was later buried on the site of his supremely Christian gesture, once the mosque had been wrested from the Mohammedans, and – now in the great church built there in its stead – later placed in a chapel where his memory is venerated as the bravest of Granada's heroes.

Below, on the left, is a detail of the large portrait of the belligerent Pulgar which hangs in a shadowy corner of the chapel. Although not painted during his lifetime it seems quite old from the holes in it, one of which can be seen next to the warrior's right elbow. In the center, a painted carving on the altarpiece shows Pulgar's hand holding the flaming torch which he nailed to the door of the mosque, along with an anagram of the words he left there, AVE MARIA. On the right, a fanciful drawing of the "heroic deed" which I found in an old Spanish school book.

To see the chapel for yourself, go behind the altar to the far left hand corner of the nave and peer through the iron bars. Pulgar is buried under the great marble slab in the middle of the floor, with these solemn words carved on it:

Here is buried the Magnificent Knight Fernando del Pulgar, Lord of Salar, who took possession of this Holy Church when this city belonged to the Moors. His Majesty ordered him to be buried here. He died on the 11th of August in the year 1531.

Other legendary figures of the 15 and 16th centuries were buried on the site of the old mosque, such as the good archbishop Hernando de Talavera who made himself loved by the Moors although he failed to convert them, the two sons of the Sultan Muley Hasan and his wife the Christian captive Isabel de Solís, who converted to their mother's original religion after the conquest, as well as the already-mentioned Ambrosio de Vico. But the exact positions of their graves have, with all the changes made since then, been forgotten...

Plaza de las Pasiegas

The marble-paved esplanade in front of the Cathedral has a curious name and also a curious history, literally "Square of the Women of Pas". The square, it seems, was previously known as Plaza de las Flores for the market held there in which, among other things, flowers were sold. But in the 19th century a new fashion gripped Granada's upper classes - wet nurses, when they were needed, not from the nearest village or farm as had been customary, but the mountains of the old Kingdom of Asturias in the north, and particularly a remote Cantabrian region of it called the "Pas" valley... And the women from *el Valle del Pas* were called *Pasiegas*, pronounced *passee-AY-gas*.

It all got started with the cruel and stupid King Fernando VII - detested in Granada for having ordered the death by garotte, in 1831, of the city's brave and defiant heroine, Mariana Pineda, who was caught plotting against him along with other revolutionaries. When the King's wife gave birth to the future Isabel II and was either unable or unwilling to breast-feed her, he ordered a young mother in good health to be brought precisely from the Pas Valley to serve as *nodriza*, or wet nurse.

One might wonder why a nearby farmer's wife couldn't have done, given the difficulty of travelling through such a rugged part of Spain to find a woman just from there. But in spite of that - or perhaps because of it, because having an Asturian woman, and if possible a genuine *pasiega* to nurse your baby and then care for it over the next two years, was a sure sign of a family's wealth - the aristocracy and eventually the bourgeoisie all followed suit.

It is often said that these women were thought to have better milk, like cows, because they came from a place of fertile pastures famous for its cattle, butter and cheese. But the real reason was an historical one - Asturians have always taken pride in the fact that their particular corner of Spain is the only one never to be overrun by the Moors in the 8th century. It was from a place there - now a religious shrine - called Covadonga that the Christians soon after launched the slow-motion reconquest of Spain under their leader, the legendary Pelayo.

This was what first attracted the Royal Family, which often had need of wet nurses: that the women of Asturias and neighbouring Cantabria, and especially the ones from the remote Valley of Pas, were certain to have "clean blood" untainted, over all those centuries, by heathens. Being able to prove one's racial purity or *limpieza de sangre* was since the days of the Inquisition of great social importance, with so many Moors and Jews converted under pressure to Christianity and then murkily disappearing into the ethnic mainstream as "new Christians", and marrying "old" ones.

Being a native of the old Kingdom of Asturias, therefore, was the best guarantee that the heir to your throne or estate would not be suckled on "*leche de mora ni de judia*"... For one thing - among many other possible calamities - when a woman fed her own child and also another's, those two children were traditionally treated as quasi-siblings, *hermanos de leche*, and expected to take care of one another later in life.

What attracted the *pasiegas*, of course, were the bountiful wages. All the new mother had to do was leave her baby with a neighbour who had one of her own to suckle and get on a cart carrying the region's famous cheeses and fabrics to the south, always with a newborn puppy cradled in her arms to "keep the milk flowing". After two or three years of service in the palace or manour, the young women went home with enough savings to set up a business in their village or build a new house. Since a nanny was often called back by her patrons to visit the child she had cared for, and who often loved her like a veritable mother if not more, it was - as well as all the gifts received - an additional chance to ask her charge's highly-placed father for special favours and even assistance in court cases over, for example, land ownership.

By the end of the 19th century the *pasiegas* mania hit Granada's bourgeoisie too, and because the newly-arrived wet nurses positioned themselves in front of the Cathedral to await wealthy patrons, the square's old name was replaced in their honour - perhaps mockingly at first, given the natives' notoriously evil tongues or *mala follá*, as this enduring *granadino* trait is known. But, as with all things in Andalucia, the irony was soon forgotten and - somehow - the incongruous name was made official. By then the term *pasiega* had become generical, since many of the *nodrizas* or *amas de leche* were also from Galicia and the Basque Country, where even the Roman legions were unable to enter.

In this photo of the Cathedral square I have inserted a picture of a group of *pasiegas* in their traditional costumes, taken just around the time the invention of formula milk put them suddenly out of business. King Alfonso XIII, who was deposed in 1931 to make way for the Republic, was one of the last royals to feed at the breast of a "pasiega", whom he adored, and our great poet Federico García Lorca, who was nursed on one's breasts himself, wrote about Granada's *nodrizas* nostalgically. But according to him it was less for the quality of their milk than the folkore they transmitted to the upper-class children who would otherwise have remained ignorant of Spain's vast repertory of popular songs and legends. The idea is typically *lorqueño*, but it makes sense too!

"Gran Vía of Sugar"

Leaving the Alcaicería, the Royal Chapel and La Madraza behind, we go up the steps to the handsome cast-iron gate protecting the Cathedral, and emerge from the archaic world of kings and queens and Moorish mosques onto the shockingly prosaic Gran Vía, with its turn-of-the-century mercantile buildings.

The curious traveller will want to get across it as quickly as possible and head for those romantic little streets one can see peeking out among the banks and travel agencies on the other side. But if you're interested in the effects of unbridled capitalism on impoverished parts of southern Europe, read this fascinating parable of how Granada's heritage was decimated for the sake of a few decades of *nouveau riche* self-aggrandizement.

Granada's history with sugar goes back to the Middle Ages, when the Moors planted cane on the coast. Local production almost disappeared in the 16th century when much cheaper imports began to arrive from Spain's overseas colonies, Cuba and the Philippines. But when in 1898 Spain's last remnants of empire melted away, the price of sugar soared, making it profitable not only to relaunch sugar cane planting on the coast, which continues until today in the region of Salobreña, but also to grow and mill sugar beets on the much higher and cooler plain of Granada. The tall brick smokestacks which still stand to the south and west of the city (used for burning off the waste material) are relics from this ephemeral period.

The new wealth which this boom created enabled the direct beneficiaries - the *hijos de la remolacha*, or "sons of the sugar beet" as they were mockingly called - to create a flashy monument to their social enhancement in the form of a broad, straight avenue lined with 4-storey buildings which, for the period in Granada, were unbelievably high, luxurious and modern, boasting latrines on every floor, running water and in the most extravagant ones, lifts.

The city's intellectual set protested, but in vain. The developers argued that their avenue would sanitize the old city with its stinking streets and outbreaks of cholera, but the undeniable effect of the *Gran Via del Azúcar*, as it was nicknamed, was to plough a trough half a mile long right through a labyrinth of Moorish and Renaissance palaces, leaving in its wake two now obsolete and decrepit rows of pretentious façades, complete with curlicues around the windows and stucco frosting on the top.

The industry went into decline in the Depression and died out altogether when rising overheads made it, once more, impossible to compete with cheap sugar from tropical countries. But the damage to Granada's heritage was irreparably done.

As you scurry across the Gran Vía, cast a quick glance at the marble statue atop the fountain at the intersection with *Calle Reyes Católicos*. It represents the "Catholic Queen" Isabel giving Columbus her permission to make his journey, and was sculpted in Rome for the Fourth Centennial of the Discovery of America in 1892 and, until the Gran Vía was built, initially installed on the promenade by the Genil River.

The official name of the place is *La Plaza Isabel la Católica*, but the *granadinos* amusingly call it "La Plaza de Colón" - Columbus Square - since there's no doubt in their minds that the real hero was the sailor and not the Queen, who merely signed the chit entitling him to obtain the ships and supplies. Her share of the glory seems even slighter when one considers that she strong-armed the townsfolk of the port from which Columbus sailed into building the three ships free of charge, as well as borrowing the hard cash she gave him from a Valencian *converso* Jew - the Luis de Santángel whose name is engraved on the pedestal – and who was a great supporter of the expedition because, he passionately believed, it would bring Christianity to the Asians. In exchange, the financier hoped to get royal gratitude in the form of special privileges, which turned out to be even more useful than he had imagined. Five years later when he and his family were directly threatened by the heresy trials of the Inquisition, in which one of his cousins was sentenced to beheading for having practiced Judaism secretly, he requested from king Fernando and received a precious "clean blood certificate" which effectively gave him the same protection as that enjoyed by "old Christians".

Albaicín, jasmine and secrets...

Granada lies at the foot of the snowy mountain range called the Sierra Nevada, in the place where its western slope reaches the plain. The last hills stretch out like two long claws splayed on either side of the River Darro, which carries the melted snow onto the sun-swept farmlands. The hill overshadowing the east bank is the Alhambra, and the one on the west the Albaicín.

Prehistoric peoples are known to have lived on both of these naturally protected ridges. But the first evidence we have of a fortified citadel is on the crown of the western hill. After the native Iberians came the Romans, who created a theater, a forum and baths. But the place came to be the extraordinary monument which it is today because, in the Dark Ages, the Moors chose it as their stronghold.

The new fortress on the hill was called "the castle" or Alcazaba. But as the knights pushed slowly south, taking the Moorish cities one by one, their inhabitants fled to Granada, finding refuge in new satellite villages outside the walls of the castle. These settlements were often given names which evoked the dwellers' original town. When in the 13th century the people of Baeza (a city near Jaen originally called *Beatia* by the Romans) built their huts to the north of the castle gates, this suburb became known as *al-Bayazin* - "the place of the people of Baeza" - just as the quarter where the Alhambra Palace Hotel and the Manuel de Falla Musem stand today is called La Antequerela, for the Moors of Antequera who sought refuge there when they were forced to flee to the east.

After the center of power moved from the alcazaba to Alhambra on the left bank of the river, it fell into ruin. The fort and the hill itself were called for centuries the "old fortress" - in Arabic *Alcazaba Kadima* – but the name that prevailed was the one of the *extra-muros* village, the Spanish transformation of which is *El Albaicín*.

Here, in the times of the splendour of the Alhambra, lived the populace of Granada, on the other side of the river from the palace. Historians say that the Albaicín in the Middle Ages was much like the citadel of Fez in Morocco today: a honeycomb of tiny houses, narrow alleyways and teeming humanity, contained within crumbling fortress walls.

When Granada fell to the Christians, many of the Moors fled or were expelled, leaving the quarter largely uninhabited, and it became customary for the city's new inhabitants to buy or take over clusters of the tiny houses and build a small palace or villa on the site. Having all the space they needed, they had the local *morisco* tradesmen - the Moors who had converted to Christianity - build them enclosed gardens with bubbling fountains like those in the courtyards of the Alhambra. These gardens were called in Arabic *karm* - vineyard - which the Spaniards changed to the girl's name *carmen*, coming to signify not only the garden but everything within the enclosure, including the home.

But apart from the luxurious *carmenes* scattered about the alleyways of the hill, the Albaicín was, until quite recently, a very poor quarter with unpaved streets, peopled with tradesmen, field labourers and gypsies. In the first half of the 20th century, when the exotic element of Spanish culture became fashionable, artists and intellectuals settled here, inevitably followed in more recent years by a varied assortment of *granadinos* and foreigners, attracted by the tranquillity and charm. Living in the Albaicín was, and still is, like living in a picturesque hill town only a stone's throw from the "real" city.

Those who come here and neglect to explore this "paradise closed to many", as a 17th century poet called it, have, in the spiritual sense, simply not been to Granada. I have written the following pages because the road to paradise is, like the streets of the Albaicín, steep and twisting, and because the curious traveller will, like me, want to decipher this puzzle of whitewashed towers and crumbling brick walls overflowing, in the words of another poet, with "jasmine and secrets"

The most popular road of access to the Albaicín is called the *Calle de la Calderería Nueva* – "The Street of the New Cauldron Factory" - *nueva* or "new" because the alley which bisects it from below is called the *Calle de la Calderería Vieja,* the old cauldron factory…

The *granadinos* simply call it *La Calderería*. Whenever I begin to climb this narrow and tortuous street shaped like a mountain flood - wide at the bottom and tapering as it begins to climb - I feel as if I were crossing the frontier between the two warring kingdoms of reality and romance. No monumental gate ever stood here, and yet the perspective seems to announce something lying beyond, some mysterious citadel - which is precisely what the Albaicín is.

I therefore advise the curious traveller to initiate his visit of discovery through the Calderería and not by one of the many tiny alleys which permeate the foot of the hill, or even by the *Carril de la Lona*, the *Cuesta del Chapiz* or the *Cuesta de Alhacaba*, which, due to their steepness and lack of shade, are better for the return journey.

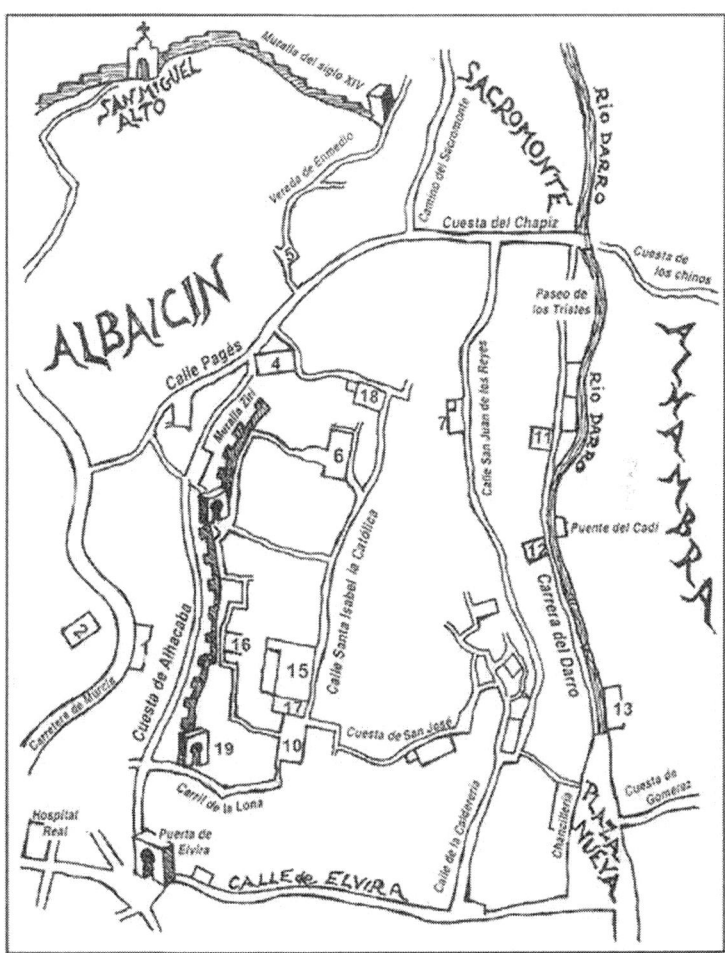

1. Mirador de San Cristóbal 2. Iglesia de San Cristóbal 3. Plaza Larga
4. Colegiata de San Salvador 5. Placeta de Albaida 6. Mirador de San Nicolás
7. Iglesia de San Juan de los Reyes 8. Placeta de Carvajales 9. Iglesia de
San José 10. Plaza de San Miguel Bajo 11. Casa de Castril 12. Bañuelo
13. Iglesia de Santa Ana 14. Casa de Porras 15. Convento de Santa Isabel
la Católica 16. Palacio de Dar al-Horra 17. Iglesia de San Miguel Bajo
18. Convento de Las Tomasas 19. Puerta de Monaita

Calle de la Calderería

If this atmospheric, bustling little street were in New York it would be called "Little Morocco", what with its thicket of Arab tea shops, restaurants and pastry makers. Since the 1980's, at least, Granada has been a center for Muslims, not only those coming from Arab countries but also converts of Spanish and even British nationality. There are several small mosques sprinkled around the district, so discreetly as to be unnoticeable, while on the top of the hill, stands the much newer Great Mosque of Granada.

The tea shops, or *teterías*, have become very popular over the years, since they offer something quite rare in Spain: a very quiet, comfortable, discreetly lit place to sip not alcohol but one of many varieties of herbal infusions and teas. Some are distinctly Moorish in atmosphere, while others play Vivaldi and Mozart... They are invariably packed with students, mostly female, on Saturday nights.

The Calderería ends at the Church of San Gregorio, standing on the site where the medieval Christian community of Granada is said to have had their temple during the Moorish reign. Leaving behind us the hustle and bustle of this charming but busy little street, we climb the wide steps alongside the church, called the *Cuesta de San Gregorio*, taking the first corner on the right, the *Cuesta de las Arremangadas*, a curious name which literally means, "the slope of the skirt-hoisting women", because this alleyway begins down to the right as a very steep and rough flight of steps, which women in the times of long skirts had a hard time negotiating. We stop short of the notorious staircase and turn left on the *Calle del Beso*, "Street of the Kiss". The Moorish-style door on the right, at number 10, is where the first pages of this book were written, in a room facing the Alhambra...

The sentimental story of the Street of the Kiss

This "street", only a few hundred feet long, is at one elbow-shaped point so narrow that you can almost touch both sides of it with your elbows as you pass – perhaps it should have been called the Street of the Elbow! The intriguing name is romantic, but not so amorous as one might have imagined, or hoped.

In the 18th century it was still called the Calle del Conde de Cabra, for the aristocrat who appropriated this part of the Albaicín after the reconquest. On it lived a man and his wife who had a beautiful young daughter who was so angelical that all the people in the quarter loved her. One morning when the mother took a bowl of warm milk to her bed, as was her custom, she was horrified to find the girl inert. "Oh, God!", the poor woman cried, "She's dead!". Everyone in the quarter was stricken with grief, until the next day when the mother leaned down to bestow a parting kiss on the child's face as she lay in her coffin – and the girl's eyes slowly began to open. She in fact had fainted, but the unsophisticated folk of the Albaicín were sure that it was all a miracle and renamed the place "The Street of the Kiss".

The Calle del Beso takes us out onto a junction where stands a 16th century palace known in Granada as the *Casa de Porras*, with a simple but vividly sculptured façade. Here lived a noble family whose surname was Porras, until the place became tenement house. The city bought it some time ago and it is now used for cultural events such as art shows and jazz concerts. During my first weeks at the Calle del Beso, I thought that the constant stamping of the students of the flamenco class came from some industrial machine, until I went in one day to see some paintings and discovered a room full of women busily hammering the floor with their heels.

On our right as we climb the stairs are the towering garden walls, overflowing with bougainvillaea, of the *Carmen de los Cipreses*, which was a haunt of the city's intellectuals in Lorca's day.

We return to the Cuesta de San Gregorio, one street higher up the slope. Now we continue up this street, which bends to the left. We take the first street to the right, following it until we reach the Placeta de Carvajales.

This shady, secluded square is unknown to most mortals, even those who live in the Albaicín, and deserves a special visit for the stunning perspective it affords of the Alhambra -instead of seeing the palace all stretched out horizontally, you look up at it from one side, creating an especially romantic effect, which I have tried to capture in the illustration. This is one of the few places from which one can see the *Puerta de las Armas*, once the main entrance to the palace.

Minaret or Alminar of San José

Now we go back on our footsteps, down the Cuesta de San Gregorio again. When we reach the corner at which we began (after leaving the Casa de Porras) we take the broad, irregular staircase-street on the right, which leads up to the ***Iglesia de San José***. This church stands on the site of what was once the Mosque of the Hermits, of which it retains the original minaret, now surmounted by a brick bell tower. It is one of Granada's most ancient Islamic treasures, composed of irregularly-shaped stones with a pretty "horse-shoe" arched window half-way up, and curiously nicknamed *el alminar de San José*, "the minaret of San José". Near its foot is the usual mosque fountain for the ritual ablutions.

It is said that the minaret of the Great Mosque (which once stood on the site of the Cathedral) was very similar in style and proportions to this one. A few days after the Christians took Granada, Isabel and Fernando had a Mass celebrated here to launch the place on its new vocation as a church. I imagine the two of them and their courtesans and priests, on a winter's day, kneeling in their brocaded cloaks before the makeshift altar which had been set up among the Moorish columns and arches of their finally defeated enemies.

Plaza de San Miguel Bajo

We continue up the Cuesta de San José until we come to the *Plaza de San Miguel Bajo*, which is one of the most popular squares in the Albaicín, for its open-air cafés. It is called "Saint Michael the Low" even though it is on one of Granada's highest points, because, as we know, there is another Church of Saint Michael atop a mountain overlooking the city, making the temple which stands on this charming plaza at least comparatively low. The church is one of the jewels of Granada's post-conquest architecture - the façade was designed by Diego de Siloé, who created so many other buildings of the period - but it unfortunately only opens for Sunday Mass. It was expropriated by the State and closed up 150 years ago, but has now been handsomely restored, with the baroque woodwork painted in warm reds and browns, offset by the austerely whitewashed walls and finely inlaid Moorish or *mudéjar* ceiling.

On the side wall, facing the Plaza, we see the original Moorish aljibe or underground water cistern set in a pointed arch which curiously stands on two small white Roman columns, undoubtedly found in the ruins of an ancient palace.

The vaulted roof of this cistern can be seen protruding from the floor inside the church, like a large swelling, as if the mosque, after having been buried in the bowels of the earth, had tried to come back to claim its rightful place.

The vanished palace of King Badis

Medieval cities grew like mushrooms, without any form of planning, creating a dense tangle of streets which covered every bit of free space, even around great palaces and temples. Whenever we find a plaza of this size in such a place, we can be fairly sure that it was the site of some large building which was demolished before the Renaissance and which, later on, administrators imbued with the new notions of urban development decided should become a plaza or park.

We know that in the vicinity of the Plaza de San Miguel stood the castle of the Zirid dynasty which reigned in Granada in the 11th century, known as the Casa del Gallo – House of the Rooster, for the weathercock said to once stand on its roof. This, with the proximity of the alleyway of the same name and the remains of a mosque, later transformed into the church which we have just visited, all suggest that the current plaza fills the space left by the legendary castle of King Badis.

The legendary palace of the Zirids had vanished long before the Christians took Granada, though, probably at the hands of the Nasrids, since it was an old tradition that each new dynasty of Moors ritually tore down the palaces of the routed rival.

Christ of the Clamps

At the far end of the square stands a stone statue of Christ on the Cross called El Cristo de las Azucenas, "Christ of the Lilies", but popularly - and curiously - known as the *Cristo de las Lañas*, or the "Christ of the Clamps"... A year after Spain's Republic was proclaimed, in 1932, an army General (not Franco) attempted a *coup d'état* to prevent what he claimed was a Marxist takeover of his country. The putsch failed, but so outraged Spain's Republicans that it touched off a wave of anti-clerical vandalism, the Catholic Church being closely associated with the ruling, anti-democratic classes.

In Granada, the Church of San Nicolás was one burned to the ground by a gang of local Republicans, leaving only the roofless walls. They pushed over the stone cross standing in front of it too, and on the way back down the hill, for good measure, smashed the 17th century crucifix in front of the Church of San Miguel Bajo.

The fragments were lovingly carried away and hidden in homes all around, until the Civil War was over when the effigy could safely be repaired and re-installed, with the iron "clamps" of its affectionate nickname now holding together torso and limbs. In those days, it should be said, water brought from outside the home was stored in huge earthenware pots, *tinajas*, and, in like manner, after the end-of-year *matanza* or pig-slaughtering, the pork not used for curing hams and stuffing sausages was first cooked and then stored, in its own congealed fat, in smaller amphoras called *orzas*. Whenever these fragile vessels cracked or broke, a tradesman called a *lañero* was called to repair them, and it was one of these who restored the shattered Christ. The effect, although certainly unintentional, was to accentuate the Lord's sacrifice by inflicting yet more wounds upon his dying body.

When I remember first coming across the Plaza de San Miguel Bajo, one starry night in 1962, the crucifix stood on its own in the center, but a decade later, as if punished for obstructing the godless miracle of modern progress called automobile traffic, it was relegated to the south-east corner where it is now, enclosed in a wrought-iron fence bristling with pointed spikes.

In 2008, however, after showing worrisome signs of decay, the Christ was restored - so efficiently that the distinctive clamps, blackened by age, were removed and the chunks of stone seamlessly cemented together without them. Althought the *albaicineros* seem to think it's an improvement, by force of habit they go on calling the effigy the *Cristo de las Lañas*, because that is what has, over the years, given the effigy its fame. Since only the old-timers who remember the clamps understand why the name perdures, I have dug up, for the benefit of the curious traveller, some old pictures of what the Christ looked like, both after it was smashed and after it was pieced together, with its unsightly but also supremely evocative iron fixtures...

Cristo de las Azucenas,
Plaza de San Miguel

Next, the Christ now, more handsome, but without the clamps...

I should add that the Christ of the Lilies began its four centuries of life on the other side of the square, facing the Moorish *aljibe*, where it was moved up and down whenever it got in the way, and even turned around, now with its face to the church and then its back, which is how we see it in this postcard dated 1950.

Strangely, in this picture the clamps are not at all visible. They were probably either retouched by the postcard publisher or covered in a thick coat of whitewash, like everything else…

Plaza de San Miguel Bajo, 1950

It's the picture I'm fondest of, though, because the Christ is just as I discovered it that starry night, overlooking the moonlit plaza, truly like the King of the World.

On the far side of the plaza from the church (to the right of the Christ) a narrow street leads down to a belvedere overlooking the city called the *Mirador de la Lona*. The slope which plunges down from it to the right is also called the *Carril de la Lona*. There was once workshop here which made sails for ships, and the bolts of canvas - *lona* - were unrolled and stitched together on the slope, which is particularly broad at the top, giving the place its name. It is said that the sails for the "invincible" Spanish Armada were made here, in the 17th century.

Now we are going to walk to the most famous viewpoint of the quarter, the *Mirador* – or "belvedere" - of San Nicolás. The most direct way to get there is along the *Calle de Santa Isabel la Real*, which begins in front of the Church of San Miguel, taking us past the convent of the same name. It was founded by Queen Isabel after the conquest. The sagging but monumental gate is always open and you should step into the cobble-stoned courtyard, to see the magnificent Gothic door on the side of the church, built in the grand "style of Toledo", complete with the yoke and arrows symbolizing the union of the Christian kingdoms. If you come on Sunday morning you can enter the lavishly decorated church to attend Mass, and see the coiffed nuns sitting like motionless butterflies behind the massive iron grill which separates them from the world.

For 500 years, no one was allowed to enter the Convent except the nuns themselves and the Bishop, but its magnificent interior has recently been fully restored, as a result of which scheduled and guided visits can be enjoyed. As one of the first visitors, I can testify that the *mudéjar* ceilings, the richly-painted *azulejos*, or tiles, and the many carvings and statues are true wonders of the purest *arte granadino*.

From the convent, walk straight ahead for several hundred yards, take the left (upper) fork and, then, the flight of steps leading up to *Mirador de San Nicolás*. The alternative route is along the *Callejón del Gallo*, the "Alley of the Cock", which leads off the Plaza de San Miguel, on the west or right hand side as you stand with your back to the church. It turns right, then left, then right again, where it becomes the *Callejón de las Monjas*, the Alley of the Nuns, since this was the old way of getting to the convent. After the first corner, the street follows the inside of the old wall of the Alcazaba.

Palace of Dar al-Horra

We come to an exquisitely proportioned Moorish palace, with an elegant tower pierced by tiny arched windows, known as *Dar al-Horra*, the House of the Queen. It was built in the 15th century for Aixa, the rejected wife of the Sultan Muley Hasan, who ungratefully fell in love with the 15-year old Christian captive, Isabel de Solis.

After the conquest, Aixa went into exile with her disgraced and disconsolate son, the vanquished Sultan Boabdil, whom she rebuked with the famous words "Do not cry like a woman for that which you failed to lose like a man". Isabel, as might be expected, converted back to her original faith, spending the rest of her life in convent in the north – by which time Muley Hasan had long since died and, according to his last wishes, been buried in the snows of the mountain peak now bearing his name, *Mulhacén*, atop the Sierra Nevada.

Dar al-Horra, like so many other Moorish monuments of Granada, fell into ruin and was not very respectfully restored until the beginning of the 20th century, by the Director of the Alhambra. The Convent of Santa Isabel la Real, which stands back to back with the palace, was built on Dar-al-Horra's reputedly beautiful gardens, of which only a small part is left and, apparently, used for growing vegetables by the keeper.

The *Callejón de las Monjas* takes us under the arched aqueduct which once supplied the convent with water. This tiny bridge is famous in Granada's rich folklore because during the War of the Spanish Succession, at the beginning of the 18th century, a number of dissident politicians were hanged there and left on display to put fear into all who passed. We walk along the edge of a new park, past a disused Moorish fountain known as the *Aljibe Kadima* or "old fountain", and then (after turning left and then right) up a walled street running parallel to the old ramparts, the "street of the gypsy girl's fountain"- *Aljibe de la Gitana* - and then right along the broad street known as the *Calle de la Mina*, or "Street of the Mine". Turn left where this street becomes a narrow staircase - the *Cuesta de María de la Miel*, or "Slope of Honey Mary", thus called by the Moors for the fountain which stands on it and whose water is, it seems, especially sweet - and then right to get to Mirador de San Nicolás, with its world-famous view of the Alhambra.

Mirador de San Nicolás

The extraordinary sight before us has been immortalized in paintings and photographs, with the Moorish palace crowning the woody ridge against its backdrop of snow-covered mountains. What most people do not know, however, is that the spacious, tree-shaded belvedere on which we are standing was the site of a much older fortress, the *Alcazaba Kadima*, which has long since disappeared.

But let us identify the profusion of monuments before our eyes, rather than try to imagine those which no longer exist. From right to left (or south to north), this collection of fortifications and palaces which makes up the Alhambra is as follows:

Las Torres Bermejas - the "vermilion", or reddish towers - are really a fortress of their own, directly overlooking the city to the south. This is the most ancient part of the Alhambra, built over 2, 000 years ago by the Jewish community to defend their tiny citadel which gave Granada its name, and reconstructed on a much larger scale by the Moors to defend the southern tip of the new castle.

La Alcazaba, or "military fortress" is the series of massive towers directly in front of us, the tallest of which is the one with the bell tower, *La Torre de la Vela*. When the Christians took Granada, their first action was to place the large bell they had brought with them as a symbol of their faith - and known as *la vela* or "the sentinel" - to ring the chimes of victory. Later, the bell played a more practical role in the city's life: by means of complex series of rings, it regulated the opening and closing of the *acequias*, or irrigation canals, on the plain below (this system was perhaps the greatest legacy of the Moors, enabling them to use the water from the snows of the mountains to turn the *vega* spreading below the palace walls into a heavenly orchard). The original bell was replaced in the 18th century, but its descendant is still rung on the 2nd of January as part of the celebrations of the *Día de la Toma*, the "day of the taking" of Granada in 1492.

The *Torre de la Vela* and its sisters, right up to the Palace of Carlos V which stands massively in the background, are empty military buildings and mainly visited for the views they afford. The tall slender tower with the single arched window, which stands slightly below the rest of the mass, and plunged more deeply into the vegetation, houses the *Puerta de las Armas*, which was the main entrance to the Alhambra until the collapse of the bridge over the river which connected it to the city, after the Christian conquest. The gate itself - which we saw the top of from the Placeta de Carvajales - is hidden from our view on the south side of the tower.

The round tower which stands to the left of the Torre de las Armas is the only part of the fortress which was built by the Christians, around and on top of a smaller, square Moorish tower. It is known as *El Cubo*, which means bucket or, in this context, "round tower".

In the center and towards the back of the ensemble we see the pointed bell tower of the church of *Santa Maria de la Alhambra* and the square mass of the *Palace of Carlos Quinto*. Everything to the left of these Christian additions is known as the *Nasrid Palaces* - the elegant buildings used either for the administration of the kingdom or the pleasure of the kings, which were adjoined to the primitive fortress by the Nasrid Dynasty in the 14th century.

To begin, the great tower on the left of the Palace of Carlos Quinto - the one with the two tiers of tiny arched windows - is the *Torre de Comares*, the main hall for functions of state. Just to the right is the oratory or *mirhab* which, upon entering the palace, one visits after the Mexuar. To the left of Comares is a small, elegantly roofed tower and arched walkway, the precious *Peinador de la Reina* - "the queen's boudoir" - part of the "rooms of Carlos Quinto" which were built by the Christians on top of the Moorish bulwarks, so that the King and Queen would have a place to stay when they came to Granada, until their own palace was finished (as we shall see, it never was). To the left of this charming Renaissance version of Moorish architecture we catch an oblique glimpse of the overlapping roofs of the *Court of the Lions, La Torre de las Damas* and the four defensive towers which are part of the northern wall, leading up to the bridge which spans the gorge separating the main palace from the gardens of the *Cerro del Sol*.

The Generalife is the slender white building alone among the trees on this steep slope called "Hill of the Sun" where the court retired to hunt, and the military watch tower near the summit it is known as the *Silla del Moro* - the "Seat of the Moor". If you come in summertime you won't see much snow on the Sierra Nevada, but the rest of the year the contrast of the creamy white mountains and the towers of the castle, like gigantic cubes of brown sugar, is... well, any of a wide range of superlatives can be used and at the same time none of them renders it justice!

In this historical photograph of the Mirador as it was long before its reconstruction in 1945, a merry band of neighbourhood children are enjoying the view, just as we do today...

Mirador de San Nicolás, 1900

...and in this one, a gypsy girl poses proudly in front of the Moorish palace.

Mirador de San Nicolás, Albaicín, 1913

*Other interesting things which can be seen
from the Mirador de San Nicolás*

The almost vertical slope beneath the palace is also interesting, but not for architectural reasons. We can see the ruins of long defensive walls snaking up and down among the greenery, and - straight ahead of us and just below the round tower - a huge cavity of bare earth which plunges down towards the river bed, like the gap left in a cake after one wedge has been removed. It is known as *el socavón del Cubo*, "the hole of the round tower". A powder-house at the foot of the Alhambra, on the edge of the river, blew up in the year 1590, with such a blast that several parts of the palace were damaged and the course of the river was changed by the landslide.

Immediately below, looking down the eastern slope of the Albaicín at our feet, we can see the spires of the churches of *Santa Ana*, the pretty minaret-like one on the right with the green and white tiles, and *San Pedro*, the church which picturesquely overhangs the river gorge on the Carrera del Darro. Both were mosques before the conquest of the city.

Immediately to our right, separated from the esplanade by a staircase, is a handsome old house with watch tower and the words *Carmen de Apperley* written over the door. This was the home of an English portrait painter who came to live in the Albaicín after World War I and married a local girl, whom he painted in several sensuous and un-Victorian paintings which are widely reproduced in Granada, posing semi-nude against the view of the Alhambra seen through the arches of the tower.

Beyond the church, to the left when we face the palace, is, according to the people who built it, "the first mosque built in Spain by Spanish Muslims". There are many Spanish converts in Granada and their *mezquita*, inaugurated in 2003, is studiously discreet and Andalucian in appearance. When the project was announced several decades before, however, local persons of a conservative, not to say reactionary mentality deplored what they interpreted as being the return to Spain of the very enemy which the glorious Catholic Monarchs had toiled to expel. And when the construction permit was finally granted, it had to almost immediately be suspended for a reason which is very common in this part of the city - as soon as they dug down a few feet to lay the foundations, remains of the early Roman fortress, and a bit deeper Iberian, fortress were discovered, requiring the attention of the university's archaeologists before the project could continue. Since then, the directors of the *Mezquita Mayor*, or Great Mosque, have shown their respect for the local inhabitants by refraining from using loudspeakers when the traditional call to prayer is chanted from the smallish minaret which effectively means that very few people, Muslims included, hear it. The mosque is so tucked away in the labyrinth of streets that it's hard to get a proper photograph of the minaret, and this one I took of it, at the end of the alley behind the San Nicolas church, is about the only angle I could find.

Visitors are welcome to enter and can watch the faithful at prayer through the large door, always open, as you can see in my drawing below. I go there to enjoy the view of the Alhambra when the Mirador gets too crowded with noisy tourists and other merry-makers, which is, unfortunately, most of the time, and simply to enjoy the charming Mediterranean garden.

The view from San Nicolás is best just before sundown, when the towers turn ruddily incandescent and the snows take on a pinkish hue. Another unforgettable moment is at night when the whole castle is splendidly illuminated. There can be no better way to end an evening of wine and tapas than to sit for a while with your legs dangling over the parapet of San Nicolás, that is if you can find a place among the young people who gather there.

From San Nicolás to Plaza Larga

The Church of San Nicolás was burned, along with many others, by the anti-clerical *republicanos* during the Civil War, and only recently restored. The fact that it was once a mosque can be seen by the *aljibe* (covered well) and fountain, once used for ritual washing, which stands beside it on the plaza. Because of the stupendous view, ideal for the background of romantic photographs, the church is very popular among the *granadinos* for the celebration of weddings, and on a Saturday afternoon you may well run into a crowd of gay young people milling about there in their best finery.

We will now walk back into what I call the "heart" of the Albaicín since it is the part which gave the whole citadel its name - the lively suburb outside the walls of the old fortress, with its market streets and tradesmen.

We cross the broad square behind the church, passing in front of the neighbourhood library (where I did much of my research for this book) and go down the narrow street on the far side, which takes us to what is left of the wall of the old *alcazaba*. The square tower we come to was in fact one of the city gates - the *Puerta Hernán Román*, as it is popularly called - in the passageway of which the Christians installed a chapel to Granada's first bishop and patron San Cecilio, who was martyred here by the Romans. Here we see him in his niche, with the symbolic pomegranate in his hand.

What were those rows
of little holes for?

A detail which intrigues many curious travellers when contemplating the ancient walls of Granada are the horizontal rows, one above the other, of strange small holes, making the rough mortar look as if it had been strafed by a machine gun. They are the cavities left by the Moorish builders, when setting up the moulds needed to pour the liquid *argamasa*, a crude form of concrete. Two great boxes of planks were aligned on either side of the section of wall to be built for the mortar to be poured between them, and to prevent these free-standing, mobile caissons from spreading under the weight, they were attached to one another by long poles which were fitted into the planks and secured at the ends. Obviously, steel cables didn't exist then.

Just before the mixture hardened, these ties were pulled out for use further on. The holes they left disappeared under the final layer of smooth mortar which was then white-washed. But over the centuries, this finishing sheath, being thin and fragile, fell away and revealed the unsightly holes. That is why all the Moorish walls in Granada that have not been fully restored are punctured from one end to the other with hundreds of pock-marks gaps left by these wooden ties.

In the photo below, you can see how on the right end of this section of the Zirid Wall, seen from the *Carril de la Lona*, some of the original plaster still clings to the rougher surface, whereas in the rest, to the left, erosion has exposed the construction holes.

We turn left on the street of the same name as the chapel - *Callejón de San Cecilio* - and walk to the neighbouring gate, which still retains its designated purpose, the *Puerta Nueva*. This is the best preserved Moorish gate in Granada apart from the Alhambra itself, with the characteristic elbow-shaped passageway. It was called "new" by the Arabs in the 11th century, when they opened it in the wall to replace the one we have just seen (which was sealed up on the outside, creating the grotto-like cavity which the Christians used for their chapel). It is also called the *Puerta de las Pesas* - the "Gate of the Weights" - in reference to the market which has been held in the *Plaza Larga* outside it since the Middle Ages. When the King's inspectors discovered that a merchant was using rigged weights the appropriate fines were imposed and, as an example, the undersized iron slabs would be nailed to the wall, and until the recent over-restoration we could still see a few of them rusting away above the outer side of the gate.

Plaza Larga, heart of the Albaicín

We step through the L-shaped gate and into the Plaza Larga, the "long square". If the Albaicín - in reality not one but several quarters sprawling over a very large hill - has a center, this would have to be it. I have always loved this plaza, with its secret, shady feeling, which might have been the one Lorca evoked in his poem which says *"and the night became intimate, like a tiny plaza"*. On summer nights it is full of restaurant tables with people drinking and laughing under the trees, and children running to and fro among the gypsy matrons sitting tightly side by side on the public benches, as if they were their living room sofas. On Saturday mornings it is full of stalls selling cheap clothes and vegetables, much as it was centuries ago.

Two market and shopping streets lead off it: the *Calle del Agua*, opposite as we enter the plaza and so named because in Moorish times there was a public bath here; and, to the right, the *Calle de los Panaderos* - Street of the Bakers - which takes us to one of Granada's less known but most ancient monuments...

Colegiata del Salvador

Here, until 1492, stood the great mosque of the Albaicín, which, according to the foreigners who visited Granada after the conquest, was even more beautiful than the Great Mosque in the city below.

Isabel and Fernando converted the Muslim building into a church and missionary school - *colegiata* - for the conversion of the Moors. The only part of the mosque which their builders spared was the courtyard and fountain of ablutions, the *Patio de los Limoneros*, or "patio of the lemon trees". It is one of Granada's most ancient Moorish monuments, in the plain but well-proportioned style of the Almohad dynasty which reigned between the 12th and 13th centuries. You must enter the church (which was gutted during the 1936 war and recently restored) to visit the patio, after paying a modest fee, ostensibly to enter the small museum of religious statuary.

We will find here none of the aesthetic satisfactions which await us in the Courtyard of the Lions, since what we see is dismayingly simple, even rustic: three colonnades of roughly-cut stone columns and arches around a central well. But it is interesting to compare the two because it shows us how the

Spanish Muslim civilization evolved, in just a few centuries, from the austerity of the fanatical Berber warriors to the decadence of the Nasrid rulers, who were more entranced with the pleasures of the senses than of the spirit.

The mission was a humiliating failure, with the Moors – who didn't want to be converted - stoning the priests who, terrified, fled, on several occasions, to the safety of the Christian part of town around the Cathedral.

If you walk around the church you will come to the place of the Moorish gate, *Bib-al-Bonoud*, or "Gate of the Banners", of which remains only the large square tower standing behind the convent called *Convento de las Tomasas*, further down the hill. The gate was given this name because each time a new sultan of Granada was chosen, the first celebratory banner was flown atop it. But it is more famous as the place where the first *morisco* uprising began, against the attempts to force the local people to convert, contrary to the promises made in the treaty of surrender.

If you still have the energy, you might want to press on to visit the Sacromonte, which is only a short walk from the Colegiata del Salvador. Or you can go half way down the hill to visit the…

Church of San Juan de los Reyes

This church (which stands on the street of the same name, *Calle de San Juan de los Reyes*) has a special, if largely forgotten place in the city's history. Originally the Mosque of the Converts, many of the city's Christians became Muslims here, usually under pressure of one kind or the other. This is why it was the very first mosque in Granada to be sanctified by Isabel and Fernando, just three days after they took the city, and they made a point of giving it their own name : the "Church of Saint John of the Monarchs". As might be expected, the new mosque-church soon became the site of mass reconversions of the city's "Arabized" Christians, who quickly went back to the faith of their forefathers.

Eventually a Gothic church was built to replace the Moorish building, but it was expropriated by the State in the 19th century. Today this abandoned shell's only distinction is the minaret which the Christians, as usual, topped off with a belfry. This *alminar* was made under the 13th century Almohad dynasty, with lace-like brick relief, very similar in style to the great Moorish tower of Seville's cathedral, known as *La Giralda* and with the same inner ramp instead of stairs, twisting to the top counter-clockwise to the place from which the call to prayer rang out over the city. It is not visible from the street, so you must leave the Calle San Juan de los Reyes and walk past the front of the church, up the hill, to see this relic of Granada's Islamic past, forgotten among the fig trees and crumbling walls.

It's not very pleasant to stroll along this street, due to the cars and motorcycles which move along it constantly. It also becomes extremely narrow at one point, just wide enough for a normal car, so that people driving big vans find themselves either having to back out or take the chance of leaving bits of metal on the roadside after squeezing through, and you can clearly see the grooves in the walls on either side which they have left... Archaeological excavations made in the area have shown that the Calle San Juan de los Reyes was once a Roman road, which connected Granada to the city of Guadix.

At the Plaza Nueva end there still were several time-honoured brothels, when I began writing this book in my *pied-*

à-terre on the Calle del Beso, overlooking the Calle de San Juan de los Reyes. The ladies, who apart from the garish make-up looked like stocky grandmothers, stood on the sidewalk waiting for the customers, and I could hear them raucously discussing the day's trade, or lack of it, from my desk by the window, just as their predecessors, the legendary *rameras*, must have done centuries ago....

In memory of Granada's rameras and expósitos

Prostitution, in Christian Granada up to the not so distant past, was so widespread, and so generally accepted to be a public necessity, that the city's prelates unofficially condoned it, to the point that some of the wealthier churchmen even had financial interests in brothels around the city.

But the Bishop drew the line at Easter, saying that it was unacceptable to have harlots openly plying their trade on Good Friday. So the *rameras*, as they were known for the leafy branches – *ramas* - which they put in their windows to show that they were ready for business, were herded out of the city at the appropriate moment and lodged for a week in outlying farms. It became a popular tradition that, when they returned, the men of the city came out to welcome them with delirious cries of joy, in an impromptu carnival. Another well-entrenched institution of the times were the *expósitos* - the abandoned or "exposed" foundlings whom unwed mothers - usually destitute servants on their way to becoming *rameras* - left on the steps of the city's churches.

The *expósitos* were placed in church orphanages, where they provided a bountiful supply of well-indoctrinated candidates for the lower levels of the clergy and the civil service. Many of them were given the surname Expósito, "foundling", just as in Italy they were named Esposito, in France Dieudonné, "God-given", and in Portugal, *de Jesus* – "of, or belonging to, Jesus".

Down the Cuesta de la Alhacaba

Starting from the top of the Albaicín at Plaza Larga, let us go back down to the lower city on the western side, by the legendary Cuesta de la Alhacaba. I will describe this street from top to bottom for reasons of comfort, since it is very steep, leading up from the city in a single, unbroken slope. In fact, its name translates literally as "the slope of the slope", since its original Arabic name *al-acaba* means "the slope", to which the Spanish then added their qualifier *la cuesta* meaning the same thing.

As we let ourselves be carried down by the force of gravity, we enjoy a splendid view of the ramparts of the old fortress on our left, unbroken by gates from the Puerta Nueva, which we just visited in Plaza Larga. Above on our right we see the squat, brown cubes of the Church of San Cristobal and the spectacular belvedere of the same name.

We pass the beginning of the Carril de la Lona, which leads up on the left to the Plaza San Miguel Bajo. If we go half way up, we will get an impressive view of one of Granada's mightiest and most ancient Arab gates, the *Puerta de la Monaita* (*monaita* being a corruption of the Arabic word for "threshing floor").

Puerta de Elvira to Paseo de los Tristes

We continue to the bottom of the slope and come out in front of medieval Granada's mightiest Arab gate and official entrance point, the *Puerta de Elvira*. It was Granada's triumphal arch for all of the city's invaders: the Catholic Monarchs paraded solemnly through it when they conquered the city on January 2, 1492, and three centuries later they were followed by the Napoleonic army. Like many medieval gates, it was originally a massive fortress in its own right, with the characteristic monumental gate followed by, in this case, two narrow passageways. But once Granada fell to the Christians the gate as a fortification became obsolete and much of its stones were carried away to build a monastery.

Then with the French invasion, in the 19th century, Napoleon's General Sébastiani, a fellow Corsican who had installed himself luxuriously in the Alhambra Palace, feared that this could be an obstacle for the rapid deployment of troops in case of a popular uprising on the Calle de Elvira, and had the whole labyrinth of inner constructions torn down - except for the inner gate leading up to Cuesta de Alhacaba, which was too steep for his canons to be dragged anyway. What the French didn't desecrate the *granadinos* did, though, and it was finally demolished by the city council in 1879 in the name of "modernization". This curious etching shows it still in place a few years beforehand.

Why is the gate called *"Puerta de Elvira"*?

Elvira, as we know, was the Arab way of pronouncing the old name which the Romans gave to Granada: *Iliberis*, which in turn has its origin in the prehistoric *Ilbyr*. Therefore it might seem that the translation of *Puerta de Elvira* would be "Gate of Granada", which is contradictory if we remember that medieval gates on major roads were always called by the name of the town they led to rather than from. The infernally complicated explanation for this, put as clearly as possible, is as follows:

When the Arabs invaded Spain in the 8th century, they used the name Elvira to refer not to the city of Iliberis itself but to the entire region or *cora*, which they administered from a new city they founded to the west of Granada called by them *Madinat Elvira* or "City of Elvira", while referring to the old Roman city as *Madinat Garnata*, Garnata being the name of the Jewish citadel which was then its heart.

Elvira's ruins are buried near the foot of the isolated rock which rises from the plain to the west of Granada, still called Sierra de Elvira. In any case, Madinat Elvira was abandoned at the turn of the millennium with the advent of the Zirids, a tribe originating in Tunisia, which preferred to use the old Roman city, now called *Garnata/Granada*, as their capital, probably because it was easier to defend and had abundant water coming from the mountains.

Therefore it is clear that the name of the gate does not refer to the ancient city of Iliberis/Elvira, now Granada, but to the *Madinat Elvira* founded by the Arabs, and which has long since disappeared.

We have only to step through the gate to find ourselves on the main artery of the Moorish city, the *Calle de Elvira*, which winds narrowly along the southern foot of the Albaicín to Plaza Nueva. There are several antique shops on the end closest to Plaza Nueva, and it is the starting point for the picturesque *Calle de la Calderería Nueva*.

But let us return a moment to the Puerta de Elvira. As was often the case in medieval, fortified cities, the esplanade outside the main gate was a very busy place, with fairs, merchants and also graveyards, as archaeologists confirmed when the underground parking lot – *Parking Triunfo* - was dug, just down the road from the Elvira Gate. The Christians built several major buildings here, including a monastery for the conversion of the Moors (now a military barracks) and the *Hospital Real*, the "Royal Hospital" which King Fernando created to attend to the many sick, wounded and insane people who filled the streets of Granada after the conquest.

The hospital later became famous as a center for the treatment of syphilis, which the Spanish sailors are said to have brought back from America, causing so much suffering in the particularly virulent form it took at the beginning. While the thought of having a hospital at hand is comforting, we would do well to remember that until the 19th century, hospitals were, as the name indicates, essentially places which offered hospitality to the dying, who usually had little hope of being cured, but whose souls could be saved from Hell by priests and nuns. The very name of the main hospital in Paris has since the Middle Ages been "Hôtel Dieu", for example, even though its vocation has changed from a spiritual to a physical one.

Today this stately Renaissance palace standing outside the old city walls of Granada, and which in no way resembles a hospital, is the University's administrative center and called the *Rectorado*, as well as a being used for cultural exhibits. Visitors can wander, free of charge, through its majestic halls and elegant courtyards, and visit the soaring Gothic chapel in its center, where so many patients bid farewell to the world. And there is, I think, no better place than here to speak of two very moving moments in the very exciting history of Granada.

Saint John of God and the
Triumph of the Virgin

The most famous "patient" of the mad-house at the Hospital Real later became Granada's own saint, the founder of the now worldwide Hospitaller Order of Saint John of God. His story gives us a vivid glimpse of life in 16th century Spain and, especially, in the recently conquered city.

Saint John was born in Portugal as *João Cidade* or "John of the City", and roamed the peninsula and Europe as a soldier of fortune - he went as far as Vienna with the army of Carlos Quinto to fight the Turks - and itinerant book-peddler, until he came to Granada. Here, he was "re-born" at the hands of one of the time's many fiery street preachers, who often offered the poor their only ray of hope in that time of war and disease, given that the Princes of the Church had proven disappointingly powerless to remedy their sufferings.

While listening to the fateful sermon, John "heard" God ordering him to care for the sick, an experience which sent him into a fit so violent that he was locked up with the *locos* in the Hospital Real for several months. He soon became a familiar figure on the filthy streets of the city, often carrying home dying beggars on his shoulders.

With the alms he collected he created his own hospital, which after his death multiplied into the great Order now active throughout the world. On the street which leads down from the park below the Hospital Real - the *Calle San Juan de Dios* - is the modern hospital and baroque church dedicated to his memory. The site of his tiny bookstore, next to the Arab gate on the Calle de Elvira, is marked by a neo-Gothic chapel.

Another less touching but much more bizarre reminder of the irrational world of the times is the statue of the Virgin Mary known as *El Triunfo de la Inmaculada*, which stands atop a column in the public park to which it gives its name, *Jardin del Triunfo*, just down the hill from the Hospital Real. Towards the end of the 16th century a bloody debate raged through the cities of southern Spain about the Mother of Christ. The issue was not her virginity (as many local people still believe) but whether or not she was born free of sin, "immaculate", making her different to other mortals whose sinful condition is innate or original.

The belief in the "immaculate conception" had been alive for centuries but since there was no mention of such a thing in the Gospels, the Church had not yet confirmed it as rigorous "dogma", only "doctrine", which allowed each person to believe or disbelieve as they chose. The fanatical *inmaculistas* wanted the Church to make it dogma, motivated in many cases by the fact that many of them were recent converts to Christianity who were at pains to prove the sincerity of their new faith. On the other side, the more conservative and cautious *maculistas* felt that Mary's purity was already sufficiently proven and refused to believe in an additional claim because it wasn't mentioned in the Gospels. But the masses took the side of the fanatics, partly because many simple folk found the whole thing too complicated to understand and thought it was a heretical attempt to deny the virgin birth of Christ. The Church, for its part, was only too glad to have a popular outburst of faith, having lost much prestige in the battle with the Lutherans in northern Europe, and – as I have said – having been widely accused of failing to relieve the sufferings of its flock. So the Pope finally found a way of defending the Immaculate Conception without making it Dogma, by forbidding the *maculistas* from criticizing the *inmaculistas* in public. It was then that statues of the Virgin were erected all over Andalucia and called *triunfos*, or "triumphs", since it was generally accepted that Mary had triumphed over her presumed detractors.

It wasn't until 1854 that the Vatican finally calculated nine months before the birth of Mary on the 8th of September and decreed that the 8th of December should be celebrated as the Day of the Immaculate Conception, requiring it to be accepted as Dogma by all Catholics. Today it is one of Spain's most popular holidays, but for hedonistic rather than religious reasons. It happens to fall just after the *Fiesta de la Constitución*, the day when democratic Spain got its first constitution, on 6th December, 1978, and when there is a Saturday or Sunday in the middle the country shuts down for a *puente* or "bridge", a long weekend of five days – for those lucky enough to be civil servants, school teachers or office workers. It's a great time for visiting distant relatives and doing mountain sports. People either call it *el Puente de la Inmaculada* or *el Puente de la Constitución*, depending on how pious or political they are.

Granada's statue, bristling like a hedgehog with iron rods meant to resemble holy rays and perched atop a sort of kitschy candelabra, was first placed in front of the Elvira Gate where everyone would be sure to see it. When the public park was created (under Franco) on the site of the city's old bull ring, this laughable bit of iconography (which one author has said should really have been called the Triumph of the Church), was moved in front of the long row of Mussolini-style fountains at the top of the park.

What is the cake called "pionono"?

A more endearing, and far more enduring trace of the Conception polemic that, unknown to most, still survives in local folklore is Granada's most famous pastry, curiously called a *pionono*.

A *pionono*, which you can enjoy with a cup of coffee in any *pastelería* of the city, tastes a lot like a *baba au rhum*, and unlike many Spanish sweets it is both light and refreshing, neither over-sweet nor over-sticky. The recipe itself is of Moorish origin, but a new version was produced in the 19th century to celebrate Pope Pius the Ninth's acknowledgement of the Virgin Mary's innate purity, and christened with his Italian title: *Pio Nono*. It was also reshaped as an upright cylinder intended to resemble his head, which is portrayed below.

Granadinos are eternally grateful to Pius Ninth for his saintly action, but others blame him for being the Pope who, under great military pressure, gave up the Papal States, in 1870.

Plaza Nueva and Plaza de Santa Ana

The River Darro is a short river with a long etymology. The Romans called it *Dat Aurum*, Latin for "gives gold", which in vulgar Latin became Dauro, which the Moors then arabized as *hadarro* and which after the conquest was abbreviated to Darro. We know there was gold here because until the mid-20th century people panned for nuggets in the stream where it flows beneath the tiny bridge, Puente de Cabrera. The river, really a creek, starts at a mountain spring not far away and flows between the Alhambra and the Albaicín and across the city to join the River Genil in the southern part of Granada.

But most of its course is now underground. In the 16th century, soon after the conquest, the square now known to all as Plaza Nueva was gradually covered, with the result that today the river flows beneath it through a tunnel, unseen. However, the huge space is really composed of two "plazas", not just one. The northeast corner is properly named Plaza de Santa Ana for the Church of Santa Ana which stands there, although most *granadinos* - and many street maps - mistakenly call the whole esplanade "Plaza Nueva".

The reason for this is that the church once stood on its own little clearing, cut off from the rest of what was then a field because of the stream which flowed, uncovered, down the middle of it and, also, a cluster of houses and public buildings, including a hospital (which in those days meant a place where the homeless were brought not to be cured but to die a Christian death, after confessing).

Forgotten by most *granadinos* today, another church, the Iglesia de San Gil, occupied the diagonally opposite corner of the current plaza with its own clearing in front for ceremonial occasions, the Plaza de San Gil. When it became necessary to provide more breathing space for the Chancellory, this old plaza was extended northwards, clearing away yet another labyrinth of houses and covering the river as it went, until this new square or "Plaza Nueva" merged with the Plaza de Santa Ana. An iron fence was put around the Santa Ana church yard as a boundary for a while, but then removed because it got in the way...

Today there is no visible sign of where the Plaza Nueva ends and the Plaza de Santa Ana begins, except that the houses on both sides of the upstream end of the square are numbered as belonging to the Plaza de Santa Ana. Which one is which between them only God knows, and even He might not! I decided to telephone the church pretending to be an ignorant visitor, and asked the priest point-blank where his church was located in Granada, to which he answered, "On Plaza Nueva". Upon further questioning he "confessed" that it was really Plaza de Santa Ana but no one called it that... Such are the mysteries of Granada!

To make them a little less mysterious, here are the two plazas as shown on the 16th century pictorial map of Ambrosio de Vico, a veritable gold mine for all lovers of Granada's history.

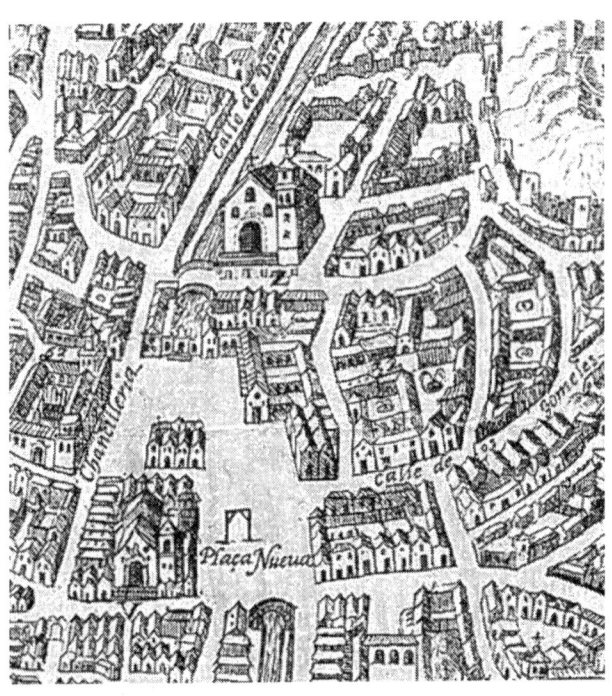

At top is the easily recognizable Santa Ana church, with its old Moorish bridge spanning the river in front of it, as well as the jumble of streets that then stood to its south. The strip of empty space in front of it was the original Plaza de Santa Ana, where you see the large letter **Z**, which on Ambrosio's map stands for the church itself.

At the bottom left of this detail of the map is, marked with a **V**, the vanished Iglesia de San Gil - church of Saint Gilles. Amusingly, it stood in the exact part of our modern Plaza Nueva now full of the sidewalk cafés where we all enjoy a glass of wine now and then, to gaze at the world going by... (After this ruinous church was demolished in the 19th century, the parish of San Gil was merged with that of Santa Ana, making the current church's official name "Iglesia de San Gil y de Santa Ana".)

On the left (west) side of the square is, as marked, the "Chancilleria", the great classical palace which today dominates the entire square. There is also a strange cluster of houses in the middle of the space, all on its own, but cities then were like mushroom patches that spread wherever they could.

In the bottom center, the admirable Ambrosio took care to add, as an admonition, a gallows, but without anyone hanging from it as he showed in the nearby Plaza de Bibarrambla. Just above and to the right of this symbol of justice, or injustice, we see the famous Cuesta (slope) de Gomérez, here written as "Calle de los Gomeles", the picturesque street which stretches up through up through the Alhambra forest to the palace. (The castle's ramparts are visible in the upper right hand corner of my small detail of this extraordinary work of art, as well as just of cartography.)

In the upper left hand corner flows the Darro, with the riverside promenade on its right bank given as "Calle de Darro" rather than the current Carrera del Darro. At the bottom again, the street that leads away to the left from the vanished Saint Gilles church is the tumultuous Calle de Elvira, whose name (not shown here) was the same then as now.

Soon after the Castilians took over the city, they set about making it easier for their troops - needed in case of a very possible Turkish invasion to redeem the Moorish kingdom or Islam - to get up and down to the fortress by attaching a new bridge to the old Moorish one which then was the only way of crossing the Darro without getting your feet wet. After that another bridge followed and yet another, until there were four bridges forming a wide ramp. But this was still too narrow for the crowds bustling back and forth, so in 1515 it was decided to cover the entire space, forming what is essentially today's esplanade.

During the 19th century, the river was covered from Plaza Nueva all the way across town to the Genil, over the protests of the city's intelligentsia who claimed that "a city without water is a city without soul". Whether it lost its soul or not, the center of Granada must have been very pretty, with its winding river crossed at every turn by narrow, hooped bridges, of which we are about to see the two surviving examples upstream from the church.

Plaza Nueva became the setting for great events, such as the transferral of the remains of Isabel and Fernando from the Monastery of San Francisco in the Alhambra to the shining new Royal Chapel, with the solemn procession descending the Cuesta de Gomérez to fill the square with pomp and ceremony of a kind which has never been seen since. Even the city's *moriscos* took part, wearing their ceremonial costumes. They had nothing to thank the Catholic Monarchs for, but everyone, and especially in Granada, loves a good parade and a chance to show their grief, or joy.

Just after the conquest, the fearsome Cardinal Cisneros, confessor of the Queen and future General Inquisitor, had the thousands of Arabic-language books he found in the *Madraza*, or Islamic University - most of which were in fact translations from scholarly works written in Greek and Latin - publicly burned here because he thought, or said he thought, that they were "all Korans".

Today Plaza Nueva is one of the city's most pleasant squares, overhung by the main tower of the Alhambra - *La Torre de la Vela* - and bustling with sidewalk cafés and people young and old, but mostly young, going to and fro. As we look up the elongated plaza towards the Alhambra, we have the steep, picturesque *Cuesta de Gomérez* on our right, which climbs to the entrance of the Moorish palace.

On our left is the imposing 16th century building which today houses the Provincial Courthouse, the *Audiencia Provincial*. It draws most attention for its huge Italian-style "pineapples" bristling on the roof, although they were a later addition and are criticized by purists as being out of place in a Renaissance façade (we like them just the same). The palace was originally the *Chancillería Real*, the Royal Chancellery, built after the conquest for administering the Kingdom of Castile's vast new territories which included the central and eastern parts of southern Spain and the Canary Islands, until it became the courthouse in the mid-19th century.

At the end of the square stands the picturesque Church of Santa Ana, built, like so many of Granada's churches, on the site of a mosque. It is one of the city's finest examples of the 16th century *mudéjar* style inspired by the architecture of the Moors.

Peeking up on the hill behind the church, here in my photograph, is the Alhambra's Torre de la Vela, which, as its name suggests, seems to be watching over the city...

The charming bell tower, which replaced and perhaps resembled the original minaret, has an especially oriental appearance, with its coloured tiles arranged in geometrical patterns, and exquisite "horseshoe" arches covering the tiny windows of the inner staircase. Rising from the tower's roof, the spire with its ornamental cross bears a representation of the copper spheres said by the Muslims to symbolize the universe, the *yammur*.

The ones atop the nave of the church, as well as being larger, are easier to see in my photograph below, taken early in the morning with the dawn etching them against the sky.

In Muslim countries these beautiful globes were replaced in the 16th century by the crescent moon we all know, reducing them to an anachronism only found, as far as the author knows, in Spain. The *yammur* shown below on the left, displayed in a museum, is said to be the only surviving one of its kind extant in Spain, taken from a demolished mosque. On the right we see an obviously counterfeit one, created to show the triumph of one faith over the other since, similar to the *yammur* on the Santa Ana church, it has a Christian cross and weathervane on top. However, the belltower itself is a genuine minaret of the Almohad period and belongs to the very historical church of San Juan de los Reyes, which we have already visited.

Casa de los Pisa, and "el loco de Dios" again

Looking to the left as we stand facing upstream, we see a narrow street leading up to a small palace with a massive door framed in beautifully carved stone, called *La Casa de los Pisa*. This 16th century home belonged to the aristocratic Pisa family, who were given a large tract of land in the Albaicín for the role they played in the taking of Granada. Later, they became famous due to their enduring friendship with John of God, who spent his last moments among them.

When John was dying - of fatigue and hardship - a kind lady of the Pisa family persuaded him to spend his final weeks here, because at first he was unwilling to be separated from his own patients in his hospital on the Cuesta de Gomérez nearby. The "Casa de los Pisa", as it is called, is now a museum with a splendid 16th century patio and a wealth of relics and exhibits of a religious nature, since it is the shrine of the great saint which John of God soon became. To our modern eyes, the whole thing seems shockingly luxurious and showy for the celebration of a man who rejected every form of comfort and ostentation.

This is because John with his Christian selflessness became exalted to cult-figure proportions, leading his wealthier followers to cover his relics with gifts in the hope of obtaining miraculous favours. The small, low rooms of the palace resemble the interior of jewellery boxes, plushly lined with red velvet, panelled with ornately carved mahogany, decorated with richly gilded statues.

The room in which John died is particularly surprising. A life-like wooden statue of the saint shows him kneeling in prayer before his bed, and the guide (who when I went there was also a priest) explains that the tiny, neatly outlined section of floor on which he kneels, covered in crude terra cotta tiles, is the original one - in the baroque period, when the whole house was lavishly re-decorated, the rest of the floor was covered in much finer, burnished tiles. It's as if the priests loved his simplicity but didn't really believe in it, for cultural reasons - because simplicity was equated with poverty, and poverty with inferiority. But I suppose that if it weren't that way, we wouldn't have so many fabulous churches and palaces to admire today, just cast-concrete monoliths built "for the working classes"…

River Darro and its bridges

Now we are ready to take one of the most picturesque and romantic walks in all of Spain, along the *Carrera del Darro*, the cobble-stoned street which overhangs the river and which was once one of Granada's main arteries, leading to the vanished Gate of Guadix and, from there, to the town of that name in eastern Andalucia. First we pass old Granada's last remaining arched bridges. They were built not by the Moors, as is often believed, but after the conquest, and called *Puente de Cabrera* and *Puente de Espinosa*; their original Moorish counterparts downstream were sadly destroyed when the river below Plaza Nueva was covered in the 19th century. You can cross either of these slender footbridges to explore the seedy streets which crawl up the foot of the Alhambra hill, in the shadowy quarter known as *La Churra*, with their faded, elegantly painted façades.

Next we see a crumbling, tower-like construction on the far bank of the river, with the remaining bit of an arch jutting out above the trickle of a stream, as you can see in the drawing above. This "bridge" which was really part of the city wall with a "chemin de ronde" or passageway on top for soldiers and horsemen, is the centerpiece of one of Granada's most picturesque scenes, immortalized by 19th century engravers and painters with their craze for ruins, and popularly known as the *Puente del Cadí*, or "Bridge of the Governor", perhaps because there are two spiral staircases inside the tower, one for going up and the other for going down, which – in combination with another two in the disappeared tower on the other side of the stream – made it possible to use the viaduct as a foot-bridge.

The Moors built this *Puente del Cadí* as part of a great city wall which encompassed both the old fortress (today's Albaicín) overlooking the right bank of the river, and the newer Alhambra on the left. It was also used to travel directly from one citadel to the other, leading led down from the Albaicín and bridging the stream; from there, a ramp (the remains of which can be seen jutting up among the bushes) rose directly to the main gate of the Alhambra, the *Puerta de las Armas* (which we can glimpse if we stand on our tiptoes at the door of the *Bañuelo*, which we will visit next).

The Puente del Cadí collapsed in the 17th century, and in view of the fact that the Christians preferred to go up to the Alhambra by the much more comfortable Cuesta de Gomérez, the remaining tower and bit-of-arch would probably have been demolished at that time, were it not for the fact that there was already a rich man's villa or "carmen" on top of it. At least, that is what the most famous 19th century picture we have of the monument suggests. In the engraving by the English artist David Roberts, shown below, we can clearly see – allowing for the artist's voluntary and very romantic distortions, making everything in the scene seem much bigger and taller than it was – that the tower had become the pedestal of a well-positioned house with balconies all around. Even if it was really much smaller than Roberts made it look, it would still have been an eagle's nest which any romantic, from that century or this one, would love to live in!

Although not immediately noticeable, some curious markings on the monument give us a more complete idea of its original defensive purpose. The deep slots we see in the inner side of the arch, which I have photographed below, were carved into the stone to anchor the crossed bars of the iron grill which kept intruders from entering the citadel by means of the river bed. This perspective shows how the path from the bridge led straight up to the towers of the castle.

Here, you can see how the arch once spanned the river, with the foot bridge called Puente de Espinosa in the background, and the walkway on the far right.

El Bañuelo, the public bath

The *Bañuelo*, as it is called, is one of the few remaining Arab baths in the city, and in Spain. The Christians took care to stamp out the Moorish institution of the public bath. Washing was considered unhealthy, because dangerous germs could enter the body if the pores were kept open. It was also widely believed to be unmanly because, the Spaniards claimed, it reduced virility, proof of which they claimed was the cowardliness of the Moors in battle.

This *hammam* - known to the Moors as the "Bath of the Walnut Tree" and built in the 11th century to serve the mosque which then stood next to it - was only spared because it was, once again, part of a private home. It is one of the most ancient and complete Moorish baths still conserved in Spain.

You enter through a small patio full of potted flowers and enter the bath's shadowy, vaulted rooms, perforated with star-shaped steam vents - tiny hinged windows which were lifted when the heat became uncomfortable for the bathers. Of special interest are the terra cotta water pipes visible in one corner, curiously resembling segments of bamboo, and the capitals of the supporting columns, some of which are Roman and others taken from the ruins of the great palace of the Caliphs of Cordoba, *Medina Zahara.*

When you visit the Alcazaba, the old fortress of the Alhambra, and are enjoying the splendid view of the Albaicín below, you will be able to look down onto the domed roofs of the Bañuelo with their steam vents, if you search them out carefully in the labyrinth of streets...

Two convents, and the Casa de Castril

A few steps on we come to a bend in the river, where we see two long façades separated by a broad Moorish-looking tower with tiled roof and arched windows, all of which forms a great bulk which seems to sag under its own weight and antiquity. Both of these edifices were built immediately after the Christian conquest, the Franciscan *Convento de la Concepción*, standing on the site of a Moorish hospital or *maristán*, and the *Convento de Santa Catalina de Zafra*, originally a Moorish palace given by the Catholic Monarchs to their Secretary, Hernando de Zafra from whose hands it went to the Dominican Order. It still contains, in a hidden corner of its labyrinthine interior, a ruinous Moorish patio of the same period as the Alhambra.

These vestiges of the old Granada always make me think that the two religions, after so many centuries of rivalry and hatred, have at last melted into a crumbling but somehow convivial mass. Even the handsome alabaster baptismal font in the convent church, which we see on our right as we step through the door, if we are lucky enough to find it open, was once the fountain dish of a courtyard where prayers were said, with brow pressed to the ground and body turned in the direction of Mecca. You may notice, as you pass by, signs announcing *Venta de Dulces*, literally "sweets for sale". Most of the cloistered nuns of Granada make traditional marzipans and flaky, cream-filled pastries, with distinctive names such as bacon from Heaven, little cheeses of Bethlehem, saints' bones, and chestnuts of Santa Isabel. But they all have one thing in common, namely that they are very sweet! In the shadowy entrance hall of the Convento de Zafra, and around the corner from the Convento de San Bernardo too, you simply have to ring a bell, tell the nun whose silhouette appears behind a grill what you want and wait until the rotating window turns toward you with a bag of "dulces" on it, placing the requested sum of money in its stead.

By far the most beautiful monument of the riverside is the one that follows, the *Casa de Castril*, which currently houses Granada's archaeological museum, thus making it doubly attractive to the curious traveller. It is home to magnificent collections of prehistoric, ancient and medieval artworks found in the region, with extraordinary examples of the cultures of the Iberians, Visigoths and Moors, including the lamp of the Great Mosque of Granada. Those who have visited my town, Montefrio, will take special interest in the prehistoric remains discovered in *Las Peñas de los Gitanos*, particularly the slate scratched with the stick man representing a hunter, called the *piedra de Montefrío*.

The palace in itself is a jewel of *granadino* architecture, with its elegant and secluded courtyard, surrounded by columns and wooden balustrades. The small but very distinctive façade is carved, encrusted really, with a delightfully exuberant version of the early Renaissance style.

Among the cherubs and phoenixes is depicted the coat-of-arms granted to the same Hernando de Zafra (the palace is named for the village of which his descendants were the lords) for his services in the drawing up of the surrender treaty. Zafra's coat of arms, as we can see just above the door, is carved with a square tower representing the Tower of Comares, the Alhambra's hall of state, because, during the siege of the city, the loyal Zafra had to enter it secretly with the document which he had drawn up, in order to obtain Boabdil's signature.

Below is an enlargement of what is certainly the oldest known depiction of the symbolic tower, realistic enough to be easily recognized.

A curious, sealed-up balcony can be seen on the upper corner of the façade with a large inscription above it reading ESPERANDO LA DEL CIELO, literally "awaiting that which is found in Heaven". None of the often far-fetched explanations for this ensemble have been proven, but the one that seems most convincing to me is the following.

When Zafra's descendants built the Casa de Castril, they had to clear away the ruins of a Moorish palace which was famous in Granada for a tragic love story, so in true Renaissance style the decoration of the façade was made to allude to it. The Moor who owned the palace had a lovely daughter whom he kept locked away on the top floor, but a notorious, well-born rake managed to get messages through to her declaring his love. One night the father surprised the suitor's lackey delivering a letter in her room and, thinking that the messenger was the author of the amorous message, had him hanged from the balcony, in spite of the young man's pitiful pleas for mercy.

Since the cruel father refused to listen, the victim could only cry out to Allah, "I shall await Your divine justice in Heaven", and this is apparently the meaning of the inscription. The girl was forbidden to ever appear in public again and the balcony bricked up, so that she soon went mad and finally took her own life, and to perpetuate the legend all this was shown on the new façade.

The most commonly told version of this tale among tourist guides is that it took place not during the Moorish period but in the 16th century, the villain being none other than Zafra's heir and grandson (also called Hernando de Zafra). This revisionistic updating of the story may I think be discounted as rubbish, since no man hoping to get into Heaven - not even the reputedly unloveable Zafra - would have carved a memorial to his own crime, on the very front of his own home! With the war against Granada's Mohammedans still fresh in Spanish memories, the balcony with its pathetic inscription was more likely a way of showing, once more, how cruel and unjust Christianity's main enemies were.

From here on there are no monuments of any special importance of their own, but, rather, a feast of beauty at its most romantic pitch: the plunging river gorge, a *mudéjar* church - San Pedro - hanging on the edge of the precipice overlooking the stream, the wooded slope on the other side rising almost vertically to the Alhambra's faceless towers....

Downstream along the Darro, a decrepit-looking house a few steps before getting to Plaza de Santa Ana has a similar, although certainly not as ancient coat-of-arms over the door as the one we have just seen, in which are carved, much more clearly, the eternal symbols of the Christians' triumph over the "heathen" inhabitants of the city, and the Alhambra.

Here are graphically assembled, starting at top left, the Holy Cross that protected the knights on their way to Granada, the Alhambra itself shown as a typical castle, the keys which were extracted from the Moorish king by Zafra in exchange for the deceptively generous treaty, and in the lower right what seems to be a farm with pigs and palm trees, perhaps representing the domain he was granted by the Monarchs for his services.

In the next picture of *La Riberilla*, as the ancient stretch of riverside is sometimes fondly called, we can just barely see the stream flowing under the one-arched footbridge...

Paseo de los Tristes

The street leads into a broad esplanade known as the *Paseo de los Tristes*, the "Road of the Grieving ", because this was the old path of the funeral processions which went up to the cemetery on the Alhambra hill. Officially, it is called the *Plaza del Padre Manjón*, the priest who, at the end of the 19th century, founded the school for poor children of the Sacromonte. The good man's bust stands in the middle of the square, but up near the far end.

In the 18th and 19th centuries the plaza was the site of primitive bullfights and public festivities, with crowds so large that the river had to be covered with scaffolding and bleachers for everyone to have a seat. The picturesque lookout tower which overlooks the esplanade at the narrow, downstream end is called *La Casa de las Chirimías* and was built in 1609, with Granada's coats of arms on the front, decorated with the symbolic pomegranate. The name *chirimía* comes from a wooden flute which was played, along with trumpets and drums, to accompany bullfights. The musicians stood in the highest floor of the tower, in the two arches, while the master of ceremonies and other dignitaries sat on the ground floor. The floor in the middle was reserved for the judges and tribune, in the persons of the Lord Mayor and the "Twenty-four Squires", the *Caballeros Veinticuatro* who sat on the city council. It must have been like a Goya painting, with so much pageantry and noise!

[Another such building once stood on the south side of Plaza Bibarrambla, where the city's main events were held, including the *autodafés* described earlier. It was called La Casa de los Miradores and was designed by the famous 16th century architect Diego de Siloé, as a very elegant palace whose façade was entirely composed of gracefully arched balconies, to accommodate the local dignitaries and their families. Unfortunately the building was destroyed by fire in the 19th century.]

Crossing the stream by the Paseo de los Tristes is the *Bridge of Chirimías*, the last version of which was built in 1882. But it no longer leads anywhere except to the ghostly ruin of a sort of haunted house in the style of a dignified French villa, with its grey roof like an old maid's bonnet, totally out of place against the medieval and oriental background of the Alhambra Hill. It is said to have been built as a hotel in the early 20th century, but soon had to close down because, being sunk in the river gorge in a place which the sun seldom reached, the damp invaded its rooms from the surrounding woods, creating so much mildew that the *granadinos* contemptuously baptized it the "Hotel Reuma", for the rheumatism it was said to cause in the guests' already creaky bones. Lovers of Granada have clamoured for it to be demolished for many years because its style clashes with the Alhambra, but the years passed and now it has become such a familiar and nostalgic sight that most people prefer to keep it. There are even plans to transform it into some sort of cultural center, using modern technology to overcome the dreaded *humedad*.

Nowadays, tourists and *granadinos* alike come to the Paseo de los Tristes for its outdoor cafés, enabling the curious traveller to sip a well-iced *vino de verano* as he gazes up at the towers of the Alhambra, which seem to be hanging in the sky like so many Chinese lanterns...

From here, we can take three different paths, each of which has its own charm and interest.

We can follow in the steps of the grievers of yesteryear by crossing the bridge at the end of the plaza and going up the hill to the Alhambra on the broad footpath known as the *Cuesta de los Chinos* - the "Slope of the Pebbles", because it's paved with smooth stones from the river bed (*chino* in Spanish means both Chinese and pebble). This is a pleasantly bucolic way of reaching the Alhambra and takes us directly below the ramparts and under the bridge which connects the main palace to the Generalife gardens.

But if the curious traveller wants to escape from Granada's joyous crowds altogether, he or she can - after crossing the same bridge at the end of the plaza - take the long path which continues upstream, through the woods to the *Fuente del Avellano*, the "Spring of the Hazelnut Tree", famous for the literary gatherings which took place there in the early part of the 20th century, attended by poets and writers such as Federico García Lorca and Angel Ganivet.

The third path takes us up the Cuesta del Chapiz, which turns left at the end of the plaza, and into the Sacromonte...

Sacromonte, gypsies
and martyrs

This unique part of Granada is famous for the gypsy caves, but the gypsies were neither the first nor the last people to live in them. Long before the Oriental nomads arrived in Spain, the Arabs had discovered that the soft stone of the hill was ideal for carving out underground homes, and the gypsies simply moved into them after the Moors departed. In the 19th century, writers and artists of the Romantic Movement, most of them English and French travellers in search of picturesque oddities, immortalized the gypsies of the Sacromonte, who also inspired poets and musicians such as Lorca and Falla.

When I first stayed in Granada as a student, in 1961, the place was a filthy slum with gypsy kids running naked on the dirt paths. Since then, the traditional inhabitants - forced out of their caves by massive flooding and landslides, especially in the very rainy winter of 1963 - were moved away to new low-income housing projects in the north of the city, leaving the stage free for the next migratory wave: that of the rich hippies and life-stylers from the industrialized, or if you wish rich, countries.

The paths are nowadays paved and the caves have kitchens, toilets and Internet connections. I know one computerized Englishman, a fellow translator who rents his very attractive grotto tucked away among the cactus trees for a price comparable to that of a flat in the center. The owner, a painter who lives in the cave next door, is... Japanese!

We can discover this picturesque and scenic quarter of Granada by climbing a little higher along the Cuesta de Chapiz until we reach, on our left, the Placeta de Albaida, which we cross, taking on the far right hand side the Cuesta de los Chinos (another "Slope of the Pebbles" than the one which goes up to the Alhambra) until we reach the winding walkway called the Vereda de Enmedio, which overlooks the city like a balcony, with superb views of the Albaicín and the Alhambra.

Here we will undoubtedly catch a glimpse of the local fauna I have described, along with the few old gypsies who stayed on or returned after the flooding because, quite sensibly, they didn't want to live in dreary flats.

But the only real street of the quarter is the *Camino del Sacromonte* - the first turn on the right when you go up the *Cuesta de Chapiz* - along which you will find the updated version of the gypsy flamenco caves or *zambras*, where busloads of tourists are given a glass of table wine and an hour of song-and-dance which varies greatly in quality. The truth of the matter is that the performers in these places are invariably excellent singers and dancers, and guitarists too, but are sometimes told by the cabaret owners to "play up" to the tourists in a rather embarrassing way.

You can climb all the way up to the rather lonely *Abadía del Sacromonte*, the "abbey" which is the long brick building which we see on top of the hill, famous in all of Spain for its *Via Crucis*, Way of the Cross. Along the winding road you will see the Stations of the Cross, each surrounded with a cluster of crucifixes contributed, over the centuries, by Granada's guilds of craftsmen. They say that when pilgrimage to the shrine was at its peak, in the 17th century, there were more than 1,000 stone crucifixes on the hill, creating a sort of forest which, with the passing of time and the general decline of religious devotion, has largely disappeared.

At the summit we come to the Abbey and its church, standing among a strange jumble of domes, crucifixes and small constructions which seem to have sprouted out of the hard soil like mushrooms. Some of them are nothing more than entrances to the underground grottoes, that lead down into a twisting passageway, with on either side cavities carved in the rock that contain the relics which were discovered there centuries ago, the most famous of which are the bones of San Cecilio, and a painted carving of his head. There is even a large stone on the floor of a chapel which, according to tradition, can help single women who kneel to kiss it find a husband, which explains why it shines with such a glowing patina.

But catacombs are always fun to visit even when they don't contain anything of real interest, and you might think this is just another of them, if you hadn't read the next chapter of this book first, that is. Do so and you will understand that in Granada, everything has its strange secret.

The story of how the "mountain" came to merit the name of "sacred" tells us much about the pathetic fate of Granada's *moriscos* who, even though they converted from Islam were never fully accepted by the "old Christians", and it also gives us an idea of the inexorable decline of the Catholic Church that began in the Age of Reason.

The bizarre story of
the "leaden books"

At the end of the 16th century, two *moriscos* dreamt up the idea of forging some texts - known as the *libros plúmbeos* or "leaden books" because they were enclosed in sheets of lead - which they then "found" in a cave of the hill, in the hope of improving their sorry lot as Christians of Arab origin, given that after the bloody Moorish uprising of 1568, any trust the old Christians may have had in the religious sincerity of the new Christians had sunk to its most abysmal point.

These tablets preposterously described, in Arabic, the martyrdom of Granada's first bishop and patron saint, San Cecilio, presented as a pre-Islamic Arab who had introduced himself into the peninsula at the time of the Roman colony and converted to the faith of the persecuted Christians, sharing the same fate as them.

The hoax was cleverly designed to drum up sympathy for those beleaguered *moriscos* who had not been expelled after the rebellion, and for many years the lie worked, at least for the Church, which lost no time in building an enormous abbey in the "sacred" place, as a center for *romerías* or mass pilgrimages. To paraphrase one of the many authors who have written on the subject, "the false discovery dramatically stimulated the religious fervour of the *granadinos*, in a century when faith in the Catholic doctrine was being weakened by the new reform movements then raging everywhere".

The Vatican finally denounced the counterfeited Arab texts, but it took a very long time to do it, precisely because the two *moriscos* had also "found", along with the leaden plates, the supposed relics of the saint who had been brutally executed in the 3rd century.

The churches of Andalucian towns did a thriving trade with the bones, locks of hair and other anatomical parts of outstanding Christians, even buying and selling whole corpses which were then displayed (and in some cases are still displayed) in glass-covered coffins, since the presence in a church of holy relics increased its prestige in the eyes of the faithful, who in turn increased their donations. This type of commerce seems despicable to us today, but in those superstitious times it was seen as being quite normal: the faithful needed miracles, and the relics improved their chances of getting them. The two *moriscos'* daring attempt to advance their political interests by making an opportune discovery was in itself nothing new, since centuries earlier the remains of Saint James (Santiago) were found in much more incredible circumstances in Galicia, just when the military drive of the Reconquest was most badly in need of a new religious site to defend.

When the Vatican did intervene - almost a century later - it did so with characteristic shrewdness, hanging on to the part of the story which served its purposes and dumping the rest: the Pope declared that the "books" which claimed that the saint was an Arab were fake, but that the relics found with them were genuine. In this way it shook off the embarrassing link with Christendom's traditional enemy while keeping alive what had then become the centerpiece of the highly popular shrine of the Sacromonte.

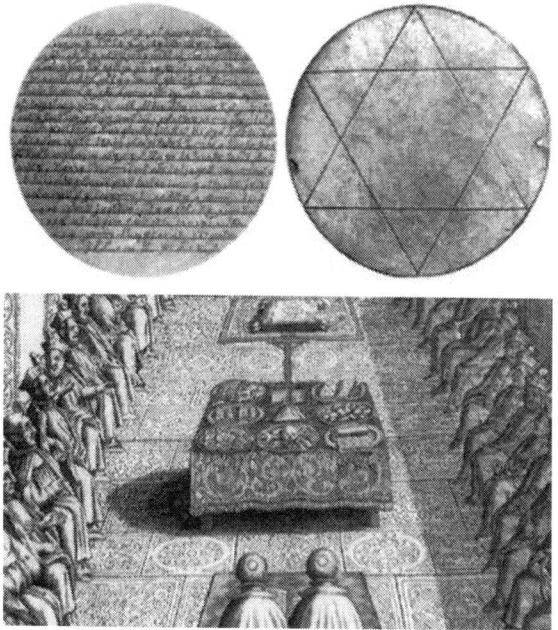

Several centuries later, the Holy See finally returned the fraudulent texts to the city, so that today the *granadinos* can gaze upon this strange remnant of their past, the desperate attempt of a community to save itself from extinction.

ALHAMBRA AND GENERALIFE

The romantic mirage
of the Alhambra

My mother used to tell a very different sort of story about the Alhambra which makes more sense to me now that I have lived so long in Spain. While she was spending the winter of 1960 in Montefrio, she befriended the young son of her next door neighbour, who used to come to watch her painting every afternoon when he got home from school. She was shocked to discover that the boy, who was 12 or 13, had never visited the Alhambra and offered to take him herself the next time she went to town. Since he had never been to Granada either, except to visit his grandmother in hospital, the outing was a big event in his life.

But as they walked through the legendary rooms of the palace, she noticed that he seemed to grow sadder and more silent, rather than enchanted, as she had naively expected. Finally, she got him to admit why he was so crestfallen. It was because the walls were not covered in gold and jewels, as all the songs and stories he had heard seemed to suggest, but only in colourless plaster. His illusions had been shattered forever, and for all we know he has never since desired to go back to the place.

I myself have visited the Alhambra many times with the greatest pleasure but, without wishing to shock the readers, I can understand just what he meant. The walls were never covered in gold and jewels, of course, but they were richly painted and hung with fabulous tapestries - yet all we see now are the exquisitely carved, but drab, plaster motifs. And the palatine buildings themselves are by our standards really quite flimsy and rudimentary, as if the Moors had simply recreated their desert tents in brick and alabaster. The only original features of the architecture are the decorative elements: the tapestry-like relief work covering the walls, with floral motifs and the text of the Koran, and the stylized "stalactites" hanging from the ceilings. The structural components: the arches and columns, the fountains and baths and the inner gardens, were all adapted from the Roman models which the Arabs so admired.

So in all honesty I have had to ask myself why we are so enamoured of the place, to put it in down-to-earth terms. Well, the answer is precisely that there is nothing down-to-earth about the Alhambra, because its magic is caused by a combination of felicitous circumstances which is simply impossible to reproduce. The Alhambra Palace is an ephemeral architectural "happening" which draws its strength not only from structures and forms, but also from the surrounding nature, the radiant light, the wild irregularity of the terrain, and, of course, the legend.

Because we, unlike that little boy from Montefrio in the year 1960, know about the legend - we know what the Alhambra represents. The culmination of seven centuries of Moorish culture in Spain, an exotic element which, like a transplanted organ, survived for a while in the foreign body and then was rejected, expelled, leaving only a few towers and gardens and fountains. This is what predisposes us to value the Alhambra's aesthetic message, makes us willing to fill in the gaps, imagine the past splendours, sympathize with the departed Sultans who were too weak to hang on to their paradise. The little boy was not jaded enough with his own Western culture - based on progress, strength, reason, solidity - to find any charm in this mirage frozen in time, this inconsequential gesture *par excellence* which we call the Alhambra of Granada.

The way up to the Alhambra

The Cuesta de Gomérez, now lined with souvenir and craftwork shops, was the Christians' main way of getting to the Palace of Carlos Quinto in the Alhambra, climbing up through the ravine between the *Cerro de los Mártires* and the *Cerro de la Sabica*. The Moors used it too, as well as the Puerta de las Armas, and called it "the Slope of Gomérez" because, being so close to the palace, it was inhabited by the Sultan's bodyguards, chosen from a fierce tribe of Berber warriors called the Gomeras.

[It is interesting to know that these warriors ruled over the Canary island called La Gomera, to which they also gave their name, which in Spain took on the Visigothic suffix *ez* meaning "son of". When King Boabdil surrendered the city to the Monarchs in 1492, he gave them these fearless bodyguards as part of the agreement, and some of them were recruited to accompany Columbus on his first journey to America. We know that a few stayed one, because there are families with their surname today in the Dominican Republic.]

We go through a great monumental gate in Florentine style, created under Carlos Quinto to take the place of a smaller Moorish gate. It is popularly known as the *Puerta de las Granadas*, the "Gate of the Pomegranates", and is decorated with the stone carvings of three huge fruits bursting with seeds. The original name of the city (*Garnata* or *Granata*) is only an approximate homonym of the Spanish word for pomegranate and believed to originally mean "fortress", but under the Christians the fruit became Granada's symbol nevertheless.

[Gates such as this one were built in all the towns which were on the path of the new king when he travelled south to be married in Seville in 1526, before preceding to Granada. The one in Madrid became known for a blazing sun painted on its façade, and although it was demolished in our times to make way for a business building, its popular name became associated with this crossroads at the center of the city, which we still call the *Puerta del Sol.*]

Now, we enter the Alhambra forest, irrigated everywhere with babbling *acequias* and delightfully cool in summer. The trees are tall but noticeably young as trees go, which is because they were all planted by the Christians, not the Moors. In medieval times the hill had to be stripped of all vegetation for military reasons – there could be no bushes for any attackers to hide behind. This part of the castle grounds was originally the site of a cemetery where noble Moors were buried, such as the Sultan al-Ahmar, founder of the Nasrid dynasty.

As soon as we go through the gate, we leave the main road and take the footpath on the left, where the 16th century marble cross makes it clear to all those who enter that they are in the home of Christians and not Mohammedans...

This takes us past the Renaissance fountain, picturesquely weather-worn, known as the *Pilar de Carlos Quinto*, to the towering *Puerta de la Justicia*, the "Gate of Justice ", with the Hand of Fatima engraved above its arch, whose five fingers symbolize the Koranic fundaments of single deity, prayer, fasting, charity and pilgrimage to Mecca. The key carved in relief over the inner arch symbolizes Allah's power to open the gates of heaven. The Madonna above the third arch was placed there soon after the conquest by the Catholic Monarchs, and, of course, jars irreconcilably with the rest. In any case, it is only a replica of the original, which has been stored away.

The Moorish gate that moved

Those who aspire to a more intimate knowledge of the city's history should, on some other occasion, take the main road up through the woods. On the left, forgotten among the trees and mossy stones, stands the *Arco de las Orejas*, the "gate of the ears" which once stood near the Plaza Bibarrambla in the city center. By the 19th century it had long since fallen into disuse and become a picturesque bird's nest of garrets and topsy-turvy dwelling places.

Then, at the turn of the 20th century, four entrepreneurs, who have since become deservedly infamous, wanted this decrepit obstacle to (their) economic progress torn down, and they naturally won out over the protests of the city's artists and writers. Like the footbridges over the Darro, the gate was removed, and the only consolation of the "lovers of Granada" was to keep the stones of the original construction and, many years later, have them reassembled here in the Alhambra Forest, where the skeleton of the gate now stands. The gap created by the demolition, a few steps from the Plaza de Bibarrambla, became a street with the same proportions as the gate and called *Callejón del Arco de las Orejas*. Although the established name of the gate was *Bib-Rambla*, "Gate of the Strand", it got its popular name, "Arch of the Ears", because, during the Moorish period, the ears and other extremities of law-breakers were cut off in the square and then nailed to its walls for all to see. An English writer known for his love of Granada has said that the same should have been done with the ears of the four entrepreneurs.

Here is a photograph taken in 1870 of the gate, looking through its arches to the Plaza from the Calle Salamanca, which remains a busy shopping street today.

Even though the art of photography was still new, Granada had its own portrait shop as you can see from the sign on the left, and I would imagine the picture itself was taken to advertise its services. The passers-by have, for that purpose, been arranged in a motionless row in front of the door, to show what this new invention could do.

Granada's "other" writer...

Further up the hill leading to the Alhambra stands the curious statue to the leader of Granada's intellectual movement at the turn of the century, the writer Angel Ganivet, whose dignified bust gazes down at the bronze deer spouting water from its mouth.

I say "other" because Lorca, with his irresistibly universal, and popular, appeal, naturally eclipses all the city's other *literati*. Also, the tormented figure of Angel Ganivet was anything but a symbol of the sensual, exotic Andalucia which Lorca projected. But he was just as *granadino* as Lorca, with the difference that he was more cerebral and austere. We foreigners fancy that Spanish intellectuals are all passion and spontaneity, but in fact most of them are of the tormented, navel-staring and distinctly solemn sort.

Ganivet was however far from being "typically Spanish", in any sense of the term. During his very short life – even shorter than Lorca's – he mastered five languages and produced almost all of his opus in... Finland! He was the author of the erudite *Idearium Español*, a biting analysis of the history of his compatriots, whom Ganivet contemptuously accused of "living on a peninsula but thinking like islanders", by which he meant that they were backward and living in a vanished past. He was a friend of other ferocious critics of the demoralized Spain of his time such as Pío Baroja and Miguel de Unanumo, and a leading member of what is known as the "generation of 98", the fateful year of 1898 marking the loss of Spain's last great colonies in the Pacific and Caribbean, the "pearl" of which was Cuba. The villain was of course the growing mercantile and military power of the United States of America, which easily swept aside the archaic and postulating heirs to the once-great Spanish Empire.

Ganivet, born to a well-off family of flour-millers, left Granada forever at the age of 22. After finishing his studies in Madrid he was appointed, more for his linguistic talents than his diplomatic ones, to the consular service in Antwerp and Helsinki, taking with him his mistress and the mother of his child, the temperamental Amelia. But in Helsinki he fell in love with their Russian neighbour, the language teacher Masha, in whose arms he discovered an intellectual sort of woman he had never known before. Unfortunately he ended up without any woman at all, because Amelia's fits of jealousy so frightened Masha that she fled the country, and afterwards Amelia, who was no model of fidelity either, ran off with another man.

Ganivet, deeply disenchanted with love and life, was transferred to the Spanish Consulate in Riga, on the other side of the Baltic Sea. There, during an endless winter night, when he was only 33 years of age, this ill-starred but brilliant Andalucian threw himself into the freezing waters of the city's river. After living in Granada, one can hardly blame him!

The Latvians pulled him out, but he jumped in again and died. It seems that his natural tendency to depression – his father also committed suicide, when Angel was a child – was greatly aggravated by syphilis, which he may have caught in the brothels of La Manigua, Granada's old red light district, which I will describe further on...

As we press on up the hill, we pass the venerable Washington Irving Hotel, built in the 19th century. It was Granada's first lodging house comfortable enough for the wealthy Americans and Europeans doing the grand tour of Europe who ventured this far south from civilization. We continue up the hill to the entrance to the Palace.

Angel Ganivet

In the Alhambra Alta

Monastery and Parador of San Francisco

We walk up the long, winding path lined with huge cypress trees to the sign saying *Generalife* straight ahead and *Palacios Nazaries* to the left. We turn left for the palaces and go over the *Puente Nuevo*, or "New Bridge". The original path from the main palace to the Generalife was through a military gate down in the ravine, but when the Alhambra became a National Monument, in 1870, and was arranged to receive visitors, the two areas were more comfortably connected by the bridge.

At the same time, underground pipes were installed to do the job of the original aqueduct which supplied the palace with water, and which we can see on our left as we cross. Its continuation (identified by the sign *Acequia Real* – "Royal Canal" - is visible on the far side of the bridge, broken off to make way for the foot path which now intersects it.

We are in the *Alhambra Alta*, the high part of the citadel which, as its Arab name -*Madinat al-Hamra* - indicates, was a city in itself. The path takes us through gardens planted among archaeological excavations of tradesmen's workshops, servants' quarters, stables, noble houses and military barracks.

We pass on our left a sign calling our attention to the *Puerta de los Siete Suelos*, "The Gate of the Seven Floors". The Christians named the gate for a vanished seven-storied watch tower, although its Moorish name was Gate of the Wells, for the underground reservoirs which stood nearby. The gate is famous because it was through it that last Sultan of Granada, Boabdil, rode out to declare his surrender to the Christians camped in Santa Fe - one of the conditions of which was, precisely, that this gate be sealed forever, which it was. Further along, below us on the left in a great pit, are the excavated ruins of the palace belonging to the Abencerraje family, the rebellious nobles whose fate we shall learn of further on.

In an arch of the sculpted hedge, on our right, we catch sight of the steeple of the *Parador de San Francisco*, one of Spain's finest hotels and flagship of the *parador* chain. It was previously a Franciscan monastery built over and around the remnants of a Moorish palace that belonged to a member of the royal family. The monks lived in the palace until the 18th century when it was largely demolished and replaced with the current building, which was abandoned after the State expropriation of church property. Its large bell tower overlooks a low building nestled among orange trees and aromatic bushes, giving the place a timeless, secluded charm of its own.

Since the Paradors are also national monuments, visitors are allowed to see the historical part of the hotel, even if they're not staying there, a long rectangular space which is curiously open to the sky. This was originally the nave of the monastery church, whose roof collapsed at the end of the 18th century and, with the abandonment of the place in the 19th century was never rebuilt.

We - and here I think I speak for all true lovers of beauty - are immediately struck by the lavishly decorated, if faded, Moorish alcove at the far end of the nave, facing us like a great, open seashell. But before going further we should pause a moment to picture in our minds just how this extraordinary building became what it is today. As with so many places in Granada, the successive transformations can be hard to follow, so bear with me...

First, in the 14th century, there was here, within the Alhambra citadel, an aristocratic Moorish home belonging to a Prince of the Nasrid dynasty,. Immediately after the conquest

Isabel decreed that it should house a Franciscan monastery, since she had pledged, during the siege of Granada, that her first action would be to thus pay homage to her beloved saint. The monastery also became her tomb, because she and Fernando died before their great mausoleum, the Royal Chapel, could be made ready, and they were temporarily buried - on the Queen's own written instructions - in the monastery church, whose Moorish architecture was then still unchanged.

Their bones were some years later transferred to their final resting place in the Royal Chapel, and the Moorish building was demolished and rebuilt in the 18th century. But in memory of its royal guests, the by-then legendary alcove was spared, and allowed to retain its function as the chancel of the monastery church. The place of the graves is marked with a great marble tombstone on the floor which reads *Queen Isabel the Catholic was buried here from 1504 and her husband King Fernando from 1516. Their remains were taken to the Royal Chapel in 1521.*

The vaulted ceilings of the Moorish alcove are sumptuously decorated with the same "stalactites" or *mocárabes* we see in the Alhambra, and the walls engraved with the eternal plaster-tapestry of abstract motifs and holy inscriptions in Arabic. The very fact that the Christians allowed these Muslim symbols - which include the words "Allah is the only God" - to adorn their Monarchs' tomb is in itself a remarkable tribute to the artistic talent of their fallen adversaries.

On the left side of the roofless nave there is a tiny chapel (originally, of course, part of the church), which has been lovingly preserved, with its baroque altar piece and *mudéjar* or Moorish-style wooden ceiling, from which hangs a handsome incense burner taken from one of the city's mosques.

To the right of the former church is the monks' cloister, which is now the Parador's most charming space, complete with its two-tiered rows of graceful Renaissance arches and richly coloured floor tiles. The cloister was built on the site of the inner garden of the Moorish palace, which, it is said, was similar in style to the Generalife's. The only trace of its existence is the water channel or *acequia* which still runs next to the central fountain. As you know from the foreword, this is a sentimental place for the author because it's where the seed that became this book was planted.

When we see such an enchanting place, discreetly fitted out as a luxurious and elegant hotel, it is hard to believe that, after the damage caused to the monastery, first by Napoleon's troops and then the State expropriation, it was then allowed to be used as a tenement house and, when it was falling into ruin, as a donkey stable. Thanks to the intervention of Granada's artists and intellectuals, and notably the Alhambra's director, Leopoldo Torres Balbás, it escaped demolition in the early part of the 20th century and was fully restored, to prepare the ramshackle wreck for its new life first as a retirement home for artists and intellectuals, and later as the Alhambra's grand hotel.

This picture shows the former monastery after it was first restored, when it became a rest home in the 1930's.

This is what today's magnificent and well-appointed hotel patio - once the monastery cloister - looked like before the restoration began...

It is even more interesting to visit this unusual building when we think that, in all likelihood, Christopher Columbus stayed here on his return from America, when the monks still lived in the original Moorish building. We know, at least, that he hunted with King Fernando in the surrounding woods. The Queen was known for her great frugality, and it is said that one night she invited Columbus to stay for dinner, saying "Admiral, please eat with us tonight, because we're having chicken". And there is good reason to believe that she uttered these humble words here, in what is today the luxurious Parador.

Church of Santa María de la Alhambra

We leave the Parador and walk down the broad *Calle Real* – "Royal Street" -passing, on our right, the incontestably ugly church of *Santa Maria de la Alhambra*, built on the site of the palace mosque. The column with the marble inscription on top, standing before the church, commemorates the martyrdom of two Franciscans who, it says, were slain by the Moors when they recklessly undertook to preach the gospel in front of the mosque, in the year 1397, almost a century before the Christian conquest of the city.

The adventure of the two friars has much to teach us about medieval fanaticism. They set out from their monastery in Cordoba to preach in the land of the Mohammedans, knowing that they would be sure to find holy martyrdom. Once they arrived at the seat of the Moorish realm, Granada, they hid in a cave where they spent several days readying their spirits for the ordeal that awaited them. One would take turns tying the other to a tree and attacking him violently with lashes and rods. When they had been sufficiently hardened they went to the Great Mosque of the Alhambra (on the site of the church we have before us), where they beseeched the Moors going in to pray to give up their Satanic beliefs. Incredibly, for several days the only reaction of the Moors was to order them to leave the kingdom, but finally King Mohammed's patience ran out and, unsheathing his scimitar, he left his palace to personally give them what they were seeking, with his own royal hand.

Puerta del Vino

At the foot of the slope we come to the most ancient part of the Alhambra, the *Alcazaba* or fortress, a cluster of enormous towers overlooking the city. They have no particular decorative or aesthetic value, which is why we can only walk around and over, but not inside them.

Leaving the Palace of Carlos Quinto and walking towards these towers, we see on our left a small but particularly beautiful, reddish-coloured Moorish gate standing curiously on its own on the esplanade. This is the *Puerta del Vino*, the "Gate of Wine", one of the oldest constructions of the Alhambra and the subject of several well-known paintings, as well as the title of a musical piece by Debussy. Since the Arabs did not - or were not supposed to - drink wine, the name is believed to be a mistranslation. In fact it was called, in Moorish times, the "Red Gate" because of the reddish stone of the arch, but the Arabic words for *red* and *wine* are so similar that they got mixed up by the new occupants of the palace. We can I think disregard the far-fetched explanation propagated by some tourist guides to the effect that in the 16th century the wine drunk by the inhabitants of the hill was delivered here.

The *Puerta del Vino* was once connected to the outer wall and separated the city of the Alhambra Alta from the fortress and royal palaces, but due to the many changes made in this area since the conquest, it was left standing all on its own without any apparent relation to the fortifications. Proof, however, that it was a major point of passage is the grisly fact that when the Moors killed the son of the King of Castile in a battle near Granada, his body was triumphantly exhibited before it for all the passers-by to see, like a hunting trophy.

Linguistic confusion

Many of Granada's Spanish place names taken from Arabic originals are the result of haphazard translations. After the conquest, many of the old place names were mistranslated into Spanish, usually because in Arabic a slight difference of inflection can change a word's entire meaning, and few Spaniards had a scholarly knowledge of the tongue. As well as the *Gate of Wine*, really the *Red Gate*, this occurred with the *Puerta de la Justicia* - "Gate of Justice". The word for justice, or law - *charia* - was confused with the very similar word for esplanade, in reference to the flat area within the walls of the Alhambra (the current site of the Palace of Carlos Quinto) to which the gate led. Its real name in Arabic, therefore, is Gate of the Esplanade.

There are two opposing translations for the name Albaicín. Although it was traditionally thought that it meant "quarter of the falconers", research has shown that the Albaicín was the quarter of the people of Baeza, since the refugees from this town, captured by the Christians, founded the outlying village which eventually gave its name to the whole citadel. This curiously means that the root of the name of this intrinsically Moorish quarter is the original Latin name of the old Roman city, *Beatia*, which the Arabs adapted as *Baeza*.

Some historians have even challenged the standard translation of Alhambra as "red palace", claiming that the currently ochre towers could not have been called red, even when (as some suggest) seen at sunset or during a fire that broke out below, for the good reason that like all Moorish palaces they were always whitewashed. They contend that the name actually refers to the founder of the Nasrid Dynasty, *al-Ahmar*, which literally means "The Red" because he was famous for his reddish beard. Therefore Alhambra would mean "Red-Beard's Castle" rather than "Red Castle", a theory strengthened by the fact that other Moorish towns and castles were commonly named for the people associated with them, such as Gibraltar, Calatayud, Valladolid, Guadix and even the royal citadel whose ruins were discovered near Cordoba, *Medina al-Zahara*, which was itself an early predecessor of Granada's Alhambra.

Also, the generally accepted translation of Generalife – "Garden of the Architect" – due to the Arabic-derived Spanish word *alarife*, meaning "construction foreman" seems highly improbable. It is more likely that the meaning is "Heavenly Garden of the Sultan", since *arif* means "chief" or "leader", not architect. When Arabic-origin words like *alarife* entered the Spanish language they often took on meanings of their own.

[Another reason for mistranslations was the custom of adapting Arabic words to those which most resembled them in Spanish, as in the case of the broad bean, known in Spanish as a *judía* - "Jewess" - simply because it resembles another word for bean, *alubia*, which itself comes from the Arabic *al-ubiya*. After 25 years of living in Spain, I still smile to myself when someone calls a bean stew "a bowl of Jewesses"...]

The Christians in their ignorance of Arabic believed that the name of one of the halls of the Alhambra, the *Sala de la Barca* or "Hall of the Ship", referred to the hull-shaped ceiling, only because of the similarity between the Arabic *baraka* - "good luck" - and the Spanish *barca*. But the proper translation is Hall of the Blessing, due to the text inscribed on its walls which recommends the Sultan who built it to Allah. Those familiar with the Arab world know that when someone is said to have *baraka*, it is because God is protecting him with good luck.

And there is the mysterious meaning of the name of the city itself. All we can be sure of is that when the Arabs arrived they found a community of Jews living below the hill on which the Alhambra now stands, and referred to it in their writings as *Garnata-al-Yahud*, "of the Jews". The Christians eventually adapted the name to the Spanish word for pomegranate, *granada*, even though it had no relation to the Arabic name for the fruit (*romá*).

But it was natural for the Christians to use the word which was phonetically most similar to their own Castilian tongue, as a result of which, ever since the conquest, the squareish fruit with its spikey crest has been depicted on shields, mosaics, seals and official documents as the symbol of the city - and, of course, on the monumental Puerta de las Granadas which we have just seen.

Lorenzo wonders about... *Grenata*

On my recent travels through the French countryside just north of the western Pyrenees I came across two towns both curiously called *Grenade*, which is the French name for our city of Granada. One is *Grenade-sur-Garonne* and the other *Grenade-sur-l'Adour* - in a region ill-suited for the farming of pomegranates - and both derive their names from the Latin-based Occitan word *Grenata*, meaning a place rich in grains, with bountiful harvests of wheat. And south of the eastern Pyrenees there is the Catalonian farming town Granadella, and yet another in Extremadura, Granadilla, whose medieval name was Granada until it had to be altered to avoid confusion with the recently reconquered city of the Alhambra.

Could it not be that the Jewish farming village which the Arabs discovered on the left bank of the river was called by a name derived from a similar Roman word? I previously accepted the explanation that the origin may be an Oriental word meaning fortress or shrine, but now I find myself leaning towards this less poetic but more logical one.

Just look at the well-watered plain, *La Vega de Granada*, stretching away from the city to the west. It was for the ancient inhabitants a huge oasis in a dry and rugged land that provided them with food all year round. Nothing more natural, then, than for the place to have been gratefully called the Latin equivalent of our granary or "breadbasket".

...and *Iriberri*

Another intriguing place-name theory has been proposed for Iliberis, the name given by the Romans for the citadel they built on the Albaicín hill. Following Roman custom, it was a Latinized version of the place's original name in one of the prehistoric languages which are now lost - all but for one, the tongue of the Basques, who are now believed to have been the original Iberians, descended directly from the native people of the peninsula. We know from the vast majority of Spanish and French Basque toponyms that these shepherds and woodsmen were fond of descriptive names for places (and later, when surnames were invented, for the families that came from them) such as "good river" for Bayonne (*bai*-river+*on*-good). Given that there are places and families called *Iriberri* or *Iriberry*, "New Town", could not *Ilbyr-Ilibiri-Iliberis* come from that ancient name, Iri+berri, "town+new", indicating that it was founded by a tribe of Basques who had, without leaving any documented traces because they had no writing, wandered as far south as Granada? The fact that "iri" was originally "ili" makes the similarity between "old Basque" for New Town, "iliberri" and the Latin Iliberis.

Patio de los Aljibes

Facing the twin towers and high up on our left on the ivy-covered wall is a large marble plaque. It commemorates the heroism of the invalid soldier who cut the wick of the series of bombs which Napoleon's troops had prepared to blow up the entire palace, when, humiliated, they left Granada in 1812.

The broad, sandy esplanade which we cross next is known as the Patio de los Aljibes, which means "Plaza of the Cisterns", although there is nothing in sight which resembles a water tank. However, just under the surface there is – unknown to most - a huge and ancient cistern, of such proportions that, when it was built 500 years ago, its interior was compared to the nave of a church. Soon after Granada was taken from the Moors, the new master of the Alhambra, an illustrious grandee called Iñigo López de Mendoza of whom I shall speak further on, decided to build in what was then a ravine separating the Nasrid Palaces and the Alcazaba, a brick-and-mortar underground tank with a roof supported by rows of sturdy arches, for the purpose of storing the water that was channelled down from the mountains and through the citadel. The Spaniards feared that if the Turks invaded Spain, they might lay siege to the Alhambra and cut off the water supply at the source. With the new *aljibe*, or cistern (an Arabic-derived word which is pronounced *al-HEE-bay*), the soldiers quartered in the fortress could hold out for over an entire year.

When Carlos Quinto ordered his great palace to be built, 30 years after the cistern (although the name of the place says "cisterns" there was in fact only one), the roof of the construction was gradually buried under the debris thrown there by the workers, which over time filled up the entire ravine. The new esplanade was useful for holding military ceremonies, fairs and even bullfights, but it also took away destroyed much of the setting's charm, since it put the three surrounding monuments – the fortress, the Moorish gate and the Carlos Quinto palace – on the same level as the terrain, rather than majestically overlooking it as they had done before.

The cistern was made especially large, with its capacity of 1,600 cubic meters, so that, as well as being consumed by the few thousand people who lived in the citadel, it could supply the many thousands in the city below. Since the Turkish threat eventually faded away, this additional function became a profitable business. The precious liquid was sold by the jug-full to the picturesquely-attired "aguadores" – water vendors – who carried it through the streets on their colourfully-harnessed donkeys, crying out as they went *"¡Agua de la Alhambra!"*. That meant that by comparison with water from the city's wells it was very cold, given that the cistern was only filled once a year, in January when the mountain stream was at its lowest temperature, and, stored in the massive underground cistern, more or less stayed that way right through the stifling months of July and August. For a *granadino* trying to "beat the heat", drinking a glass of "Alhambra water", carefully poured out by an *aguador* was like, today, cooling off with an ice-cold lemonade or beer, and at a similar cost.

The next picture is the roof of the cistern, which now serves as a resting-place for tourists, with its entrance door for the yearly cleaners on the left and, in the background, the Carlos Quinto Palace and Puerta del Vino; and a view of a section of the cistern's interior (not open to the public) with its monumental arcades, and some rain water which has leaked through the roof and gathered at the bottom...

The large plaza we see today - or to put it more realistically, the bare and unsightly yard - is best known as the setting for the historic flamenco contest organized by Lorca and Falla in 1928. It was the first official impetus towards elevating this complex form to flamenco's current artistic status. The idea that uneducated people could create great music was still a revolutionary one, and the *Concurso del Cante Jondo* -"contest of the Deep Chant" - created such a stir that one old gypsy walked across half of Andalucia to sing for the *señoritos*, "the gentlemen", in the palace of the *rey moro*.

Alcazaba, military fortress

We proceed towards the gate between the two towers, have our ticket punched and climb a long staircase to the top of the round tower (built by the Christians) and known as *El Cubo*. This is undoubtedly the best spot for enjoying the splendid panorama, because the tower overlooks not only all of the higher, Moorish part of the city, but the low-lying Cathedral quarter as well.

The view that unfolds before us as we step up to the parapet is simply a thing of magic, like a scene from the Thousand and One Nights. The Albaicín lies directly in front, a vast mound of white walls, tiled roofs, flowering gardens and Oriental towers. We can see down into its labyrinth of alleyways and streets, and using the church steeples as landmarks retrace our wanderings through this ancient Moorish *medina*.

Starting at the bottom left is the church of San Gregorio; half-way up the hill, the church of San José with its minaret-bell tower distinguished by the Moorish horseshoe-shaped arched window; and on top, the church of San Miguel Bajo. On the highest point of the right side of hill is the Mirador de San Nicolas, with its long balcony and tall white church - we can see the crowds of tourists and young people sitting on the parapet like a multi-coloured caterpillar, gazing over the river valley towards us and the palace. Far up on the mountain on the right the church of San Miguel Alto overlooks the city, where the great wall built by the masters of the Alhambra marches over the arid hills. On the very far right is the Sacromonte and the gypsy caves, with their winding trails and cactus trees. All that is lacking, if you're a Lorca lover like me, are the double silhouettes of "mules and shadows of mules" which he evoked in his poem to this quintessentially *granadino* place.

And down among the roofs of the city, immediately to our left, rises the Cathedral's square bell tower, its round dome covered in enamelled tiles and, splaying out below, its fan-shaped buttresses. The deep groove of the Calle de los Reyes Católicos winds like the river which it covers through the old city center: Plaza Bibarrambla, Alcaicería, Puerta Real...

What makes this place unique, however, is the bird's eye view which it gives us of the fascinating remains and monuments lying on either side of the gorge. Directly below us we see the church of San Pedro standing on its promontory above the river. On the far side of the church and to the left of the steeple is the Casa de Castril, the Renaissance palace housing the Archaeological Museum, with its graceful courtyard and two massive cypress trees rising from the far right corner. To the left of this building, facing the river, are the two convents - *Convento de la Concepción* and *Convento de Zafra* - which date back to the conquest. Moving up the river to the right we see the long plaza called the *Paseo de los Tristes*.

And from our vantage point we have a unique view of what was in Moorish times the Alhambra's main entrance, the *Puerta de las Armas*. To see it, let us walk to the left side of the platform and look towards the next tower on the ramparts. This is the *Torre de las Armas*, and contains the gate of the same name. We can see the inner side of the gate at its foot, with the long ramp running inside the wall towards us, and the remains of the fortified wall - covered in moss and bushes and lying on the hillside like a ruined staircase - which connected this gate to the bridge over the river, the *Puente del Cadí*. Seen from above, this favourite subject of Romantic painters is barely visible, an oblong stump covered in vegetation.

In this picture I took from the belltower of the Church of San Miguel Bajo, the legendary but long-disused "Gate of Arms" is in the center, just above the trees.

Just across the river from the bridge and slightly to the left is the *Bañuelo*, the Arab bath, which when seen from the *Carrera del Darro* looks like a non-descript two-storey white building. But now, to our delight, we can admire its Moorish roof, with its rows of rounded-rectangular, reddish domes, perforated with the tiny ventilation windows we have already admired from inside. Most visitors miss this evocatively Oriental detail when looking down on the city from the Alhambra - with so much to captivate the eye, it is quite understandable! - but the curious traveller will be well rewarded for hunting it out among the jumble of antiquities.

I have repeated below my photograph of the bath seen from above which is part of the chapter devoted to the Bañuelo, to make it easier for you to pick it out in the jigsaw puzzle of rooftops which surround it.

We continue our visit of the Alcazaba, following the signs through the Plaza de Armas, the main courtyard of the castle to which led the gate of the same name, containing the excavated foundations of the original military barracks and stables, and then into the Torre de la Vela, where we climb to the top of this great tower. Below on the right we can see part of the arch of the *Puerta de las Armas* peeking over the lower wall.

The rather historical photograph below, taken of me on the Alcazaba fortress when I was a student in Granada, shows the Albaicín with remarkable clarity. The Church of San Cristóbal is on the left just next to my chin, the Mirador of San Nicolás on the far right, and behind my shirt collar rises the Sierra de Parapanda in the distance.

Granada, winter of 1961

The sign-posted path leads us from the Torre de la Vela out along the southern wall, where there is a charming garden of date palms and orange trees. You are advised to rest a while on one of the benches before moving on to the most spectacular part of the visit, the Nasrid Palaces. But before we reach them, we will unavoidably pass in front of the ***Palacio de Carlos Quinto***, as it is known.

The *Casa Real de la Alhambra*, "Royal House of the Alhambra", which is its original and official name, is a massive Italian-style building which sits squatly in the middle of the Alhambra, creating an unfortunately brutal contrast with the delicate Moorish surroundings. The fact is that, here, this imposing monument depresses rather than impresses, bluntly reminding us that material - and military - power always takes precedence over the hedonistic fantasies of the spirit.

Who was "Carlos Quinto"?

First of all, asks the truly curious traveller, who was this guy whose name keeps popping up all the time in Granada? Before answering the question, I must increase your confusion by specifying that in Spain, although he has always been known as Carlos Quinto (Charles the Fifth), his real title was King Charles I. He was the grandson of Isabel and Fernando, whose daughter Juana married the Habsburg prince Philip, whose home was in Ghent, where Charles was born. Philip came to live in Castile with his wife, the Queen Juana, but there was great fear that a foreigner might inherit the throne, and this is thought to have been the cause of his sudden death after drinking a glass of chilled water...

Whether the handsome Philip was assassinated or not, Juana went mad with grief and had to be shut away for the rest of her long life. Her son Charles was brought up by his grandparents in Ghent, and when he reached the age to become King was sent to Spain to take his mother's place as Charles I of Castile.

But, soon after, he inherited from his grandfather the throne of the Holy Roman Empire (which was the ostentatious name given to Germany), as Charles V, in Spanish *Carlos Quinto*. He always used this second, and in political terms inferior title - Spain was then the first world power - for the simple reason that, while his insane mother lived, and even though she was hidden away in the cell of a monastery, sleeping on the floor in her own excrement, she continued to be the Queen. Charles, therefore, although recognized as King, was in reality the Regent until she died, just several months before his own abdication forty years later.

The young King married his cousin Isabel of Portugal, in Seville, and then brought her, with a huge following of courtesans and dignitaries, to Granada for their honeymoon in 1526. Unexpectedly, Charles not only fell in love with his bride – highly unusual in state marriages – but also with the city, which still resembled the Moorish *medina* it had been before the conquest. He was particularly impressed by the abundance of water flowing everywhere, unlike Castile where it had to be brought by hand from distant wells and carried in ox-carts along dusty roads to be sold to those who could afford it. Instead, there were ingenious channels which brought the water down from the sierra to fill deep *aljibes* or underground cisterns where the people could fill their jugs, and to water the orchards below on the plain. It must have reminded him of his native Flanders and the fertile Burgundy of his youth, so different from the arid and austere country which he had inherited from his grandmother's uncouth and unruly family, the Trastámaras.

These very life-like carved portraits of Carlos and his bride, displayed near the altar of the Royal Chapel, show his prominent lower jaw, due to an hereditary overbite, and also that Isabel was, as famed to be, a beautiful young woman, although fated to die young.

Carlos dreamed of having his own sumptuous palace in Granada so that he could come down to stay in this beautiful land whenever his royal duties allowed it. But, Carlos being a very serious King, there also had to be a strong political reason for building such a grandiose monument. Granada was not just a very healthy and pleasant place to spend a holiday, it was for Catholics everywhere Spain's "New Jerusalem", torn by Carlos' pious grand-parents from the hands of the *mahometanos*, a symbol of triumphant faith where so many churches, monasteries and convents had been built that all over Spain, and abroad too, it was being proudly called...*Cristianópolis!*

Today it seems strange that the city which fascinates us for its Moorish heritage could have, in other times, represented something so different. Simply, religion no longer has much influence over our tastes and preferences. When the young Diego Velazquez, the painter of *Las Meninas*, visited Granada on his way from Madrid to Italy via the port of Malaga, the only drawing he made wasn't of the Alhambra (which nothing suggests he even visited) but the new Cathedral, considered at the time to be as fine an example of the new style as Saint Peter's of Rome, the aesthetic model for all men of erudition. If Velazquez knew about the existence of the old Moorish Palace at all, it would have been as the quaint residence of a despicable and vanquished enemy, not at all as a landmark of universal art.

So Carlos decided to have a great palace built for himself, next to the enclosed patios and ponds of the Moorish kings, which he planned to use for outdoor events. But he wanted his palace to have the modern European comforts befitting a man of the Renaissance, with amenities such as doors, windows and fireplaces, for those winter nights when the wind blows down from the *sierra*...

This was quite understandable, since the Moorish palaces, if one considers them as everyday living places, are more similar to tents than real shelters against the winters of a region which half the year is quite cold. To finance the construction, the King levied yet another tax on the city's beleaguered *moriscos*, who agreed to pay rather than face further repression.

Even though we may find the palace, in these surroundings, rather obtrusive, it is historically important for several reasons: not only was it the first great building in the Renaissance style built outside of Italy, but it was also the first full-fledged royal palace ever to have been built in Christian Spain, given that

Charles' forefathers had all lived in uncomfortable, rugged fortresses and monasteries in the north.

But the project went sour from the very beginning. First, during the otherwise idyllic summer the Monarchs spent in Granada, there was an earthquake which frightened Isabel so badly that she could not later be persuaded to return. And once the work began, the tribute of the *moriscos* soon proved to be insufficient to finance a building of that scale, as a result of which the pace of the work had to be geared to the collection of the tax.

The construction ended up taking no less than 110 years, twice that of Notre Dame Cathedral! The man who was to be the occupant of the house, Charles, died when the work was still "only" in its thirtieth year, and in its fortieth year, just when the workers were going to lay the rafters, the main source of funds dried up with the expulsion of the *moriscos* towards other parts of Spain, where they received a cold welcome, in reprisal for the rebellion of 1568.

Nevertheless, the work moved forward unstoppably, swallowing up generation after generation of workers. It is awesome to read the account of the construction: the first architect, Pedro Machuca, devoted his whole life to one part of the palace, and after his death was replaced by his son, until he also died of old age and was replaced by another, who continued until his death... until the whole thing was abandoned when Spain's economy collapsed in the 18th century. The gaping carcass that survived, just because it was so solid, was finally given a roof and fitted out under the Franco dictatorship, not to be a royal palace but a national museum. In fact, no king of Spain ever lived there at all.

The photos below show the palace still without its roof at the end of the 19th century, with the top of the circular colonnade jutting up into the sky; and as it is today, after the mid-20th century restoration. The steeple in the background belongs to Santa María de la Alhambra.

The palace's massive façade is distinguished by its Renaissance roughened or "rusticated" convex stones.

But it's most popularly for its huge bronze rings for tying horses to, which, in view of their size and height, must have been, like their heroic masters, of mythological proportions. The famous circular courtyard is surrounded with tall columns which give it a strongly Roman and imperial look - a veritable temple to the God of Power...

I must confess that the only thing which gives me any aesthetic satisfaction in this building are the reliefs on the bases of the columns around the main door, carved by an Italian master with great delicacy and realism. They depict the Emperor's many battles throughout Europe and the Mediterranean against those Mohammedans and Protestants who to his ever-lasting disappointment refused to embrace the Catholic faith.

The net effect of all this on the curious traveller, in spite of the fact that we are assured that the architect, Pedro Machuca, was a disciple of Michelangelo, is less than enthralling, so after glancing at the bleak, monumental circular courtyard we shall eagerly move on to the fairy-tale palaces of marzipan which, after all, are what we have journeyed so far to see...

Still, there are hidden jewels of European (in this case baroque) art in the Alhambra, like these dolphins in the Adarve Garden, even if almost nobody notices them!

The Nasrid Palaces of the Alhambra

Nazarí, or "Nasrid", is the name given to the last dynasty which ruled over Granada, founded in the early 13th century by Yusuf ben Nasr. This was the "glorious twilight" of the Moorish presence in Spain, during which the Emirs only survived because they accepted the sovereignty of the Christians in all but internal matters.

Therefore we should not let ourselves be deluded by the "official version" put out by ill-informed tour guides and glossy travel magazines, which make a business of singing the glories of Moorish Spain. We would be simply wrong to think that the monument we are about to visit was the center of Moorish power at its height, simply because the luxurious palaces which the last rulers of Granada built here reflect nothing more glorious than their desire to publicly enjoy what they could, in the private knowledge that "all was lost". If they behaved with arrogance, it was partly bravado, to convince their subjects, and their enemies, that their splendour would last forever. For historians, the Nasrid Kingdom is a synonym of hedonistic decadence, proving once more that cultures produce their best art when they're on the way out.

Unfortunately, also, the history of Granada is often presented, for political and commercial reasons, as having occurred on an enchanted planet of its own that was immune to events and developments elsewhere, which is far from being the truth. Therefore, to explain to you how the Moors' Iberian adventure came to its ignominious end, before you step inside the Nasrid Palaces which were their fabulous swan song, I have drawn up an as-short-as-possible history of the preceding millennium in Spain, with some whimsical illustrations for the purpose of lightness…

With the collapse of the Roman Empire, the colony of Hispania, like all of Western Europe, was invaded by peoples whom the Romans contemptuously called "barbarians", because they spoke languages which, to the refined Latin ear, sounded like an endless *ba-ba-ba*. The first Barbarians who took advantage of the crumbling of the Empire were the Alans, the Sueves and the Vandals.

It is even said that it was the Vandals who gave their name in Arabic to what is now Spain, although it finally came to mean the southern part of the country, Andalucia. The Vandals, after sacking the peninsula, crossed the Straits of Gibraltar to Africa and Carthage. There, they caused such terror that the place from where these savages had come became known as "land of the vandals", in Arabic *al-Andalus*.

But the only Barbarians who put down roots in Hispania were the Visigoths, who came from the Black Sea where they began their short history as Goths. The legend has it that the Goths were divided into two groups when, fleeing other barbaric tribes, they tried to cross the frozen Danube on foot. The ice broke in the middle, leaving half of them on the west side and forcing the other half back onto the east one. Those who got across to the west were known as Ostrogoths and the ones who stayed in the east, until they found another way of crossing, were the Visigoths.

They didn't arrive in the Empire as invaders, but as useful allies of the Romans, who they gave them the task of crushing the other Germanic tribes which had spread over all of Europe and the Iberian Peninsula. They were mercenaries, but once their job was done they chose Hispania as their new home, ruling over it for two very chaotic centuries.

The reign of the very violent Visigoths, or *visigodos* as they were known here, was catastrophic for the inhabitants of the old Roman colony. For example, they didn't believe in dynastic succession but instead had each new king chosen by a council of nobles, which although it sounds democratic led to fierce physical struggles among the candidates in which the strongest always won.

[The only admirable thing the Visigoths seemed to have done was make jewellery out of gold and coarsely-cut gems, in a strong, simple style which seems curiously modern to us. The Archaeological Museum of Madrid has among its treasures one of their greatest creations, the ceremonial crown suspended above the head of King Recesvinto.]

But it was the Visigoths who set Spain free, even if they did so as tyrants. Hispania was still a colony nominally dependent on Rome when they arrived, but once they took power they effectively became the first kings of a new country. Even more important, in spite of being adepts of an early sect of Christianity called Arianism which had already been condemned by the Catholic Church as heretical, they soon converted to the Roman church of the natives. This meant that, when King Recaredo renounced Arianism and converted in the year 587, he became the first "Catholic King" in a line which led to Isabel and Fernando, who always boasted of their Visigothic rather than Roman origins.

The strife created by the rule of the Visigoths left the field open for other invaders, who this time came from Arabia. After the death of the Prophet Mohammed, his followers launched a vast campaign of conquest which reached as far as India to the east, Somalia to the south and, to the west, the old Roman colony of Mauritania.

The peoples of this North African region were also called barbarians by the Romans, giving them their current name, Berbers. The Arabs quickly converted them to Islam and herded them into their armies, for the assault on their main goal, the rich country which lay on the other side of the Strait of Gibraltar.

Spaniards call the invaders of the historic year of 711 *moros*, Moors, because they came from the Kingdom of Mor, but in reality the soldiers were from many far-flung places, such as Egypt and Syria, and they fought as much amongst one another as with the Christian enemy. The only link that bound them together was their religion, but since many had just recently been converted, it still had less strength than their tribal loyalties.

The Moors soon got their chance to enter the peninsula. After the death of the Visigothic king Witiza, the throne was seized by a rival, Rodrigo. King Witiza's son naturally wanted the throne for himself, and sought help from a fellow Visigoth who lived in his castle on the North African coast, and who set about recruiting an army of Berbers to come to the pretender's rescue.

The Moors weren't long in seizing the opportunity. The Moorish general Tarik landed with his troops at the foot of the Rock of Gibraltar, giving it its name which in Arabic means "Tarik's mountain" – *Jabal-Tarik*. After Tarik had won a single battle in favour of the dead Visigothic king's son, the Moors forget their agreement and decided to stay on and conquer everything that lay before them.

And in each city they were received not as enemies but as liberators. The wretched subjects of the Visigoths hoped that the Moors would rid them of their tyrants, especially the Jews, whom the Visigoths, upon becoming Catholics, had attempted to baptize by force. This well of resentment made it possible for the invaders to subjugate almost the entire peninsula in about as long as it took them to ride over it on their horses.

The vanquished Visigoths took refuge in the mountains of the north, where they soon launched the series of very short battles and very long truces which, a thousand years later, historians called the Reconquest. They recovered the northern third of the peninsula with little difficulty, because the Moors decided to pull back and entrench themselves to the south and east of the cities of Toledo and Zaragoza.

During the first three centuries, then, the Christians and Moors were separated by a vast central plateau, a no-man's land which the Arabs called *Castilya* because it was scattered with the enemy's castles. The Moorish part, al-Andalus, was shared among the various tribes, largely hostile to one another, while the feudal Lords of Castille, Navarra and Aragón in the north went on with their endless fights over succession and land.

The memory of the Moor's long stay in Spain is cherished and mourned by today's Arabs, not only because it was a "promised land" full of wealth where their Emirates flourished, but also because it was discovered at the most important moment in their history, when their religion was still in its youth. Mohammed died without leaving a male heir, and the resulting power vacuum enabled the Caliphate to fall under the rule of a powerful Arabian family, the Hummeyads, who for strategic and mercantile reasons had moved their court from Mecca to Damascus. In less than a century, a rival family in Baghdad, the Abassids, challenged the legitimacy of the Hummeyads, claiming that the throne belonged to them because they were the descendants of Abbas, the uncle of the Prophet, which meant that the very blood of Mohammed flowed in their veins. The long-term effect of the schism that this caused was the creation of two antagonistic sects, Sunnites and Shiites, but the more immediate one was that the Abassids massacred the Hummeyads and moved the center of the Caliphate to Baghdad. Only one Hummeyad managed to escape alive, and disguised as a shepherd he fled to the distant Cordoba where he found support among the partisans of his family, who put him on the throne as Prince Abderramán I. Even today, he is known to the Arabs as *Abderraman Addakhel*, "he who sought shelter".

The feats of the Hummeyads brought unbelievable glory to the Moorish realm in Spain. Cordoba soon became the largest city of Europe, with street lamps, running water, a multitude of public baths and its enormous Mosque.

In less than two centuries, the Emir who then reigned, Abderraman III, pronounced himself to be the Caliph - the supreme leader of all of Islam – although there already was one in Bagdad. Among other achievements, Abderraman stamped out the rebellion of the Mozarabs, the old Christians who had remained in al-Andalus after the Moors invaded, and he built an enormous palace, or "palatine city", in the hills near Cordoba, called Medina Zahara, named "City of Sarah" for his favourite wife.

The new Caliphate of Cordoba had to defend itself not only from the Christians in the north, but also the old Caliphate in Baghdad, as well as a third Caliphate which had been founded in Tunis by the Fatimid sect of Islam.

Thanks to the strength and prestige of Abderraman's great military chief, known as *al-Mansur* by the Arabs and *Almanzor* by the Spaniards, the Moors of Cordoba were able to remain united and ward off attacks from the enemies of the Caliphate. And to fully understand the lust for glory and revenge that drove the men of that time, both Christians and Moors, we can do no better than to consider the story of...

...the bells of Santiago

On one of his terrifying raids in the north, the chief Almanzor got as far as Santiago de Compostella, the great shrine of the Reconquest, where he humiliated the Christians so badly that they waited several centuries to take their revenge, and in the most spectacular fashion.

The city surrendered to the dreaded Moor, who rode straight to the Cathedral and without dismounting went inside to let his horse drink the holy water from the baptismal font, causing horror among the Christians.

He then ordered the bells to be taken down from the steeples and had them sent to Cordoba – hundreds of miles to the south – where their clappers were removed and oil lamps hung around the rims so that they could, as trophies of war, light up the Great Mosque. This was what the Moors did whenever they could lay their hands on what they saw as being the hated symbol of Christianity, the bell.

Almost two and a half centuries later, King Fernando III reconquered Cordoba from the Moors. The first thing he did was to enter the Mosque on his horse and have the bells taken down and stripped of their lamps – which, for the Christians, were the hated symbol of Islam – and have them dragged back, over mountains and plains, to their ancient home in Galicia.

The death of Almanzor led to the collapse of the Caliphate, and in the year 1031 the old Arab elite was driven out by the Berber peasantry, who sacked and burned the great palace of Medina Zahara. The Moorish kingdom was split into dozens of self-serving factions, or *taifas*, each with its own *reyezuelo* or little king, Seville, Badajoz, Zaragoza, Toledo... and Granada, which under the Zirid dynasty built a great fortress on the southern end of the Albaicín hill. Each of the chieftains wanted to rule over his corner of the country, and grab as much land as he could from his neighbours, all in the noble pursuit of adventure and war.

The picturesque multi-state of the *taifas* barely lasted half a century and only deserves its place in history for marking the end of a great Empire. But, for us, with our love of cultural over military values, it was distinguished by an unusually high level of refinement and open-mindedness. Harsh religious laws were relaxed if not flouted, and the "little kings" in their luxurious courts all strove to attract the most illustrious poets and scientists who under their protection were even allowed to study Greek philosophy, since many of them longed to give Islam a more humanistic, rational dimension, just as had been done with Christianity. But the less educated people, the Muslim clerics and the common people, mistrusted any attempt at change. The masses rebelled against the Sultans, who were forced to silence, and even imprison and exile the humanistic reformers whom they had sheltered in their midst.

The "little kings" also enjoyed practicing the arts of war. The larger states gaily swallowed up the smaller ones, to such a point that the *taifa* of Toledo expanded to include the territory of three of Spain's current provinces, while the *taifa* of Cordoba was hacked down to barely the size of the city and its outlying areas. Each king maintained friendly relations with one or the other of the Christian kingdoms, and pledged loyalty to him in exchange for his support against his antagonistic Moorish neighbours. In the meantime, the military power of the

Castilians, with the Crusader movement gathering force in the rest of Europe, became greater every day.

Castile struck the first of a long series of blows in 1085, when King Alfonso VI, taking advantage of riots in Toledo, conquered the city without a drop of blood being shed. The ancient capital of the Visigoths and symbol of Iberian Christianity, but very weak taifa, had at last been recovered, causing jubilation throughout Europe. But the catastrophe terrified the Moors, and the King of Seville desperately called for reinforcements from Fez and Marrakesh.

This desperate act predictably led to a century of Berber domination and repression, since, once more, the outsiders whose mission was to save the country became its masters. The very next year the warriors of the Almoravid clan crossed the Strait of Gibraltar "like a cloud of locusts". They crushed the *taifas* one by one, and rigorously reimposed order and Koranic law. The time of freedom and tolerance was over, and the Jews and Christians had to flee from Moorish lands, mostly to Toledo. It was this exodus which gave birth to the School of Translators under the patronage of King Alfonso X "The Wise", where learned Jews, as well as Christians and Moors, translated, from Arabic into Latin, the works of ancient Greek scholars which were presumed lost since the fall of the Roman Empire.

[In reality, copies of all the classical works existed in monasteries around Europe, but since the monks considered them to be "pagan" books they kept them from public view, for fear of promoting heresy. Constantinople also kept the ancient writings, but few scholars were able or willing to cross the pirate-infested Mediterranean to consult them.]

Fifty years later, another tribe of Berbers, the Almohads, rose to power in Morocco, invaded Spain and took the place of the Almoravids. This fanatical sect, whose name means "partisans of the only God", continued the strict application of religious law, to the great regret of the people, who nostalgically looked back to the easy-going rule of the *taifas*. The Almohads are more familiar to us historically because, unlike the less creative Almoravids, they have left us fine monuments such as the Giralda, the bell tower or minaret of the Cathedral of Seville, with its brocade-like patterns of raised brickwork.

The Christian rulers had reason to fear that the Almohads wanted to take back the kingdoms of the north, and prepared their counter-attack, with help from the Frankish knights, since we are now in the time of the first crusades. In the year 1212, a mighty coalition of forces gathered to crush the Almohads near the source of the River Guadalquivir, in a place known as Las Navas de Tolosa. Once this was done, the Christian victors were free to move down the valley to Cordoba and Seville, which they took soon afterwards.

It was then that the small provincial town of Granada entered the stage of history for the first time. Since it stood high up among the rugged mountains of the south-east it was much harder for the Christians to reach, but now it was next in line, as the only Moorish city left to be conquered. The *granadinos* were terrified to find themselves face to face with such an enemy and sought the protection of a famous warrior in northern Andalucia who had lost his own castle to the Christians. His name was Nasr, although he is better known by his family's name, *al-Ahmar*.

Alhamar, as he is called in Spanish, began his reign over Granada – which then roughly included the current provinces of Granada itself, Almeria and Malaga – by making a very clever diplomatic move. He realized that it was useless to oppose the Christians and that he would have to submit to their will. He therefore made himself the vassal of the Castilian king, promising to pay him a huge tribute in gold (equivalent to one fifth of the kingdom's tax revenues) and also to defend him in war, even if it meant fighting against his Moorish brothers. Fernando III knighted him, and when he attacked Seville in 1248, the warriors of Alhamar fought alongside the Christians. After the death of *Fernando el Santo* as Spaniards have called Fernando III since he was beatified, a delegation of Nasrid warriors was sent from the Alhambra to follow his funeral procession like all the other vassals of Castile.

The *granadinos* also depended on their new masters economically. The Christians had cut off the trade route across the Straits of Gibraltar which left them without the necessary shipments of grain and cattle from Morocco, which now had to be imported from the Christian north. This food trade and the yearly payment of the infamous *parias*, made in gold brought by the Moors from Sudan, were very profitable for Castile and zealously controlled. Periodically, one of the Sultans would refuse to pay the tribute, until the Castilians punished him with a devastating raid and seized what was owed, plus recovery costs. Even so, when it suited them the Castilians would waive the payments, in exchange for Moorish support against external enemies such as, for example, Portugal.

However, by the mid-15th century the Castilians reached the decision that, profitable as it was, the old *modus vivendi* with the Moors had to come to an end, and what made them decide to break their bond with Granada was fear of the Turks. The Ottoman Empire was becoming more powerful, and when in 1453 the Turks conquered Constantinople, the living heir of ancient Rome and the sole bulwark between West and East, a wave of panic spread through Europe. Castile, particularly, feared that the Turks might use the coastline of the Emirate of Granada to invade the peninsula, as the Barbary pirates had been doing, to plunder the seaports of property and also people, to be sold as slaves.

[The grim fact these terrifying raids continued and even increased after the Moors were finally expelled from Granada is testified by the watch-towers the Spaniards built along the long coast facing Africa, and which seem so romantic to us today as we drive between Alicante and Malaga. Sentries would take turns on these *atalayas* looking for suspicious sails on the horizon, so that the villagers could head for the hills in time. For centuries Spanish churches had a special basket for alms for "the hostages in Tunis", who were dragged from their beds in the middle of the night, sailed across the sea and either sold or kept in chains until ransom was paid.]

When the devout Isabel became Queen of Castile, she saw herself as a Joan of Arc whom God had given the divine duty of ridding her country of infidels. But, more pragmatically, the Monarchs also acted like landlords evicting old tenants because, as well as being a nuisance they were slow in paying the rent. One way or the other, they believed that the Moors' presence in Granada was *la perdición de España*, "the curse of Spain", and they were determined to put an end to it.

Mexuar and the Golden Room

Our visit, unfortunately, begins with the ugly duckling, the one room which has been disfigured out of all recognition: the *Mexuar*, (mex-oo-AR). In Moorish times, this was the reception hall where the public could accede to the royal power, and receive royal justice. However, because it was the closest building to the main esplanade, the Christians later made such heavy use of the room, first as the residence of the architects of the Palace of Carlos V and then as a royal chapel, that it was re-shaped in such a hodgepodge of styles that it has, for us, no more than a passing historical interest. When I accompany my visitors through the palace, I always notice their dismay to first find themselves in this incoherent room, instead of one of the magical spaces they identify with the Alhambra.

On the walls we see painted tiles with the motto of the Spanish Empire, PLUS ULTRA, or "always further", expressing Spain's will to spread the Catholic faith around the world so that, as they put it, "the sun would never set" on their realm. The curious wooden balustrade which crosses the room like a bridge is what is left of the choir of the Chapel of Felipe V, especially created for that king's visit in the 18th century. The platform behind it, on which the singers stood, has since disappeared.

But just beyond the mutilated Mexuar, things suddenly improve. In the Islamic tradition, there is a small mosque or oratory for prayer attached to the room. Visitors are only allowed to look through the door nowadays, because the underpinnings were beginning to crack under the weight of the crowds. In any case, the oratory we see today is a modern restoration - in fact, an elegant pastiche - since the room was wrecked by the explosion of the powder-house below in the valley at the end of the 16th century. Still, from the door we can enjoy through its graceful arches a truly fairy-tale view of the Albaicín.

Next we pass through a room with open arches overlooking the valley, the *Cuarto Dorado* or "Golden Room", where visitors waited to be admitted to the royal residence. From this charming belvedere, we step down into the small courtyard with the fountain in its center, which we cross to enter a small (small for a palace) door in a high, narrow wall, engraved with elegant arabesques.

This is nothing less than the ceremonial entrance of the Palace of Yusuf I, popularly known as the Tower of Comares. It seems strange to our Western eyes that the entrance to such a great palace should be through a discreet side door rather than a mighty gate, and with a twisting and turning corridor following it. But the Moors, imitating their desert tents whose flaps were designed to keep out the dust and wind, preferred small, labyrinthine entrances, which were also useful for preventing large numbers of people from forcing their way in all at once, in case of an uprising.

Courtyard of Myrtles, Palace of Comares

This courtyard is known as the *Patio de los Arrayanes* for the fragrant shrubs growing on either side of the pond (the name comes from the Arabic word for myrtle). On the upper floor of the long side walls lived the four legitimate wives of the Sultan. The southern façade is composed of two levels of airy and graceful arches supported by slender columns, creating the effect of a great embroidered curtain, and was the dwelling place of the Sultan's children by his official wives. These were destroyed to make for the palace of the Christian king, looming up from behind like a huge granite barge about to crush a fragile Persian dhow.

Before the myrtles were planted according to legendary description, as part of the mid-20th century restoration, this vast courtyard was called *Patio de la Alberca*, for the long pond which so artfully reflects the massive tower looming above it in the sky, with at each end a fountain set in the floor like an open water lily, in which a trickle of water breaks the silence before flowing into the watery mirror...

Two old men and a girl

The ageing Sultan Muley Hasan, aware that his vizirs disapproved of his beautiful young wife, the Christian captive Isabel de Solís, resolved to humiliate them in front of the girl while she bathed in the palace's great pond.

He ordered each one of them to drink from the water in which she had bathed, to prove their reverence. One by one they reluctantly did his bidding, except a very old vizir who, when his turn came, humbly shook his head.

When the Sultan sharply asked him why he disobeyed, the vizir answered, "My Lord, I fear that if I were to taste this water, I might be filled with lust for the lady that bathed in it". Since only old men know how dangerous such things can be, the Sultan curtly acquiesced.

The tower of the lunar windows

The Moors wrote very little about the luxurious interior of the Alhambra because such knowledge would certainly breed envy and resentment among the people, and neither have they have left us an explanation for the name *Comares*. Gallego y Burín wrote, and Granada's tourist guides have ever since repeated, that it comes from the Arabic word for stained glass, *comarías*, even though the most similar word in Arabic, *kamar*, means moon and not glass or window.

Some historians say that the name comes from the village of Comares near Malaga, where the stained glass which graced the tower's windows (until they were destroyed by the explosion of the powder-house in 1590) was purportedly made. This is hard to believe, because it would have been impractical to manufacture glass windows in a village far from Granada, given the rough roads along which they would have to be hauled.

The Lebanese novelist and historian Amin Maalouf, author of "Leon the African" (a book I recommend to the readers, specifically for the first half of the story evoking the hero's childhood in Moorish Granada, in which the above morsel about the old Sultan can be found) says that Comares comes from the Arabic word for moon, *kamar*. The name, according to Maalouf, is therefore "Tower of the Moon" because, he contends, the royal astrologers climbed up on its roof, in the company of the Sultan, to study the sky at night for advance information about his political future, which is certainly true.

But since nothing is cut-and-dry in any language, and even less in Arabic, the lunar explanation - according to the research of my own Arabist-in-residence Wijjie - may also refer to the tower's stained glass windows. This is because the Arabs, who were supreme masters of the craft, distinguish between two types of window, "solar" ones – *shamsiyatt* – that are pale or clear and meant to let in light, and "lunar" ones – *kamariyatt*, which are richly-coloured to keep the rooms shady when the sun shines directly on them. They commonly abbreviate these words to *sham*, "sun" and *kamar*, "moon", so it seems that Gallego y Burín was, once more, right in saying that Torre de Comares means "tower of the stained glass windows", even if he didn't know that in Arabic the word for stained glass is "lunar".

Leaving the courtyard and entering the great tower, we first cross a long, narrow hall called the *Sala de la Barca*, which means, in Spanish, the "Hall of the Ship". The traditional explanation is that the ceiling resembles the hull of a sailing vessel, but this a mistake caused by the similarity between the Spanish word for ship - *barca* - and the original Arabic, *baraka*, which means "blessing" - a word which is inscribed repeatedly on its walls in praise of the king who built the room. The "Hall of the Blessing" was greatly damaged in a fire at the end of the 19th century and the ceiling had to be fully remade, and as you can see, the patterned plasterwork on the walls still bears the mark of the disaster.

We now enter the great tower itself, the castle keep which overlooks Granada from its crenulated roof. Its windows, now open, were once covered with Oriental stained glass windows, but these were destroyed by the explosion of the powder-house in 1590. The tower is almost entirely occupied by the Sultan's throne room, and is called the *Torre de Comares*, "Tower of Comares".

In this room as in many others in the palace, the walls are carved everywhere with the tiny shields of the Alhambra. This coat of arms was given by the King of Castile to the Nasrid Sultan when he pledged to serve him as a faithful vassal, although the clever Moor later defiantly inscribed it with a diagonal banner reading, in Arabic, "Only Allah is the victor".

The small, narrow door we see at the end of the Sala de la Barca, looking to our left as we enter, led to a rare luxury in medieval castles, a latrine, since there were usually just earthenware pots which the servants carried away when full. This mysterious-looking door is always closed, probably because toilets, even medieval ones, are not considered to be suitable for public viewing, which is a great pity since everything is of interest to the curious traveller that tells us how people lived, and live.

In a great Christian castle in Arab lands – the inverse of the Alhambra – the detail I remember best is precisely the latrines, a row of holes carved in granite seats, set on a closed porch jutting out into the sky, where the Crusaders sat down one next to the other to relieve themselves. The excrement fell straight down the outside and onto the rocky Syrian plain below.

I imagined the Frankish knights sitting there in their chain mail and white tunics hoisted up as they discussed their latest skirmish with the Mohammedans and the booty they had brought home.

Before entering the great hall let us stop a moment to contemplate several other traces of the always-crowded palace's daily life. To our right we see a tiny oratory or *mirhab* big enough for only one person to prostrate himself. It was reserved for the Sultan so that he could leave the affairs of state in the hall to make his five daily prayers. Peeking inside, we see that it resembles the interior of a sea shell, delicately carved and enveloping.

To our left there is another mysterious little wooden door which, like the latrine, is always closed. It leads to a staircase and the winter apartment of the Sultan, in the loft just above the dome and beneath the roof, where it would have been warmed by the winter sun. We can imagine the lucky man, after a hard day's work giving orders, choosing his favourite concubine, or even wife, and going upstairs to spend the night in his private rooms which we, unfortunately again, cannot see. From there he would have stepped out onto the roof with his astrologers to study the stars for any signs of what the following day would bring.

The curious niches on either side of the archway were for water jugs, so that the presumably nervous visitors could moisten their lips before approaching the Sultan with their petitions. The Arabic inscription carved above each of these jug-nooks poetically invites the passer-by to quench his thirst, thus disproving the popular explanation which some tourist guides still give, that the shelves were for storing one's slippers before prayer-time. They are still commonly called *babucheros*, for the Arabic word for the leather pointed slippers open at the back.

As we walk around the large, square room we will notice the running strips of sacred writing that are repeated over and over again, just above the painted tiles. We can see that there are two distinct styles of writing, one above the other: the upper is in the elegant, flowing "cursive" script commonly used by the Nasrids, and in modern Arabic too. But the lower one, scarcely recognizable as calligraphy, looks more like a decorative motif, all square and angular with knots and tails linking one block to the other. This is a more ancient form of writing that the Arabic we are used to seeing, and which was favoured by the Nasrids because it was more suited for pen-and-paper, or parchment. It is only used today in some wall inscriptions because of its historical importance as the script used to set down the first Korans. Since it originated in the holy town of Kufa (modern-day Iraq) it is known as the "kufic" style.

There is always a gaggle of visitors staring down at a roped-off square of floor tiles in the center of the room, as if it were an antique carpet in Versailles Palace. These tiles are much smaller than those in the rest of the floor and more ornately painted, although in very bad repair having lost their glazed finish, and would probably never be noticed if it weren't for the rope around them.

After many years of seeing this curious scene, I at last discovered what it was all about, thanks to a newspaper article in the local daily. The explanation tells us more about the attitudes of the Alhambra's 19th century restorers than the Alhambra itself. The original marble floor of the room having been removed, or stolen, the room was paved with ordinary clay tiles. To make it look prettier, these smaller, coloured ones were taken from a wall torn down somewhere else and stuck in the center of the room, as just another part of the floor. It wasn't until much later that a visiting Muslim of some social importance complained that it was blasphemous to allow people to walk on them because they were all inscribed, albeit in tiny, rubbed-out letters, with the name of Allah, so they were cordoned off to avoid causing further offence.

But neither this nor anything else could diminish the grandeur of the dome which opens above us, like a mystical planetarium. According to Gallego y Burín, the ceiling is composed of thousands of incrusted pieces of cedar wood, which still conserve some traces of the paint of their original colours. The vast ensemble represents, geometrically, the seven heavens of Islam: God, whose symbol is barely visible in the shadows and without the colours, is in the center of the dome, surrounded by the heavenly bodies, distinguishable from their whitish colour, with one of each of the four rivers of Paradise in each corner of the base. How could water be lacking in the heaven of people from the desert?

Each time I step into the hall, I get a special *frisson*, just to think that such a thing could have survived the centuries relatively untouched - perhaps because it is so high up, safely out of the reach of plunderers and restorers.

Once more, the place is not only impressive architecturally, but also, metaphorically speaking, for the ghosts of the often tragic past which inhabit it. The Sultan and his viziers, when receiving high-ranking subjects or foreign ambassadors, would sit, each in one of the alcoves – with the Sultan in the one facing the entrance - framed by the diffused, coloured light which, as we know, before the fateful explosion poured through the stained glass windows.

The halls of power

When power changed hands, the *Torre de Comares* was the setting for three momentous events.

Here, in the last days of 1491, the Sultan Boabdil held the council which decided to surrender to the Castilians who laid siege to Granada in their camp at Santa Fe. There was little to discuss, since the Moors were all too aware of the hopelessness of their predicament.

Some of them must have at that moment remembered, with dread, the pitiful fate of the similarly besieged Moors of Malaga, not so many years earlier. The Christians had promised them that if they did not surrender immediately they would all be sold into slavery for the rest of their lives, but if they left the castle unarmed they would go free. The offer was rejected, the final battle was fought, and the promise was mercilessly kept.

The story of Malaga's *Gibralfaro* fortress has much to tell us, not only about the cruelty but also the complexity of the bitter battle being waged. Most of the inhabitants of the city, who had taken shelter within the walls, wanted to surrender to the enemy in order to avoid the punishment which they knew would be meted out. But there were among them a large group of *elches*, which was the term for renegades or turncoats who had given up Christianity to become Muslims. The *elches* knew that they would be executed for treason as soon as the Castilians laid hands on them, so, having nothing to lose, they prevented the others from surrendering the castle.

When they ran out of food, after three months, the Christians finally forced their way in, everyone was put in chains, parents and their children torn apart and herded off like cattle. As usual, everything was done according to time-honoured procedure: one third of the prisoners was sold in the marketplace, one third was delivered to the Monarchs, and one third sent as a gift to the Pope. Only a few Jews managed to escape slavery, because they had relatives in Toledo who brought the gold needed to buy their freedom.

Jerusalem, from behind

Shortly after the city was taken on the 2nd of January of 1492, legend has it that Queen Isabel received Christopher Columbus here and, as he kneeled before her, authorized him to embark on his journey across the Atlantic on behalf of Spain. She had refused to finance him on several occasions before, but this time, with Granada finally hers, she was ready to launch a new and glorious exploit for her country and for the spreading of Christianity, as well as being sure to yield great profits if he succeeded in reaching China.

There is an anecdote which, although apparently true, is seldom told simply because it is so unbelievable to us in the scientific age. The Monarchs nurtured an even wilder hope than the mass conversion of pagans and a trouble-free trade route to China from the expedition. Now that they had finally "liberated" Granada, they thought they could do the same with the very heart of Christendom, Jerusalem, which had languished under the Arabs for three centuries. Imagining that Europe and Asia were relatively close and with nothing in between to get in the way of their caravels, the Monarchs calculated that an army could, after landing in China, easily march across it to the east of Jerusalem, where with the appropriate stealth, they would be able to catch the Mohammedans unawares. Since the Crusaders had always arrived from the west, the enemy would be facing the Mediterranean, making it easy to take them from behind, in a Western-movie style ambush.

[It is, indeed, known that the Portuguese, who were by far Europe's most experienced navigators, had correctly reckoned that the earth was much larger than Columbus thought. One of their trading vessels, exploring the coast of Africa in 1488, had already discovered an eastward maritime route around the Cape of Good Hope, and they hoped – as indicated by the name they gave to the southern tip of Africa – that the shortest way to get to India was not by going west but east, as they later did with Vasco da Gama. What neither the Portuguese nor Columbus could know was that his technical error would lead him to

America, a far more valuable prize than India or China. In geography as in other realms of science, small mistakes can lead to great discoveries!]

Here again, only a season after Christians had, at long last, regained all of Spain, on March 31, 1492, Isabel and her husband Fernando, seated solemnly on their thrones, declared that all Jews who did not give up their religion and convert would be expelled from the land - thus, at a stroke, giving rise to the Sephardic diaspora throughout Europe, and mainly in the countries of the Ottoman Empire, where the often wealthy and talented refugees were welcomed.

The Jews might have escaped their fate if the Monarch's fear of losing face had not been greater than their desire for gold. They were seriously considering an offer of 30,000 ducats made by the Jewish community to have the order reversed, but the Church, in the person of its Main Inquisitor, the notorious Friar Torquemada, had a special grudge against the Israelites because many of them continued to practice Judaism even though they had officially embraced Christianity. When Torquemada heard that a deal was afoot, he burst into the Monarchs' meeting with the emissary of the Jews, holding a crucifix before him, and cried "Christ was sold by a Jew for thirty pieces of silver, and you are going to sell Spain for thirty thousand ducats!", throwing the cross at their feet before striding out.

Regretfully, the Monarchs - who badly needed the money after the many battles they had waged to win Granada - called the deal off for fear of losing face, and the order was decreed.

Courtyard of the Lions

We now enter one small door, walk a few steps in a passageway and find ourselves in the most original and best-loved part of the palace. It was likened by one of the city's 19th century visitors, Alexander Dumas, to a "dream petrified by a wizard's wand". Indeed, the delicately clustered marble columns, the fabulous honeycombs of moulded plaster draped between them, with the hooded terra cotta roofs rising all around like sentinels, seem to have a life of their own, as if they had miraculously grown there, rather than been built of innate material.

The Courtyard, or "Hall" of the Lions, as the Christian conquerors called the palace, was built by the Sultan Mohammed V in the mid-14th century. No one could have doubted that Christian supremacy was a *fait accompli*, artistically as well as in force of arms. The disenchanted occupants of the Alhambra had tired of the austere, abstract architecture imposed on them by Islam and opened their minds to the freshness of pre-Renaissance Western art, with its love of nature and sensuality.

This new attitude was stimulated by the friendship which had grown up between the Sultan and King Pedro I of Castile, who had built a palace for himself in a similar "mixed" style, within the Arab fortress of Seville, using Moorish craftsmen sent from Granada by his vassal, the Sultan.

The Courtyard of the Lions, with its two preciously-designed pavilions which jut out into the garden from either end, is far more reminiscent of the Cistercian cloisters of northern Spain than of its typically Moorish counterparts, such as the one we have just seen, the Patio de los Arrayanes. Gallego y Burín, in his classic *Guía de Granada*, speaks of the courtyard's "tremulous, organic quality", beside which the other rooms of the Alhambra seem more like four-sided Korans.

Philosophically, also, the Courtyard of the Lions is different because it represents an idealized vision of nature and its pleasures. The architects wanted to represent the Garden of Paradise as a heavenly oasis, festooning the courtyard's then brightly-painted arcades with intricate encrustations, like palm trees bearing fronds and dates. There was, also, certainly, a variety of flowers and aromatic bushes planted in clay pots around the central fountain, as in the courtyards one can visit today in the homes of the Middle East.

Mudéjar, a uniquely *granadino* style

The Courtyard of the Lions is a fusion of Oriental and Western, a new genre of its own which can best be described as the unique style of Granada, which flourished here and elsewhere after the conquest under the name *mudéjar*.

But there is more: the *Patio de los Leones* is also a radical departure from the orthodox Moorish style in that it contains the Alhambra's only examples of figurative art, whereas according to Islamic tradition only Allah has the sacred right to "create" living things.

The reason for this commandment lies in the very roots of Islam, which came into being as a reaction against the rampant idolatry of the previous polytheism of the Arab world, around which a shameless trade in effigies had grown up. When Mohammed and his zealous followers seized power, they destroyed all the idols and forbade artists to make figures of any kind, in order to prevent a possible return to the superstition of the past.

This had the immediate effect of forcing the decorators of temples and palaces to become masters of calligraphy and geometrical patterns. Although not a bad thing in itself, the prohibition virtually made it impossible for them to communicate ideas and feelings and, also, to perform what, at least in the times before photography was invented, was art's main function, the imitation of nature.

However, as in any other religion, there existed a less fanatical school of thought which interpreted the Koran as saying that while idols were blasphemous, there was nothing wrong with innocently depicting reality. The masters of the Courtyard of the Lions undoubtedly used this argument to defend themselves against the iconoclasts. But their lack of Islamic rigour would later be held against them - along with other decadent Western practices such as drinking wine - when they were finally expelled from their European paradise, saying that they had been punished by the wrath of God....

Fountain of the Lions

The fountain's twelve crudely carved lions, spouting water, have always puzzled, precisely because they flaunt the famous Koranic prohibition. There are several theories as to their origin: some scholars say they were imported from Persia, where the idolatry law was interpreted more flexibly, while others claim they were the gift of rich a Jewish merchant of Granada to the Sultan and represent the Lions of Judah. And an 11th century poem suggests that they belonged to another earlier palace, of the Zirid dynasty, which stood in the Albaicín. Whatever, the very fact that they were placed here at all demonstrates that the Sultan was not afraid to stray from the Koranic path.

The love of water

Like all desert people, the Moors of Granada venerated water, an attitude which survives among the modern Andalucians.

It's the rule of life: we adore that which we lack. Shakespeare could write a sonnet comparing his mistress' eyes to the sun, but what thrilled the Moors was the thought of a cool and inexhaustible spring, as we see in these refined verses, engraved on the fountain bowl which rests on the heads of the twelve lions.

Molten silver flows among the pearls,
as beautiful and as pure as they.
Water and marble mingle so perfectly
that no one can be sure which one races and ripples
and which remains still.
Do you not see how the water
which spills into the bowl,
then vanishes into the channels?
It is an enamoured girl
who struggles to conceal
the tears which well up in her eyes....

The three great halls around the patio

When we enter from the Courtyard of the Myrtles, we pass through the *Sala de Mocárabes*, which has the distinction of being the only room of this sublime place which has nothing of either beauty or interest in it. As its name suggests – *mocárabes* being the multi-facetted "stalactites" which were first moulded in plaster and then fitted together like the pieces of a puzzle – the ceilings were once richly decorated, until they were destroyed by the explosion of the powder-house in the 16th century, and later replaced by a very conventional baroque ceiling which is also in ill repair.

The Courtyard of the Lions is surrounded by three great spaces: the Hall of the Abencerrajes, the Hall of Kings and the Hall of the Two Sisters. Until quite recently the real function of these rooms was unknown, which left the field open to the fantasies of legend-makers. Research has now shown that Abencerrajes, being closed in on all sides, was used for wintertime receptions and feasts and Reyes, really a very long, deep arcade, for gatherings held in summer. Two Sisters was the great Hall of State where the monarch Mohammed V received his vassals and foreign ambassadors, just as his father Yusuf I had done in the great hall of the Tower of Comares.

To each sultan, his own palace

This disproves the explanation which is often heard claiming that Comares was exclusively used for public ceremonies and that Lions was the private part of the palace, only for the enjoyment of the sultan and his harem. We now know that they were two separate places each having the same functions and in fact duplicated rather than complemented one another. Before the conquest of the city they weren't even interconnected – the Monarchs had the passageway (and the construction that now fills the space between them) built to form a single palace or "Casa Real" for their own use.

Simply put, each Sultan felt the need to build his own monument to himself, if possible a grander one than that of his predecessor. The fact that "Lions", the Palace of Mohammed V, is more feminine and delicate than the sterner style of "Comares", the Palace of Yusuf I, does not mean that it had a different, more intimate purpose but that, when it was built, the artistic sensitivity of the Nasrids had been directly exposed to European culture, raising it to greater heights of subtlety and expressiveness.

One might wonder why all this was frozen in time, since there were other kings that followed Mohammed and his son before the end of the dynasty. The answer is simply "money", because with the constant attacks and demands for tribute by the Christians, the Nasrids could no longer build or rebuild anything. For our great joy, all stayed as it was in the 14th century.

Hall of the Abencerrajes

The name *Hall of the Abencerrajes* was coined after the conquest by the people of Granada, who loved to tell, from generation to generation, the tales of the amorous adventures and political intrigues of the Moorish kings. Later, Washington Irving wrote them all down in the romantic style of his day, and the huge popularity of his book, *Tales of the Alhambra*, ended up by giving them a veneer of authenticity.

This tall, narrow and richly decorated room with its central fountain imbedded in the floor is, according to legend and Washington Irving, the place where all the male members of the aristocratic Abencerraje tribe were slain, having been lured to a dinner with the Sultan Boabdil, whom they had been plotting to overthrow, although another version claims that the massacre was motivated by the Sultan's jealousy when his wife was spied trysting with a member of the rival tribe in the Generalife gardens. In reality, the vengeful king was not Boabdil but his father Muley Hasan, although there is no proof that the massacre occurred here.

When we were students we laughed at the palace guides - those energetic little men with their official caps and authoritative way of speaking, or shouting, French, English and German, all with the same Spanish accent - who ensured the incredulous tourists that the reddish iron oxide stains on the marble of the fountain bowl were the indelible blood stains of the fallen Moors...

Unfortunately, we cannot visit the Patio of the Harem, which is on the upper floor of the tower adjacent to this room, and said to be one of the most beautiful spaces of the Alhambra.

Hall of Kings

The other example of figuration is found in the Room of Kings, on the far side when we enter from Comares, which was used in summertime for royal receptions and banquets. The Christians gave it this name because of the painting of the Nasrid Kings which decorates the ceiling of one of the alcoves, while the other two have similar scenes of courtesans and warriors, painted on a surface of leather ingeniously moulded to the form of the domes.

Like the lions, there is no proof of their origin, but it is generally accepted that they are the work of a group of wandering Christians, possibly, in view of the *quattrocento* style of the painting, Italian artists. This seems logical since there was a community of Genoese traders which had been established for many years in the Great Bazaar of Granada. These foreigners may have been commissioned by the Sultan for a job which would have been impossible for an Islamic painter: to depict scenes of men, women and animals, Islamic and Christian warriors, hunting and fighting.

The central dome is painted with the portraits of the ten Nasrid kings who had then reigned - excepting two of them who were foolish enough to challenge the power of Mohammed V and have therefore been banished to oblivion.

The scene, like many walls in the palace, is adorned with repeated images of the Nasrid shield given by Castilian King Fernando III to his vassal al-Ahmar.

The lateral domes depict the chivalrous adventures of Moorish knight in enemy territory: in one scene, an Arab and Christian joust to win the hand of a Christian maiden, and in the next the Arab is shown as the victor...

Difficult as it is to imagine in such an Oriental setting, this room was used immediately after the conquest and for over a century afterwards as a church, while the old mosque of the Alhambra which had been used for years as Granada's first cathedral was being torn down and the current monstrosity built in its place, next to the Palace of Carlos V. At this transcendental point of their astonishing history, the Castilians were colonizing their own land, and it is intriguing to imagine them, with their black beards and Renaissance garments, piously chanting *Ave Marias* in this shadowy Moorish alcove next to what might be a garden out of the Rubaiyat of Omar Khayan.

Hall of the Two Sisters

The name *Sala de las Dos Hermanas*, the "Hall of the Two Sisters", was taken from a poem by one of the great poets of the Alhambra, Ibn al-Jatib, and alludes to the huge twin slabs of marble which, like "two sisters", lie alongside one another near the central fountain. Like all the marble of the Alhambra and the Generalife, they had to be dragged 100 miles over mountains and valleys from the quarries of Macael, in the southeastern corner of the peninsula.

In this great room, the curious traveller's imagination will have no need to be stimulated by far-fetched legends or vulgar metaphors to take flight. He or she will only have to look up at what are among the most beautiful ceilings ever created, even though the overhanging stalactites or *mocárabes* have almost entirely lost their brilliant colours.

This is why it is so important to visit the Alhambra on a fine day - only the diffused sunlight can restore the original chromatic effect, cascading down from the windows surrounding the "lantern" or center of the dome and playing over the luxuriant, undulating encrustations which enrobe its interior.

The sight, like an optical illusion, always makes me feel I am inside a transparent coral reef, looking up from the sea bottom at the dappled light on the water's surface. Sheer beauty, for its own sake - and all utterly meaningless. No wonder that the jaded painters and poets of the Romantic School found their spiritual home in the Alhambra.

When the petitioners went before the Sultan, they first had to pass, for greater effect, through the series of smaller rooms which led from the Sala de las Dos Hermanas to the royal alcove, overhung with a richly carved canopy of *mocárabes*. There, the monarch awaited them on his throne, mysteriously wrapped in the light of the sun which filtered through the arched windows like an aureole, creating the same effect as the central alcove of the Tower of Comares.

This suite of rooms originally overlooked first an orchard and then the river valley and the Albaicín. That is why it ends with this exquisite balcony, El Mirador de Lindaraja, which has been called the *Balcony of the Eyes of the Queen* ever since the rejected wife of Sultan Muley Hasan lived here, after being replaced by the young Christian captive. She is said to have spent her days sitting sadly in her window, gazing out over the medina that rose on the other side of the valley.

But, disappointingly, the balcony now looks onto a rather sombre garden and a dun-coloured wall. This is perhaps the worst crime committed by the heavy-handed Christians against the Alhambra: that wall was plonked there, blinding the eyes of the Queen, as it were, by the minions of Carlos Quinto, when they built the suite of rooms as his provisional residence. They were the forerunners of our current-day developers, who build their apartment blocks and cut off the view of the people living next door. As it turned out, the building was useless too, because Carlos never returned to Granada.

Two wise Kings, and two unlucky ones

The history of the Nasrid reign is perfectly reflected in the lives of the four kings to whom it fell, in pairs, to live respectively the kingdom's periods of glory and ruin: the father and son Yusuf I and Mohammed V, and the father and son Muley Hasan and Boabdil.

The first two reigned throughout almost the entire 14th century, which was when the most beautiful palaces of the Alhambra were built. Many even hoped, then, that the last remnant of Moorish power had a chance of surviving, thanks to the cleverness of the two sultans.

Yusuf and Mohammed played a relentless game of political chess with the forces surrounding them: Castilian crusaders in the North, Aragonese knights and grasping Genoese merchants in the East, and their envious fellow Moors, particularly the Marinids, just across the water in the south. And as if this were not enough, they also had to fend off the frequent palace coups staged by rival clans, such as the legendary Abencerrajes.

Yusuf I reigned from 1333 to 1354, when he was murdered by a servant while praying in the mosque, a not unusual event in the quicksands of everyday political life in the Alhambra. During his reign, Granada was deprived of its main life line with North Africa, when the Castilians gained control of the Straits of Gibraltar in 1340, leaving the kingdom heavily dependent on the enemy in the north for imports of meat and grain. The wave of bubonic plague which during that period swept across all of Europe only added to the instability.

In spite of all this, Yusuf acted with masterful diplomacy to establish a peace with Castile which, in medieval terms, proved to be very durable. The resulting prosperity enabled the Sultan to carry out major works in the city, such as his own palace, the Tower of Comares, the Gate of Justice and the Madraza, or Islamic university.

The long reign of his son Mohammed V, which stretched from 1354 to 1391, had the peculiarity of taking place in two stages, with a "forced holiday" of three years in the middle. Mohammed, like his father, enjoyed a friendly relationship with the Castilians, so friendly that Castile's traditional rivals, the Aragonese, during a flair-up of animosity between the two Christian kingdoms, used their influence within the Alhambra to have him overthrown and replaced. Mohammed fled to

Morocco, where he had to wait until the two kings in the north settled their differences and agreed to have him restored.

Mohammed gave us the finest works of Spanish Muslim art: his own palace, Lions, the elegant façade of his father's palace, Comares, and the vanished hospital or *Maristán* on the edge of the River Darro, which was also very beautiful, to judge from the drawings which were made before its demolition in the 19th century.

The two last kings of Granada, Muley Hasan and Boabdil, had the bad luck of governing, or struggling to control, a kingdom whose days were clearly numbered. But even this was not enough to make the contentious masters of the Alhambra forget their differences and join hands against the enemy. The second from the last king of Granada, Muley Hasan, deeply resented by his subjects for having slain all the male members of the Abencerraje tribe, "the flower of Granada", and cast out his wife Aixa in favour of a Christian girl, had to seek refuge in Malaga, leaving his son Boabdil to take the throne. Ungratefully, Boabdil set about fighting to prevent his father from attempting to regain his lost kingdom, and when the old Sultan abdicated in favour of his brother, Boabdil fought against his uncle too.

This sad engraving was made of him on one such occasion, with a captive's chain around his neck like a trophy.

All of this served the interests of Isabel and Fernando so well that on the two occasions when they captured Boabdil they immediately released him so that he could continue fighting against his own relatives, even helping him to win. Boabdil had been the honoured guest of the Castilian court during one of the frequent palace upheavals and they knew he would be easy to use as a puppet, to obtain the final surrender of the Alhambra.

Sala de Camas and the Bath

The route now takes us through several places of varying interest. First, we pass through the baths of the harem, known as the *Sala de Camas*, the "Room of the Beds", a two-tiered chamber with alcoves around the lower floor and a balcony around the upper one. In accordance with the Roman model copied in all Arab baths, this is the *apodyterium*, the antechamber where the sultan rested after emerging from the adjacent bath.

It is said that here, to the sound of blind musicians playing zithers and flutes in the upper gallery, the monarch observed his wives displaying themselves naked after the bath, each one hoping that he would throw her an apple, which meant that she had been chosen to spend the night with him.

However, the pleasure which this otherwise suggestive place would normally afford the curious traveller is almost totally spoiled by the garish and inauthentic overhaul performed in the 19th century, when the room was on the verge of collapsing. Nothing is left of the original decoration except the columns and the floor tiles; furthermore, the whole thing was gaudily repainted in the worst possible taste. It reminds me of a Hollywood movie set or, worse, an over-decorated Lebanese restaurant.

Next we enter the perfectly preserved Palace Baths, which the Christians did not alter or destroy because the women enjoyed using them, given that bathing was thought to make men effeminate and cowardly in battle, like the Moors! I have even read that the Spaniards spared it because they felt that at least one example of the enemy's heathen practices should be left intact, as a curiosity and moral lesson for all good Christians who visited the palace.

The palace *hammam* is functional and without much ornamentation, and is composed of a hot room, a warm room and a cold room. Slaves fed the fire below the marble floor, which became so hot that thick wooden clogs had to be used by the bathers to walk across it. When the heat became unbearable, other slaves on the roof opened the star-shaped "windows" to release the steam. The bathers then gradually cooled off in the other two rooms.

Rooms of Carlos Quinto and the Queen's Dressing Room

We climb a staircase to the *Habitaciones de Carlos Quinto*, or Rooms of Carlos Quinto, which we saw the back of from the ill-fated "eyes of the Queen". This suite was built as a provisional residence for the Emperor-King, until his own palace could be completed.

In fact, he never stayed in either place, and the only illustrious guest of the rooms was the author Washington Irving, who wrote his famous book "Tales of the Alhambra" here three centuries later, while he was posted at the US Consul in Madrid. He came to Granada in 1829 and stayed for several months in order to soak up the local lore and legends, the sort of thing American writers do even today. The palace had by then become home to a community of gypsies camping in its ruins, so Irving had lots of oral sources. The result may not be either good history or good literature, but it launched the palace as one of the wonders of the world and, forty years later, influenced the Spanish government to declare the ruin a National Monument.

At the end of the suite of rooms, which - as if still awaiting the occupant for whom they were built - are undecorated apart from the Renaissance coffered ceiling and monumental fireplace, we come to a lookout with delicately arched windows overlooking the city, called the *Tocador de la Reina*, the Queen's Boudoir or Dressing Room. This make-believe minaret was built on top of one of the Alhambra's flat-topped military towers for Carlos' wife Isabel, who, like him, stayed elsewhere during their never-to-be-repeated summer in Granada.

How the palace became a ruin

It is often said that the Christians, with their contempt for Moorish culture, wilfully disfigured and wrecked the Alhambra. But if it weren't for their perhaps ill-conceived attempts to maintain and "improve" the palace, very little of what we admire today would have survived the wear-and-tear of the centuries, which includes several major earthquakes soon after the conquest, the explosion of the arsenal in the valley and the vandalism of Napoleon's troops.

This primitive form of conservationism - ambiguously mixed with a visceral dislike of everything related to the age-old adversary - was the result of an amazing royal policy established immediately after the taking of Granada by the Catholic Monarchs. Isabel's own daughter declared, in an often quoted sentence which distinguishes her as a true woman of the Renaissance, that the "excellent memory" of the Moorish "towers and walls should not be lost".

And everything that followed confirms that the Alhambra was systematically used and cherished throughout the 16th and 17th centuries, until Spain's economic decline generally made it impossible to preserve so many of its great buildings. But there was another more specific reason for the abandonment of the Alhambra which lies in its own tumultuous history.

After the Reconquest, the Monarchs rewarded a leading nobleman, the Count of Tendilla, for services rendered during the war, giving him a number of buildings and plots of land. But at the end of the 17th century Spain was torn apart by the dynastic crisis caused by Carlos II "The Impotent", who couldn't produce a successor. The European powers were divided into two fiercely opposed camps. On one side were those who wanted the wish of the dying King to be respected, which was to leave his throne (the King could bequeath his throne to whomever he wanted, like the rest of his property) to a Bourbon. This was felt to be the wisest choice because France was the most powerful country in Europe, and Louis XIV naturally supported it. On the other side were those who felt that the King had been unduly influenced and that Spain should continue under the rule of the Habsburgs. The main opponents of the Bourbon candidate were England and Holland and, in Spain, people like the heirs of the legendary Count of Tendilla, who loathed the idea of one of their arch-enemies sitting on the throne.

The outcome of the War of Succession was favourable to the Bourbons, and when the new French king was crowned in Madrid as Felipe V he turned a cold shoulder on the losers, which included the administrators of the Alhambra, which without royal help were unable to maintain it properly.

Apart from the political vindictiveness, which was nothing new to Spain, a modern French sort of King would understandably have had little interest in conserving an old palace built by Mohammedans four centuries earlier. Stranded without funds, the Alhambra was gradually abandoned, pillaged and eventually occupied by those same gypsies whose picturesque figures can be seen in the engravings made by foreign artists in the 19th century.

El Partal and the Mosque

After twisting and turning through a series of galleries, corridors and patios, we emerge into a terraced area covered with flowers and shrubs popularly known as *el jardín del Partal*, the "Garden of the Portico". In Moorish times there was no garden here at all, but, rather, the mansions of the nobles who wanted to live close to the seat of power, almost all of which have crumbled into the earth, apart from the foundations which jut up everywhere. Not even the famous garden-cemetery survives - the *Rawda* which lay between the palace and the mosque. In fact, we are in an archaeological excavation which has been planted with flowers and trees, and which some misinformed tourists take to be a Moorish garden, as they do with the rose-bushes and cypress-lined alleys of the Generalife. In fact, the Moors only made enclosed, secluded gardens, not English or French-style ones.

There are, however, some interesting vestiges, beginning with the slender, elegant construction with the five arches - the portico or *partal* which gives the modern garden its name. It is believed to be the surviving counterpart of a similar construction which stood at the other end of the pond, so that - like the *Patio de los Arrayanes* - the same pattern of colonnades would be reflected in the water when seen from either perspective.

This half-of-a-palace, mysteriously known as the *Torre de las Damas*, the "Tower of the Ladies-in-Waiting", has survived because of its magnificent view of the city, and was used as a residence by several rulers, Moorish and Christian, until, during the Alhambra's deepest decline, it was bought by a businessman who turned it into a tenement house.

A well-known drawing dated 1833, called, precisely, *La Casa de Sánchez*, shows it as a sagging ruin (although this, remembering the Romantic predilection for ruins, may be a bit of an exaggeration by the British artist) with the pond half-filled with earth and rubble and all of its lovely arches walled up, the one on the far right being occupied by a massive baker's oven and chimney. There is even a donkey waiting to deliver the day's bread!

I have reproduced it for you below. We can see that the arches are walled up, because people were living and working inside, but we can see also that the columns which supported them were not the slender, round marble ones installed by the restorers, but simple, square brick pillars, which were clearly judged too rustic.

Later, a wealthy German bought it and removed the exquisitely inlaid wooden dome of the watchtower to take home, donating the rest to the Spanish government. His heirs later donated the dome, beautifully restored, to the Pergamon Museum in Berlin. All this gives us an idea of how tourists and souvenir-hunters made off with bits and pieces of the palace over the centuries. The gaps that they left, as well as the damage caused by fires, explosions and collapsing roofs, led to so many reparations and reconstructions that much of what we see today is, crudely put, fake. But it must once more be admitted that without the often clumsy "rebuilds", there might be very little left of the glorious place at all.

The small brick buildings to the left of the Torre de las Damas are authentically Moorish and contain interesting decorations, but are said to be in very poor repair, which is why they are closed to the public.

Just up the hill from the Torre de las Damas, and built directly on top of the fortified wall, is a mosque known as *La Mezquita del Partal*, with its elaborately tiled roof extending from the narrow body like a broad-brimmed hat. For me, this is one of the most enchanting buildings of the Alhambra, with its intimate, strongly Moorish flavour, in spite of the many changes which it has undergone, ever since it became the property of the art-loving Count of Tendilla. It gives us an idea of what the Mosque of the Olive Tree must have been like, which also crowned a defensive wall, on the site of the church of San Miguel Alto.

When we step into the narrow interior we understand why the Christians, when they entered Granada, were so amazed by the cramped dimensions of the Moorish buildings, which they found to be "two or three times smaller" than the equivalent home or temple in Castile. Like the oratory of the Mexuar, the arched windows of this irresistibly picturesque construction provide the curious traveller with a fairy-tale panorama.

Pretty, but "make-believe"

All over Europe in the 19th century, medieval castles and churches - sneered at as barbaric and allowed to decay since the Renaissance - were "restored" according to the tastes of the Romantic Movement, which favoured the elegant Gothic style, of the fantastic fairy-tale variety. Although the medieval revival spread to Spain as well, its best examples are found in France: the exterior of Paris' Notre Dame cathedral and the fortified citadel of Carcassonne, which were completely rebuilt to resemble what the people of the day thought a medieval church and castle should look like, rather than the cruder reality.

The same happened to the Alhambra: its 19th century restorers fancifully built a mosaic-covered dome on the eastern pavilion in the Courtyard of the Lions because it looked more Moorish and that was what tourists wanted to see. It was restored in the early 20th century to its original pointed shape by the palace's "saviour", the new Director of the Alhambra Leopoldo Torres Balbás, in spite of an indignant press campaign in favour of keeping the existing home-made restorations, even though everyone knew they were fake. The popular preference was to replace the rougher, plainer elements with more exotic and elaborate ones.

I have reproduced below a postcard from about 1920 showing the controversial dome and the "yammurs" – the metal rods adorned with symbolic globes – which were added to the three roofs in the picture, all of which were removed by the new Director. It's true that in the 19th century spires were also added to Notre Dame Cathedral and Mont Saint-Michel by the restorers, but they were prettier…

A distinguished Scottish watercolour painter called Muirhead Bone, on a visit to Spain after World War I, showed another side of the patio undergoing just such an unscientific overhaul, with foremen and bricklayers merrily patching everything up in typically Andalucian confusion.

Not long after Washington Irving made the Alhambra a "must" on the European Grand Tour, in the mid-19th century, a local architect called Rafael Contreras was working on a plaster replica of one of the rooms of the palace when the famous French writer Alexandre Dumas, author of the The Four Musketeers, came in. Accompanied his son and also-writer and a party of friends, he was searching for the true soul of Granada, like all the tourists of the Romantic period. He was so impressed with the handiwork of Contreras that he started a European craze for the man's stucco souvenirs, which made him rich and famous.

Before long Contreras was directing a major overhaul of the palace, replacing the old reliefs with their profusion of floral motifs and plant-like patterns, as well as the elegant calligraphy of the sacred texts, with facsimiles whose authenticity was less important than their ability to satisfy the romantic "Orientalists" from the north. When the old Arab bazaar near the Cathedral, the Alcaicería, burned down he rebuilt that too, in the kitschy style we can see today.

Contreras' prettified interpretation of Moorish achitecture was so successful that he set about training a whole army of restorers who in turn passed the required skills on to their sons and apprentices, in what became a dynasty of *alhambristas* who were given a free hand with their popular *pastiches* until an architect from Madrid, the aforementioned Torres Balbás, took over. It is to him we owe much of what the Alhambra has kept of its authenticity, because he insisted that restorations be done, as he called it, "scientifically", with religious respect for the original appearance, rather than to satisfy the demand for colourful fantasies.

Opposition in Granada to his removal of the dome in the Patio de los Leones, for example, was so fierce that were it not for the support of friends such as the composer Manuel de Falla and the art historian Gallego y Burín, Don Leopoldo might have been dismissed and sent back to Madrid in disgrace.

The truly curious traveller – and art-lover – who wants to see what the original reliefs were like should pay a visit to the Cuarto Real de Santo Domingo, hidden away in a corner of downtown Granada. Only one smallish domed hall remains of this elegant Moorish palace, but the fact that it stands on the old grounds of what became a Dominican monastery saved it from over-zealous restorations. This because the monks scarcely changed its decorations when they adapted the *qubba*, or domed room, as a chapel, and so for centuries it was preserved in its original state. [I have described the Cuarto Real de Santo Domingo further on.]

Coming back to our beloved old Alhambra, when you think of all the transformations it has undergone and which in a more discreetly sophisticated form continue until today, it is truly amazing that what we have still looks as glorious as it does!

The four towers

We stroll among the tall, dark green cypress trees, following the shady path along the wall with its massive towers, each of which is a tiny palace in itself, richly decorated inside. The *Torre de la Cautiva* was where lived the captive Christian girl Isabel de Solis - whom the Sultan took for his wife; the *Torre de las Infantas* is famous for its legend of the three Moorish princesses; the Torre del Agua is where the water enters the palace's system of channels coming from the deviation of the Darro River, over the aqueduct which the founder of the Nasrid Dynasty, al-Ahmar, installed eight miles upstream; and as for the pointed battlements, which give their name to the *Torre de los Picos*, it is interesting to note that they were in fact added after the conquest by the Christians.

It was on this upper part of the Alhambra that the French troops spitefully exploded several bombs when they left Granada, which might have destroyed the whole fortress had it not been for the crippled veteran who cut the wick in time.

On this part of the hill stood a great palace built by Sultan Yusuf III, which was allowed to crumble into ruin after a violent dispute in the 18th century over the lack of funds for its maintenance. Later, the ground was cleared for use by the monks in the nearby monastery as a fruit and vegetable orchard, reminding us that of the seven great palaces which once stood on the hill, only two have survived the ravages of time and men, Comares and Lions.

Below in the moat-like ravine called the Cuesta de los Chinos and at the foot of the Torre de los Picos once stood the *Puerta del Arrabal*, the Gate of the Suburb, which was the original access to the Generalife, rather than the bridge - Puente Nuevo - which we crossed to enter the grounds and now pass over to leave them....

Generalife, hideaway of Sultans

For many, the small white palace nestled among the trees of the mountainside - called *El Cerro del Sol*, the Hill of the Sun, because it faces the south - is the Alhambra's most charming place, in spite of the fact that it is scarcely more than a garden and has none of the architectural power or luxury of the great rooms we have seen.

The reasons for this preference are very human. The Generalife is small and intimate, filled with flowers and everywhere open to nature, and everywhere there is the sound and sparkle of running water. Seen from the Albaicín, it resembles a white schooner sailing forth from the forest, or, when the Sierra Nevada behind it is covered in snow, a sliver of ice which has ventured too close to the torrid plains and is about to melt away forever.

We do know that three such villas were built on the hillside and that this is the only one which was maintained by the Christians, perhaps because it had the best view. It was not, as is often said, a summer palace, since the Moors - like today's Andalucians - preferred to close themselves into shady rooms to escape the heat, rather than seek the open air. Rather, the "Heavenly Garden of the Sultan" was a secluded refuge - complete with its prayer room and baths - where the rulers could retreat from the clamouring demands of their subjects, who constantly made their way up from the city to ask for favours and dispensations. It was also a hunting lodge, around which deer roamed freely.

The Christians liked it too, and changed its appearance radically, as we shall see. But we should not let this detract from the poetic charm of the place. After all, the Alhambra as we see it today is nothing less than the unique creation of the people of Granada, the legacy of all the Moors, Christians and Jews who over the centuries lived either on top or in the shadow of the great hill, each one leaving his mark and contributing to give the place its depth and singularity. And it is good that it should be so. If we want to see "architecturally pure" Islamic buildings, we can always go to Fez or Marrakesh.

This said, we can begin our visit to this exquisite building which, from a strictly academic viewpoint, is a bastardization which has lost almost all of its historical value.

All the gardens through which we pass were built in the 20th century under Franco, one of the few good things he did because, if you are lucky enough to visit Granada in springtime, the roses planted there get as big as cabbages! We enter the "little palace" itself through a small courtyard, climb up a narrow staircase and are in the legendary *Patio de la Acequia* - the Courtyard of the Water Channel.

Through this long, narrow enclosure flows the *acequia* or open canal which carried water from the hills above into the palace grounds. Originally, it was similar to the pond of the Tower of Comares, with only a small fountain at either end, creating the gentle burbling sound which the Moors felt was enough to offset the enchanted silence of their inner gardens. The long arcade which runs along the southern side was in

Moorish times unbroken by apertures except for the central balcony, where there was an oratory, the *mirhab*.

This Muslim prayer room is of special interest to the curious traveller because its wall decorations are among the few authentic, unrestored plaster reliefs in the entire Alhambra, and only rivalled in Granada by their more ancient counterparts in the Cuarto Real de Santo Domingo, in the lower city. Soon after the conquest, the Christians walled up the arches around the balcony and plastered over its walls to create a private chapel for the new owners. 400 years later, in 1922, the Spanish State expropriated the Generalife and merged it with the Alhambra, at which time archaeologists restored it to its original state, opening the arches and revealing the original stucco carvings, the *yesería* for which the Moors are so famous.

Although these breathtakingly elaborate reliefs, hand-carved one by one rather than uniformly moulded as seen elsewhere, are rather worn down and frayed around the edges, their detail and even some of their original colours seem to have been preserved from the elements by the thick layer of plaster that covered them for so long. Like the carvings in the aforementioned Dominican chapel, the conspicuous absence of the Nasrid shield shows that they are older than those of the Alhambra itself, which all bear the symbol of the tenuous Moorish alliance with the Christians.

In the 19th century, on the occasion of the visit of Queen Isabel II, the Generalife's private owners, descendants of the Count of Tendilla to whom it had been given by the Monarchs, overhauled the whole thing to resemble the Tivoli Gardens in Italy, where they also had a villa, with the enlargement of the towers at either end, the piercing in the wall of the open colonnade joining them and - most radically - the installation of the two rows of intertwining fountains. They certainly aren't "authentic", but they have become such a symbol of Granada that it would be difficult to imagine the courtyard without them.

In the smaller courtyard we enter next stands the huge cypress tree - so old and bent that it has to be supported by an iron girdle - which is said to be where Boabdil's wife had her fatal rendez-vous with that Moorish knight, giving it its name, *El Ciprés de la Sultana*.

escalera del agua

Higher up the hill, we come to the *Escalera del Agua*, the "Water Steps", three successive flights of brick steps climbing up through the woods. The stone banisters on either side have been hollowed out to become water canals, which cascade joyously down towards the palace.

I am pleased, furthermore, to assure the curious traveller that this unique and supremely poetic staircase was in fact built by the Moors and has not been altered since!

Tanto monta,
monta tanto

Several of the pointed arches alongside the garden are curiously painted (in very faded colours) with the symbols of the Catholic Monarchs, the arrows and yoke, combined with the anagram of their motto, TATO MOTA.

According to popular wisdom, this is an abbreviation for *Tanto Monta el Rey como la Reina*, loosely translatable as "The King has as much power as the Queen". Isabel's kingdom, Castile, was far more important than Fernando's Aragon, and the motto reminded her that the new alliance gave equal rights to both. Sometimes it is quoted by inverting the first two words, *Tanto monta, monta tanto*, for greater effect. What a beautiful language Spanish is – of all the Romance tongues the one that most resembles Latin, so succinct and forceful.

In reality, Fernando is known to have been the one who gave all the orders, with the womanly acquiescence of Isabel who like all Spanish women then, and many now, was brought up to accept all of her husband's decisions, even when he made the wrong ones. It is significant that in all the deeds and documents of the time, the signatory was given as *rey Fernando* and not *reina Isabel.*

As for her husband's character, it was so willful and cunning that Machiavelli is supposed to have had him in mind when he wrote The Prince (and not Lorenzo di Medici, to whom the work was dedicated). And the only thing we know for sure about the motto *Tanto Monta* is that it belonged to the original coat of arms of Fernando of Aragon, not the one he later shared with Isabel, and with a quite different meaning.

Being famous for his impulsive, arrogant manner (both considered virtues in a medieval king), Fernando was compared by one his counsellors to Alexander the Great. When the bold Macedonian set out on his campaign in Asia, and passing through the Anatolian town of Gordium, he was told by the high priest that if he could untie the knot that a legendary peasant had tied to attach his ox-yoke to the ploughshare – the "Gordian knot" – he would become the conqueror of Asia. Alexander saw that the knot was too difficult to untie, so he expediently chopped it open with his sword, crying that what he had done was "just as good", in Spanish *tanto monta*, which Fernando had inscribed on his shield, along with the picture of the yoke and rope.

The "equal allies" explanation of the motto was invented in the 19th century, when nationalists set out to glorify Queen Isabel as a Spanish Joan of Arc by presenting her rather than Fernando as the driving force behind the Reconquest. Even Fernando's yoke was untied, so to speak, from his person by claiming that it represented the union of the two monarchs, dragging forward, side by side, the destiny of their new nation. The absurdity of the image of a man and woman bound together like a bull and cow was lost on the blindly patriotic Spaniards of the day, who were ready to believe any sort of "call for unity" that might prevent the collapse of their exhausted Empire.

As for the less controversial bundle of five arrows, it represents the five kingdoms of Spain which Isabel brought together, thus uniting the entire country except, of course, Granada.

foto Angel Sánchez

Cerro de los Mártires
and down to Casa de los Tiros

When seen from Mirador de San Nicolás, the Generalife and all the towers and buildings of the Alhambra seem to share the same hill, the southern end of which overlooks the city like a plateau, and the northern part suddenly climbing steeply upwards. In fact, since this long outcropping is slashed, as it were, by two deep ravines (the Cuesta de los Chinos and the Cuesta de Gomérez), the *granadinos* think of it as being three distinct *cerros*, or hills. The highest is the Cerro del Sol, where the Generalife stands, overlooking the *Cerro del Sabica*, the site of the Nasrid Palaces, the Alcazaba and the Palace of Carlos Quinto, which in turn overlooks the lowest and southernmost tip of the plateau, the *Cerro de los Mártires.*

This "hill", on our right as we walk up through the Alhambra forest from the Cuesta de Gomérez, was given its sombre name - Mount of Martyrs - by the Catholic Monarchs, in memory of the Christian captives who suffered perished in the notorious *mazmorras* or dungeons which Mohammed V installed in a number of disused wells and wheat silos carved into the rock. By day, the prisoners worked in construction, and at night were herded down into these damp, dark holes, 20 feet below the surface, and when the Monarchs came to their rescue, they counted (in the city below as well as the castle) 2,000 of them.

After the conquest, the Monarchs had a small church built here called the Hermitage of the Martyrs, which was later replaced by the monastery of the religious order of the Discalced Carmelites, which stood between the sites of the two hotels. The place, which during its several centuries of existence was known as *Convento de los Mártires*, is famous because it had as its founder and prior the mystical poet Saint John of the Cross, *San Juan de la Cuz.*

His convent was demolished at the beginning of the 19th century when the liberal (that is, anti-clerical) government expropriated all church properties, and there were a lot of them – not only religious buildings but also vast haciendas which had been bequeathed by sinful land-owners hoping to buy their way into Heaven. Some decades later, the beautiful spot overlooking Granada was bought by a wealthy Belgian who owned several mines in the region. He was also a great lover of Granada very popular among the city's artistic set, whom he entertained in the neo-classical palace and romantic gardens he had built there *Carmen de los Mártires*, "villa of the martyrs" in reference to the convent, although you can be sure that no one died there of privation!

Saint John of the Cross, small prior, great poet

All that is left to remind us of the stay of San Juan de la Cruz is a pretty ceramic plaque near the gate saying that it was here that the Prior of the monastery wrote his poem, "The Dark Night of the Soul". This means that the most widely read poem of the Spanish language – read not only in the original but also in translation, a hurdle which few poems survive - and in my opinion greatest one was written in Granada, even though the author was a northerner.

John was a monk in the Carmelite monastery of Segovia when he had mystical visions and began mortifying his flesh. He befriended a like-minded nun, who also became an inspirational poet and saint, Teresa de Avila. Together they founded a break-away "reformed" order called the unshod or "discalced" Carmelites" which, as its name suggests, was deliberately more self-abnegating than the Carmelites, because the friars and nuns refused the comfort of closed shoes and stockings to wear open sandals, even in winter. This act of rebellion so angered John's superiors that he was condemned to prison for heresy, spending a long year in a monastery dungeon from which he was only removed once a week to be flogged before the friars. Even so, he was able to write down his illuminated conversations with God on scraps of paper slipped to him by his minder. After escaping, and eventually having the "barefoot" order accepted by the Church, John began opening new monasteries, soon finding his way to Andalucia where, in that chaotic 16th century, there was greater tolerance for visionaries (such as Saint John of God, as we have seen).

At his new monastery in Granada, the *Convento de los Mártires*, he wrote The Dark Night of the Soul which, although the lover and mistress are presented as God and the human spirit, can easily be read as a rhapsodic love poem. As might be expected, John's poetry is commonly disliked by pious churchgoers and fervently admired by unrepentant sinners like Lorenzo! Even though the amorous encounter is suggested in the most delicate terms, the way the sensuous rhythm of the words reaches a crescendo of intensity and then floats serenely in a state of plenitude conveys a sensation familiar to all mortal lovers...

I have paraphrased the poem here so that the curious traveller can form an idea of these sublime verses, conceived in the shadow of what had once been an Islamic palace by the son of converted Jews who thought he was a Christian but may have been no more of one than you or me, and I say "you" in a figurative sense only.

The poet, speaking in the voice of a woman, who - the dogmatic foreword sternly informs us - is really a personification of the human soul, narrates a secret encounter with her lover, who, chastely, symbolizes God. Our heroine describes how on a dark night she became so "inflamed with love" that, while all were sleeping in her house she crept "down a secret staircase" to meet her lover, walking through the night "with no other light to guide me than the one which burned in my heart" but which was so bright that it "led me more surely than the light of the sun", to a secret meeting place in the forest. There the union takes place, between the "*amado*" and the "*amada*", the two lovers, who are fused together "by the night, more gentle than the dawn", so completely that she is transformed into him, in a sublime phrase which is untranslatable because of our lack of masculine and feminine declensions: "*Amada en el Amado transformada*". Then he falls asleep on her breast, while she strokes his hair and the wind, moving through the branches of the trees, "wounds" her throat and "suspends" all of her senses. "I stayed there, and I forgot myself, my face bent over the loved one. All things came to a stop, and I let myself go, my cares forgotten among the lilies".

I have reproduced below the Spanish original so that, even if you can't understand the words, you can enjoy the almost musical simplicity of the short lines, and the minimalistic stanzas.

La Noche Oscura del Alma

En una noche oscura,
con ansias, en amores inflamada,
¡oh dichosa ventura!,
salí sin ser notada
estando ya mi casa sosegada.

A oscuras y segura,
por la secreta escala, disfrazada,
¡oh dichosa ventura!,
a oscuras y en celada,
estando ya mi casa sosegada.

En la noche dichosa,
en secreto, que nadie me veía,
ni yo miraba cosa,
sin otra luz y guía
sino la que en el corazón ardía.

Aquésta me guiaba
más cierto que la luz de mediodía,
adonde me esperaba
quien yo bien me sabía,
en parte donde nadie parecía.

¡Oh noche que guiaste!
¡oh noche amable más que el alborada!
¡oh noche que juntaste
Amado con amada,
amada en el Amado transformada!

En mi pecho florido,
que entero para él solo se guardaba,
allí quedó dormido,
y yo le regalaba,
y el ventalle de cedros aire daba.

El aire de la almena,
cuando yo sus cabellos esparcía,
con su mano serena
en mi cuello hería
y todos mis sentidos suspendía.

Quedéme y olvidéme,
el rostro recliné sobre el Amado,
cesó todo y dejéme,
dejando mi cuidado
entre las azucenas olvidado.

The traveller who is truly curious can visit the tangled gardens of the Carmen de los Mártires (still overgrown and closed to the public when this was written) and wander through the Romantic gardens with their grottoes and hillocks and ponds, to the elegant palace which now belongs to the city and is often used for official receptions.

We continue down the slope towards the aforementioned hotel, built at the beginning of the century by an entrepreneur who like Lorca's father made a fortune in the sugar beet boom and wanted to provide his friend King Alfonso XIII with a "hunting lodge" when he visited the region. I can never resist being charmed by this orgiastic celebration of "Moorish kitsch", and one of my favourite places to watch the sun setting over Granada and the Sierra Nevada is from its terrace bar, over a gin and tonic in summer, a glass of *fino* in cooler months... Tucked away in the basement is a charming little theatre all in red and gold, where a very young Federico García Lorca gave a poetry recital in 1922.

Leaving the hotel we turn to the left and walk down a long street, the right hand side of which is a wall, until we come to the portentous façade, decorated with arches and columns salvaged from various medieval churches and Roman palaces, of the Rodriguez-Acosta Foundation, created by a local painter who devoted his considerable fortune to art and archaeology. It's all very academic and universal in focus, and if you have little time to spare you might follow my example when I take friends there - go straight to the basement to view the precious collection of miniature Iberian bronze figurines representing warriors and bulls.

We continue on past the museum. The street ends at the *Torres Bermejas*, the red, or "vermilion" towers, which form the southernmost part of the Alhambra's fortifications, although most of the walls which connected them to the rest of the castle, plunging down into the ravine, have disappeared. These massive towers were built by the Arabs on top of an earlier fort which was the center of Granada's ancient Jewish community, itself an enlargement of the original fortress built by the native Iberians.

Here then is the place where Granada began - the *Garnata-al-Yahud* which the Moors found. We should try to imagine a much smaller stronghold with primitive huts clustered around its feet, from which farmers set out every morning to till the soil of the plain below. The huge towers we see now are sealed up and neglected, weeds growing in their debris-filled patios, which we can only glimpse through rusting gates.

El Realejo and Church of Santo Domingo

We have three ways of returning to the city. The shortest is to walk down into the Alhambra forest, by taking the moss-covered ramp which begins at the foot of the towers, bringing us to the Puerta de las Granadas, the Cuesta de Gomérez and Plaza Nueva. The longest, and perhaps least interesting, is to return to the Alhambra Palace Hotel and walk south-east down the Cuesta del Caidero through a middle-class residential district and out onto the banks of the Genil. But since that traveller in us is curious to discover more of Granada's secrets, we will take the long path and rocky staircase that starts a short way to the left after leaving the Alhambra Palace Hotel, leading us to the south-west down the *Cuesta del Realejo*. It takes us into the quarter of the same name, *El Realejo*, once Granada's *judería*, or ghetto, razed to the ground by the Catholic Monarchs after they took the city. The sloping "square" at its foot, really just a widening of the street, is the *Plaza del Realejo*, once the bustling marketplace of this legendary part of the city.

If we turn left just before reaching the Plaza del Realejo, we come to a much larger and flatter and more symmetrical space called *El Campo del Príncipe*. In Moorish times, this area was taken up by palaces and gardens nestled at the foot of the Alhambra Hill. The esplanade was created after the conquest of Granada by the Catholic Monarchs for the festivities which followed the wedding of their son, Prince Juan, in 1497, and has ever since been known by the people as The Field of the Prince (even though the poor fellow died soon after, from sexual over-exertion, it is said). The bars on the southern side of the plaza, which fill the street with tables in summer, make this one of Granada's most popular spots for *el tapeo*, our way of saying "pub-crawling" - the exact translation would be "tapa-munching".

A short walk down from the Plaza del Realejo, twisting to the right, is the charmingly time-worn Church of Santo Domingo, built by the Catholic Monarchs in thanks to the Dominican Order - the driving force behind the Spanish Inquisition - for its help in the conquest of Granada. Significantly, the tombstones from the city's *rawdas*, or Islamic cemeteries were used as the church's building materials.

The tall, elegant arches create a loggia in front of the façade, originally used by the Inquisitors for their notorious autos da fé. The tribunal sat their in pomp when they judged "new Christians" or converted Jews suspected of heresy, with the unfortunate prisoners standing before them in the middle of the Plaza. They say that Torquemada himself lodged in the adjacent monastery, Santa Cruz la Real, when he visited Granada.

The balcony above the arcade, with its twin windows and door leading off to the right, reminds me of similar 16th century churches in Mexico, with their "chapel of the Indians" from which the missionaries evangelized great crowds of aspiring converts before allowing them inside. The one I saw as a boy in

Acolman, near Mexico City, had a single balcony above the gate.

The curious arrangement is typical of Mexico's colonial churches and also known as an "open chapel" - sometimes the crowds of recently baptized Catholics were so great that Mass had to be held in front of the church rather than inside. I can't help thinking that the running balcony here was designed for the Moors of Granada with just the same purpose as for the Indians of Mexico...

The rather faded paintings around the doors, although not as old as they look (1915), bear the symbols of the Catholic Monarchs, with the yoke and arrows. The statue of the mystical Fray Luis de Granada graces the small plaza on which the church stands, a mystic who was born just after the conquest and who became famous in those morally loose times for high-minded works such as his *Guide for Sinners*, which is not, as some wags have suggested, an introduction to the city's throbbing night life.

Cuarto Real de Santo Domingo

The Catholic Monarchs, as part of the surrender treaty, bought – at a price favourable to them, one may assume - the domain on which the church and its adjacent cloister were later built from its traditional owners, the Emir's wives – *las reinas moras*. This vast domain included a small Moorish palace or *qubba* – "domed hall", from the Latin *cupula* – which stood atop a tower of the old city wall, where the royal family would retire to fast and pray during Ramadan.

The Dominicans refurbished this lovely "room" (*al-qubba* is the origin of the Spanish word *alcoba* and our alcove) as a chapel, and called it the Royal Room or Cuarto Real de Santo Domingo. It's similar to, but much smaller than the Tower of Comares in the Alhambra, and decorated with the same exquisitely intricate stucco reliefs.

In this aerial view, you can see the Santo Domingo church and monastery in the upper left hand corner, and the old Moorish palace set on its ramparts at the bottom. The domain was cut in two after the Spanish State expropriated and then auctioned off Spain's Church properties in the early 19th century. Its new owners built the country house you can see in the insert on the lower right, attached to the old Moorish-palace-become-Christian-chapel, which now became their *mirador* or living-room-with-a-view.

Later, the middle section of the domain was sold, cutting it in two, for the construction of the ubiquitous apartment blocks. The remaining privately-owned part of the domain, along with the precious Moorish *qubba*, was purchased recently by the city council and fully restored – too fully, for my taste – and opened to the public. The old country house was replaced by the ultra-modern chrome-and-marble exhibition and conference hall you can see just behind the *qubba*, of which I have inserted a detail.

The "Cuesta de Aixa" shown above is the street which winds down along the walls from the palace grounds to the banks of the Genil River, which the last Moorish Queen of Granada took when she went into exile in Morocco with her disgraced son

Boabdil. Hence the name gallantly given to it by the ever-sentimental *granadinos*, "Aixa's Slope".

In this picture of the Cuesta de Aixa, the Qubba stands on its tower in the old Moorish wall, of which you can see, on the left, the stones which the Moors put there almost 1,000 years ago!

The *qubba* is believed to be older than the Nasrid Palaces of the Alhambra, because nowhere on its walls is to be seen the symbol of the Nasrid Shield given to the Sultan by the Christians and obligatorily woven into all of the reliefs there. This means that the Cuarto Real was built under the previous reign of the illustrious Almohad dynasty, and was certainly used as an architectural model for the Alhambra itself.

Perhaps the most interesting thing about the Cuarto Real de Santo Domingo is the almost organic intricacy of the plaster reliefs, compared to which its conterparts in the great rooms of the Alhambra seem flat and angular. This, it is said, is because the Almohads did all their work by hand while the Nasrids, with so many walls to cover, used moulds to reproduce the endlessly repeated words and patterns.

[It is also true that the long-forgotten Cuarto Real was spared the massive and often unscientific restorations, whose main purpose was to make the ruinous Alhambra attractive to foreign visitors, after it was declared a National Monument in 1870.]

In the panel on the left, the Cuarto's lovely incrustations resemble baroque sea shells and fruits, with a three-dimensionality which suggests that they were painstakingly carved into the hardened plaster by consummate artists, rather than pressed or poured into shape. The panel on the right displays a line of flowing "cursive" calligraphy, and, at the bottom, one of block-letter "Kufic" script, with, between them, filigreed arches of an almost ethereal complexity.

Entrance to the *qubba* is free of charge and it's a short walk from the center of town, so even if you agree with me about the brutally un-romantic restoration, it's worth the visit. One of the most ill-advised "improvements" are the two unsightly wooden mezzanines which like two rough black shelves cut in half the tall, graceful Moorish arches on either side. It seems they were installed by the Dominicans centuries ago as, respectively, a choir and a pulpit for their religious services.

When I remarked to the lady in charge that I didn't notice them when I was allowed a glimpse of the *qubba* before its restoration, she explained that these wooden platforms were removed when the private owners took over the palace from the Church, but that the restorers – 150 years later - found them in a cellar nearby and, verifying where they once belonged, zealously decided to put them back in place.

In that case, I was about to ask indignantly but didn't, why not have also kept the simple but charming Andalusian country manour, duly freshened up, and which I remembered from my first visit, rather than replacing it with what looks like a streamlined airport lobby? After all, it was part of the history of the place, too!

Ibn Tibonn, a Jewish philosopher
of Moorish Granada

At the western edge of El Realejo, just behind the Plaza de Isabel la Católica (where we see the bronze statues of the Queen and Columbus, with him kneeling before her to present his plan for sailing west across the sea) and in the triangular space formed by the crossing of Calle San Matias and Calle Pavaneras, stands a statue, tall and elegant, of a man in a sort of turban holding aloft a scroll. He's been there since 1988 and represents an illustrious 12th century philosopher, translator and teacher known simply as Tibonn (in full, Yehuda Ibn Tibonn).

There were many other scholars who lived in Spain in the Middle Ages, and the greatest of them all, Averroes (Ibn Rush'd, in Arabic) has his own statue in Cordoba. But this sculpture is special because it was conceived, financed and given to the city by the subject's direct descendant, an Italian Jew living in Mexico called Gutierrez Tibón, as the name is spelled in Spanish.

This romantic humanist dreamed his life long of one day gracing the streets of Granada, and especially the part of it where the Jews and his ancestor lived, with a fine statue to the man. The town council graciously, and gratefully had it placed on a pedestal so that, like the Statue of Liberty in New York, all those visiting El Realejo would be greeted by this beacon of learning and justice. At the age of 28 Tibonn had to flee Spain when it fell under the rule of the Almohads, great artists but hostile to Jews, eventually settling in southern France where he died forty years later.

There have been many stories of the descendants of Jews returning from America to find their ancestral home in Toledo and opening its door with a heavy key passed down from father to son over eight or nine centuries, but none of them have been proven. With the persecution which the Spanish Jews suffered from Moors and Christians alike, few traces of their presence have survived, even though they are said to have been in Granada before the Romans themselves.

Except Tibonn, because one of his descendants living on the other side of the Atlantic wanted every visitor to El Realejo to remember him. The good Gutierrez died shortly after bringing his graceful, even if fanciful, statue to Granada, and I've added his picture so the reader will remember him also.

Casa de los Tiros

Heading from El Realejo towards the Gran Vía, along the *Calle de Santa Escolástica*, we come to our last stop, and not the least spectacular: the 16th century palace known as the *Casa de los Tiros* - the "House of the Shots", because of the muskets which jut out from between its battlements, whose medieval aspect was unfortunately spoiled by the extra floor which was added in the 19th century. The story of the palace gives us a vivid idea of how cultures overlapped and intertwined in the newly conquered city, until one predominated over the other.

The saga of the Granada-Venegas family

A mosque stood on the site of the Casa de los Tiros, which, following customary practice, was temporarily used after the conquest as a church, until a Christian-style temple could be built nearby and which, before being itself demolished after the 19th century reform, gave the street its name, the Calle Santa Escolástica. The Moorish building was then bought by a Spanish nobleman who destroyed it and built his palace. His daughter and heir married a descendant of the illustrious Granada Venegas family.

Their saga is worthy of a romantic novel. Over a century before the conquest, a child of the noble Venegas family, lords of the Christian town of Luque, was captured after a battle and brought up in the Nasrid Court, becoming a good Moorish aristocrat and founding a clan whose arabized name was Bannigas. When Granada was conquered, the members of this family, who had kept alive the memory of their Christian forefather, immediately abjured Islam and converted to his faith. They then took what was considered to be their place as leading squires of the city, being, of course, exempted from the restrictions imposed on "authentic" *moriscos*.

The façade is indeed impressive, tall, austere and decorated only with five lifelike statues of Greek gods dressed as Roman warriors, each one standing on a small cornice. But even more powerful and unique is the palace's famous hall, called the *Cuadra Dorada*, with its extraordinary coffered ceiling, a sort of portrait gallery of Spain's heroes in relief. Indeed, I can think of no sight which so eloquently conveys the single-minded view that the Spanish *conquistadores* had of their sacred mission: to subjugate pagans, slaughtering those who opposed them, to obtain booty and glory for their families and monarch, and to spread the True Faith. These fierce, yet irresistibly attractive busts and their explanatory captions are inserted, like strips of motion picture film, between the richly decorated beams of the ceiling. They bear laurel wreaths, duck-billed helmets, Italian-style pointed hats, and some belligerently hold swords and lances across their shoulders. All are shown in profile, like the faces on stamps or coins, and in highly-stylized caricature, with a crude, yet polished power which is uniquely Spanish.

The expressive, almost grimacing faces alternately convey pride, arrogance, devotion, austerity, ferocity... but never meekness or self-doubt. Under constant adversity, these qualities would have been signs of unmanliness - and manliness, according to the Spanish version of Christianity, was synonymous with godliness.

Voices of the Reconquest

The masterpiece of the Casa de los Tiros combines pictures and words to sing the praises of those who struggled to rid Christendom of the Moors, from the Arab invasion in 711 to the time of the palace's construction, some 50 years after the conquest of Granada, under the reign of the Emperor-King Carlos Quinto. Reading the captions helps us understand how the Spaniards of the Reconquest saw themselves and their crusade. There is no trace of the guilt which tinges our modern-day neo-imperialistic ventures - quite to the contrary, these were saviours, men and women of virtue, who believed in the sanctity of their task, and who were revered by their contemporaries, just as we today look up to artists and humanitarians. Here is my commented translation - in which I have tried to reproduce the characteristically blunt style of the period - of some of the elegies inscribed, in large gilded letters, on the ceiling of Granada's Casa de los Tiros.

Don Fernando "The Saint", a Spaniard, King of Castile, among many other deeds took Cordoba and Seville. He was made a Saint. [Fernando III took Cordoba and Seville from the Moors, achieving sainthood for his leading role in the Reconquest]

Pelayo, a Spaniard, among his many other deeds, from his refuge in a cave struck at the Moors and began to reconquer Spain. [King Pelayo was the first of the Spanish kings after the Arab invasion who, after taking refuge in the legendary cave - Covadonga - in the mountains of Asturias, retaliated by launching the Reconquest.]

Isabel, Queen of Spain, among her many other deeds, cleared Spain, threw out the Jews and Moors and took Granada.

Diego de Vargas, a Spaniard, among his many other deeds, with a mace of olive wood, slew a great number of Moors in a single day.

Alonso, tutor of the King, a Spaniard, among his many other deeds, refusing to see his Lord dishonoured, entered the battle only with offensive weapons, knowing that he was going to die.
Garcia Gómez Carrillo, a Spaniard, among his many other deeds, let himself be torn apart by an iron hook while defending the castle of Jerez.

Olea, standard bearer of the King, a Spaniard, among his many other deeds, after his hands had been cut off, held the standard with his arms until he died.

The wife of Alvar Pérez, a Spaniard, among her many other deeds, defended, along with her ladies-in-waiting, the castle of Martos for three days, until they were rescued. [There are several heroines depicted on the ceiling, apart from Queen Isabel, and all are nameless, only being referred to as "'la mujer de... ". They were Christians, but they had owners!]

Recaredo, a Spaniard, among his many other deeds, destroyed the Arians and their heresies. [This is the only reference to the period immediately before the Arab invasion. Recaredo was the first medieval king to convert from the Arian sect of his Visigothic people to the local Catholicism, thus becoming the first in the line of Spain's Christian monarchs.]

The last hero celebrated as *"Iñigo de Mendoza, a Spaniard, among his many other deeds, vanquished the Moors in Huelma and ordered the release of all the Christians held captive in the Kingdom of Granada"* is none less than the Count of Tendilla, who took part in the conquest and remained in Granada as Governor of the Alhambra and military leader of the city. He belonged to the family of the powerful Cardinal Mendoza, and one of the first Spaniards of the Renaissance. His profile here is much more than a simple caricature, and suggests that the artist may have known him personally.

In any case, the wood carver has left us an intriguing psychological portrait of a restless, sensitive man, avid for knowledge and dressed in the accoutrements of a Greek philosopher, as if to accentuate his intellectual, and for his time aggressively modern, stance. I have tried to capture with my pen the main features of this eloquent image, since it is not easily distinguishable from the floor of the hall, and, also, because I have always felt a special affinity with the man...

Relics of the old Granada in the new

The historical places we have explored might have disappeared if they had not been located on such inaccessible hilltops and steep slopes in the northern part of the city. The southern part on the plain below also had its fortified walls and medieval gates, but that was where the *granadinos* naturally built their new city after the Reconquest, clearing away most of the antiquities.

But there are many isolated remains, and several names of streets and squares, which remind us of the old times. So when the curious traveller has wandered all over the Alhambra and the Albaicín, and if the thirst for discovery is still unquenched, he or she can go down to the center of the city to search for these vestiges of the past, which have much to teach us.

In Granada, *Centro* means the streets around Puerta Real, where the main thoroughfares Calle de los Reyes Católicos, Calle Recogidas and Acera del Darro form an upside down Y slightly twisted to the east. (Gran Vía, being "the street that goes nowhere" as it was called by its critics, is by far the widest street in the city, but less central, stretching along the foot of the Albaicín as it does.) The River Darro, which since the 19th century has flowed under the pavement, marks, from the place where it swings to the east at Puerta Real, the southern limit of what was once the fortified city. From the right bank of the river, the wall stretched westward below the Plaza Bibarrambla, where it twisted north to the slopes of the Albaicín, where the Zirid wall still stands. That is how the medieval city is shown in the famous map of Ambrosio de Vico, drawn in 1613, a century after the Reconquest.

Puerta Real, the Royal Gate that no longer exists

We can visualize the original shape of the great esplanade called Puerta Real by sitting on one of the public benches surrounding La Fuente de las Batallas, a handsome fountain standing in the center of the lozenge-shaped square. We will see that the contours of the urban landscape haven't changed much, although many of the elements which once formed it have been replaced by modern ones.

The Darro river was buried under the streets below Plaza Nueva by covering it with brick arches – known as *el embovedado* – which were then paved over as horizontally as possible, in the 19th century. The objective was less to facilitate the traffic of people and beasts of burden than – thanks to the new sanitation laws - to smother the stench of the sewage that flowed down from the Albaicín.

[The Darro, so charming today, had such a bad reputation that the *granadinos* ended up using its name generically for any drainage channel or sewer, and still do, without thinking what an insult that is for a stream that has long since become sparking clean. If you call a plumber to unplug your sink here, he will be sure to it as *el darro*, without a thought.]

But the original cover created an unsightly bump in the middle of the street which resembled a mole-tunnel, and was so high that people on one side couldn't see those on the other. But after the Civil War it was rebuilt with slabs of cast concrete rather than arches, and today it is so flat that many younger *granadinos* don't even know that there is a river flowing underneath it.

In the 16th century, then, the Darro wound its way uncovered and unembanked down from the Albaicín and through this vast esplanade, famous for its sprawling open-air food market or *rastro*, for which it was called *Plaza del Rastro*. It was where all the horses and coaches arrived from other towns, and after the visitors shook off the dust they had only to go through the old Moorish gate, the *Puerta del Rastro* –Market Gate- at the western end of the plaza and down the long, narrow *Calle de los Mesones* – "Street of the Inns" – where he could find a hot meal and a probably lice-infested bed. The Puerta del Rastro was renamed, at the beginning of the next (17th) century *Puerta Real de España*, "Royal Gate of Spain", when Granada received the visit of King Felipe IV. For the occasion, the medieval gate was re-faced with polished stone and carved with the royal shields, as well as an inscription praising the King's father Felipe III for having expelled the remaining 300,00 *moriscos* from Granada (and all of the Kingdom) in the year 1610, by definitively shipping them back to Morocco. There was still great mistrust of them for the bloody uprising in Granada and the nearby mountains four decades earlier, and it was generally felt they went on being Muslims at heart even if they pretended to be Christians. The drastic measure was further justified by widespread suspicions that the moriscos were in league with Ottoman Turks, North African "Barbary" pirates and even French Huguenots, to invade the country.

The Royal Gate was demolished in 1790, leaving only its name, for which the old market square had since become known. Thus, the plaza first gave its name to the gate, and then, two centuries later, the embellished gate gave its new, honorific name to the plaza...

The gently curving row of large buildings which we see from our bench on the right, and which once stood on the riverbank (and, originally, the city wall that ran along it) comes to an end at the Plaza del Campillo. This traditional meeting-place, almost entirely filled with café tables in the shade of its enormous shade trees, was in fact nothing more than a field that stood just inside another Moorish gate, torn down along with the wall.

In this detail of the famous map drawn by Ambrosio de Vico, we can see, on the far left, number 54, the old Moorish gate called Puerta del Rastro (later Puerta Real); in the center, number 53, the Puerta de Bibataubín and behind it the Plaza del Campillo, now much smaller and planted with shade trees; and to the right of the gate, the Castillo de Bibataubín with its round towers, which we shall visit next. The River Darro flows freely through the entire esplanade, towards the Genil, outside of this detail on the right hand side.

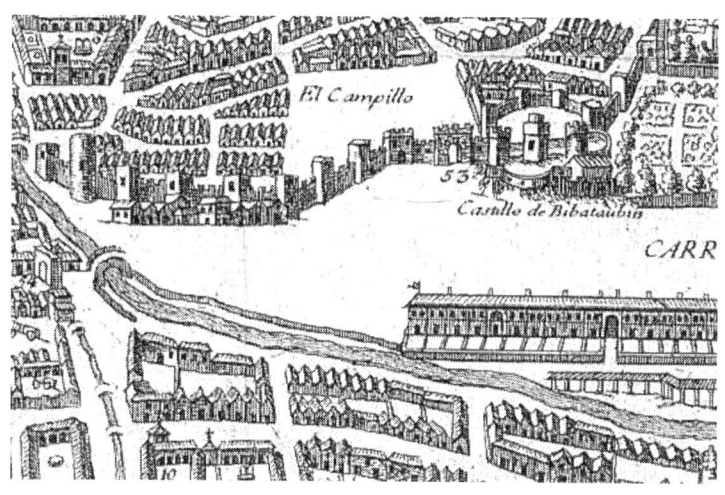

Palace of Bibataubín,
remains of a Moorish fortress

The imaginary line of the vanished wall, then, resumes after the missing part at Plaza del Campillo and its vanished gate, to next take the form of a baroque palace which, with its exuberant shapes and mouldings could be the backdrop for a Spanish *zarzuela*, or comic opera. Since the Civil War it has been the headquarters of the provincial government, but the *granadinos* have always called it by its old Arabic name, the palace of *Bibataubín*, "Gate of the Penitents", since the gate that once stood in the gap formed by the shady square we have just seen (Plaza del Campillo) led into a quarter of the Moorish town famous for its holy men, the Muslim equivalent of monks.

The palace was previously a fort or castle – and called *Castillo de Bibataubín* rather than *palacio* – which was built by the Catholic Monarchs after the conquest, in case the Moors returned with Turkish support. Much later it was torn down and an elegant military headquarters or *cuartel* built in its place. If it were not for a very curious detail we might take the building for another pretty baroque palace with curlicues and white frosting over every window, in the Sevillian style, and its two-tiered door flanked on either side by four wreathed, or twisted granite columns which, it seems, were made for the Sagrario Church next to the Cathedral but judged to be insufficiently monumental and given to the army barracks instead.

When the Monarchs built the fortress, which was much larger than the current palace, they placed four conical towers at each corner. And when, under the Bourbons, the place became a military barracks, the entire castle was demolished except – for some strange reason – the stump of one of these towers, which was used as the base for a curious appendage rising two more storeys in the air, with ornamental windows in each of its twelve sides.

We can see that it was grafted onto a pre-existing base because the bottom part is smooth and slightly conical, spreading at the bottom. In fact, it is the lower part of one of the much older towers built by the Catholic Monarchs, and it juts out from the flank of the elegant palace like an odd swelling. Some historians even think it might have been part of an older Moorish fortress.

El Campillo and the notorious "Manigua"

Adjacent to the opposite end of the palace, on the eastern corner of the Plaza del Campillo, near where the Gate of the Penitents stood, there is a restaurant which now has the name El Rey Chico (the Spanish nickname for Boabdil was "the little king" because he was very short). Before the Civil War it was a *cafeteria* (which does not mean a self-service restaurant as it does for us, but simply a café and place for drinks and snacks) called the Café Alameda, which has its place in history as Granada's most famous literary landmark. A *tertulia* or literary discussion group calling itself *El Rinconillo* – "the little corner" – gathered there to discuss poetry and art, the most famous members of which were Federico García Lorca, Manuel de

Falla and the historian to whom I owe so much, Antonio Gallego y Burín.

Until the mid-20th century, the quarter that lies just north of El Campillo was a vast red-light district (even if it didn't have red lights – just as the Spanish term for that sort of place, *barrio chino* - Chinatown – has nothing to do with China). This notorious part of town was called *La Manigua*, or "The Swamp". I only saw the last vestiges of it, but to all accounts it was a lively place with its noisy taverns and busy brothels. But the very prudish victors of the Civil War, horrified that so much dissolute behaviour could have been tolerated by the godless Republican government, set out to clean the place up, starting with the construction of a new avenue through it, which they called Calle Angel Ganivet. It is a resolutely classical street with its austere granite arcades, but it would be more in place in Madrid or Bilbao than gay Andalucía. Today it is Granada's "chic street", with several expensive jewellery and fashion shops and a smart hotel.

This had the desired effect of pushing the brothels up the hill towards the Church of San Matías, where the Manigua made its last stand until I returned to Granada in the 1980's. The only visible reminder of the old Manigua, which used to stretch all the way down to the city wall, is the name of the alley that runs behind Granada's theater, *El Teatro Isabel la Católica*. It is best known today because on it is the theatre's back entrance reserved for people like me who buy the higher seats, which requires going up a separate staircase. To get to my point, this alleyway is still called *Calle Moras*, literally "street of the Moorish girls", which is amazing when you consider the shamelessly sexist and racist origins of the name. Although few *granadinos* know it, the street was famous after the Reconquest for its Moorish prostitutes who, it seems, were greatly admired by the soldiers in the nearby barracks for their erotic arts. Since *mora* also means "mulberries", people may have conveniently decided the name was due to a mulberry tree that once stood there...

The Calle Moras is now a very smart pedestrian street of small wine bars and fashion shops and therefore of little interest to us, apart from its anachronistic name. But the building which on its south side houses the Teatro Isabel la Católica, built just after the Civil War, has an extraordinary detail which illustrates the Catholic fervour of the many *granadinos* who supported the triumphant General Franco, and in those years were still proud to show it, and which I have photographed for my book, since no one seems to notice it any more, which is easy to do because of its odd position. But if you stand on the far side of Puerta Real, you will see, peeping up from a medieval-style tower on the roof, a large and very ugly concrete statue of the Queen herself, looking southward, as if she were guarding the city against a possible return of the heathens from across the sea.

What was Granada like after the Reconquest?

If we twist around on our bench to face the other, southern side of the esplanade, we can see a narrow street coming from the Calle San Antón and whose name, *Calle del Puente Castañeda*, reminds us of the existence of the picturesque Castañeda bridge. In the etching I have shown here, you can see the river flowing towards the Genil under it , and in the background the bell towers of the Iglesia de las Angustias, framed against the snows of the Sierra Nevada.

If we could travel a few centuries in a time machine, we would easily see, high up on the left, the towers of the Alhambra and even the Convento de los Mártires, just as in the old pictures. And if we loosen the reins on our imagination a little more, we'll see a crowd of soldiers and mule-carts milling about the squat towers of the Bibataubín fortress.

Since the soldiers were always far from home, they drew a large community of prostitutes who even followed them on military campaigns, a well-organized feminine brigade that trailed along behind with their own mules and carts. Better share your mistress with others than have no wife at all, the soldiers surely thought!

And if, still on our bench, we half-close our eyes and imagine what was going on behind the now-vanished city wall, we will see *las niñas* sweeping out their huts and bringing water from the well in jugs slung on their hips. One has already started work and is leading a moustachioed sergeant by the hand towards her door, pulling back the curtain that keeps out the flies so that he can enter into the shady interior, bone-poor but clean and tidy, like all women's rooms. It is the world of Cervantes we are seeing, with all its joy and despair.

Then, in Granada as in other cities of Europe, thousands of women filled the streets of entire districts at all hours the day and night, just to find enough money to keep themselves and their children from starving. In those unforgiving times a peasant girl had only to surrender once to the master's son and get caught at it to soon find herself on the streets of one Manigua or the other.

When the soldiers and sailors brought syphilis back from the New World, there was such a deadly epidemic, especially in the early years, that the authorities rounded up all prostitutes to examine them, and if they had signs of the disease them they were locked them away in special convents. The nuns were supposed to cure and reform them, but since this was largely wishful thinking, the inevitable solution was to keep them out of the way.

Granada's convent-prison was popularly known as *Las Recogidas* and stood just south of Puerta Real at the beginning of the Calle de Recogidas (and in fact the name *recogida*, literally "withdrawn" or "taken back" was in Spain a common euphemism for "reformed prostitute"). But the institution's proper name was *Convento de Santa María Egipcíaca*, for Saint Mary of Egypt, who had herself been a prostitute in her native Alexandria before become a Christian hermit and mystic. The convent itself was demolished in the mid-20th century to make way for the new Calle Recogidas, so all that is left of it today is the name!

Mariana Pineda, Granada's heroine

The Recogidas convent held female political prisoners too, and there was one who became not only a popular heroine and martyr, but also the subject of a gripping play written by none other than Federico García Lorca, the title of which is simply her name, Mariana Pineda. She was a young 19th century revolutionary who, along with her daring (male) comrades (in Granada and all over Spain) plotted to overthrow the despotic King Fernando VII. To prepare for the day of liberation she secretly had a flag embroidered with the symbols of their cause (one of which was Masonry, which the Catholic rulers held in special horror).

But she was given away by the seamstress, imprisoned in the Recogidas convent and, after refusing to declare the names of her fellow-plotters, condemned to death and garrotted in front of the Puerta de Elvira where everyone could witness the King's justice, in the year 1831. In his play Lorca wove a love story that never existed into the political drama, although the fearless Mariana had one husband and several lovers in her short life, and several children too, one of them out of wedlock.

They say that when the nuns tried to take off her garters before going to the scaffold she pushed their hands away, disdainfully saying "I don't want to die with my stockings hanging down", and so they let her keep them on. A plaza in Granada, just above the Campillo, is named for her with high up on a pedestal a very conventional statue of what was for the times a very unconventional woman.

In this engraving, copies of which were widely sold, she is receiving the extreme unction from an exalted-looking priest, while the executioner adjusts the iron collar around the stake, against which her neck will be crushed.

The fountains of two cloisters

Until the mid-19th century there were so many churches and convents in Granada that the city was often praised as being "Cristianópolis", but most of them disappeared after the State expropriation of Church property, circa 1830. However, some of them, and also some parts of them, can still be seen.

The city's market building is called *Mercado de San Agustín* because it stands on what was once an Augustine monastery. When the building was demolished, the baroque fountain in its cloister was salvaged and placed in the center of the Plaza Bibarrambla, with its grumpy-looking "giants" holding the fountain dish on their heads, and the tiny little Neptune on the top.

Just a few streets to the south, in the *Plaza de la Trinidad*, another, much plainer fountain stands under the tall lime trees which also was part of a convent where lived the Sisters of the Trinity. The fountain stood in same spot as today - when the convent was pulled down to create the plaza, the fountain in the middle of what had been the cloister was simply left where it was, to cool the passers-by on Granada's long, hot summer afternoons.

Monastery or convent?

In Spain, the distinction between convent and monastery is looser and not at all the same as in other lands, where a convent is a place for nuns and a monastery for monks. Adhering to the ancient Latin meanings of the terms, a monastery is a place for either monks or nuns to live and pray in solitude - "mono" - and a convent is a place where either monks or nuns "convene", assemble to live and pray. Conventos are usually in the cities where the occupants can perform goods works, teach, feed and care for the poor, and monasteries far away in the countryside where the occupants meditate in silence and pray on behalf of wealthy patrons. That is why many more cloistered houses are called *conventos* than *monasterios*, even when they are full of monks.

Street of Boards and Street of Little Bridges

From Plaza de la Trinidad we walk down the gently sloping *Calle de las Tablas* which dates back to the Moorish period. It took its name – "street of the boards" – from the butchers who stood there selling their meat on makeshift wooden tables which they set up in front of the Moorish gate at the top of the street also called, in Arabic, *Puerta de las Tablas*.

At the bottom of the street we see, on the left, the *Palacio de las Columnas* – "Palace of the Columns" - a 19th century neo-classical palace which now houses the Translators' School, part of the Granada University. Half a century ago it was still the Faculty of Philosophy and Letters, where in 1961 I studied Spanish literature and Classical Arabic for a very un-academic spring term, but with lots of extra-curricular activities… As the reader may have guessed, the author had to fully mature before seriously sitting down to do his homework.

The palace-school opens onto the Calle Puentezuelas, a side street of Calle de las Tablas. Its name "little bridges" comes from the amusing fact that since it ran from east to west, perpendicularly to the ditches which carried rain water down towards the plain, people had to step over a series of small bridges not to wet their feet, at least when it was raining, which does sometimes happen in Granada.

Green Bridge and "the French Granada"

The River Darro is famous because it runs between Alhambra and Albaicín in the heart of Granada's medieval part until it flows into the River Genil on the east. The Genil, although just a stream by our standards, is part of a larger and much longer waterway that is born in the Sierra Nevada and crosses most of Andalucia before flowing into the Guadalquivir. Two old bridges span the Genil at the foot of the old Moorish city.

The first of them, coming from upstream, is the *Puente Verde*, "Green Bridge", which crosses the river near the beginning of the road that leads up into Sierra Nevada. It was originally made of wood and painted green, but when the Napoleonic troops invaded the city they rebuilt it in masonry, so that they could easily deploy their cannons and carts from one side of the river to the other in case of uprisings. But from force of habit it kept its old name, "green bridge", even though it seems strange for a bridge made of stone.

Around Granada there are other "French bridges", as the *granadinos* call them with a trace of resentment against the invader, but the tale of the Puente Verde adds insult to injury, because to build it the French cannibalized one of the city's grandest churches, claiming that it was easier and cheaper than having the stone quarried. It was also, of course, to show their republican contempt for all symbols of the old, Catholic Spain – especially in the case of this particular church, built as the shrine and burial place of the glorious military leader of the Reconquest, known ever since as El Gran Capitán.

Before the horrified eyes of populace and priests, the French had the proud bell tower of the 16th century Monastery of San Jerónimo dismantled, stone by stone, and carted across the city to the Genil. The once-tall bell tower was left cut off in the middle, and only rebuilt 150 years later during the Franco dictatorship. You can easily tell what part is new and what part is old because the stones of the lower part are burnished by centuries of Andalucian sunlight, while the new, upper ones bearing the belfry are of a distinctly lighter tone.

Here we see the two-toned belfry and the once-green bridge, which was widened to allow two-way motor traffic in 1985. Some of the belltower-stones which were carved with heraldic symbols of the noble families which paid for them were replaced and put on display in the Archaeological Museum.

Continuing downstream along the Genil, through the palm trees and aromatic bushes of the riverside garden, we come to the other old, and in this case truly ancient bridge of the river, known since time immemorial as *El Puente Romano* – "The Roman Bridge", just like the one in Cordoba and others in northern Spain. It is a typical Roman bridge with its round arches and fine proportions, although it was rebuilt by the

Moors and underwent several more overhauls down through the ages, which has destroyed much of its interest for us. Not long ago a modern bridge was built for traffic a bit further downstream, leaving for the pedestrians the older one, called the Puente Blanco, the white bridge, not (once more) for its colour but because there was a Moorish quarter nearby which bore, in Arabic, the name of "casa blanca", just like the city in Morocco. (To complicate things even further, it's also called the Puente Romano...)

Downstream from the Puente Verde, there is a lovely stroll to take along the right bank of the river, through the charming garden planted by the same French occupants. Like many other gardens planted in that time of scientific discovery, it began life as a carefully-labelled botanical garden, but when the fad faded became just a lovely little riverside park, with many species of Mediterranean trees and semi-tropical shrubs.

The French were also pioneers of urbanistic improvement, and made this part of Granada the most pleasant part of town for residents, rather than just tourists, to stroll in of an evening, thanks to the tree-lined boulevard that run parallel to the river. The furthest upstream is the *Paseo de la Bomba* (which owes its curious name to a small metal fountain among the gardens which people thought resembled the floating mines used in World War I). The broad promenade bends to the south with the river, at which point it becomes the *Paseo del Salón*, originally called by the French "Salle de Séjour" or living-room since it was intended to give the upper classes a chance to show off their fine carriages in an exclusive setting. There is even a French-style kiosk, once a bandstand, with tables set out on the river bank where one can stop for refreshments, just like ones in the Bois de Boulogne!

Continuing our walk downstream, at the monumental fountain called *Fuente de las Granadas*, "Fountain of the Pomegranates", the boulevard forks to the right and enters the city center by an even leafier avenue, the *Carrera del Genil*, "Road of the Genil", which the *granadinos* affectionately call by its informal name, *Carrera de la Virgen*, "Road of the Virgin", because on it is the great church of *Nuestra Señora de las Angustias*, Granada's patron saint. I always think of the *Carrera de la Virgen* as Granada's little Champs-Elysées, except that it is much more pleasant to stroll on, with its overhanging bower of shade trees and well-worn flagstones polished to a sheen by generations of Spanish sweethearts, so cool under the foot in summer.

After crossing the river, we proceed downstream on the left bank of the Genil (but not as close to it as before), until we reach the ultra-modern *Palacio de Congresos*. Here, we will walk through the playgrounds and down near the water's edge, to visit the first of two Moorish monuments which grace this part of the city.

Ermita de San Sebastián

The first is by far the most precious, but also the most neglected by the oft-ungrateful *granadinos*, who have a tendency to think that with the Alhambra and the Royal Chapel they have more than enough *patrimonio*, as historical heritage is called in Spanish, without worrying about restoring all the other antiquities that pop up, or, for the ones that were always there, refuse to be bulldozed away.

The name that this small, and from a distance unimpressive-looking building has had since the Reconquest is "Hermitage of Saint Sebastian", which only partly reflects its real identity. It was in the time of the Almohads a *murabit*, or as it is called in Spanish-Arabic a *morabito*, a place where hermits lived and meditated in prayer, a sort of Muslim monastery. There were many such *morabitos* in Moorish Spain and people would come to feed the wise men and ask for their help and advice, like living saints. But since these buildings were too small to be of any use to the Christians, they crumbled away – with the sole exception of this one, simply because it was turned into a church. Ironically, the God that saved the mosque was Christian.

From the outside, it looks like a small square house with a four-sided tile roof (added in the 19th century to cover up the dome) and a belfry which unmistakably marked it as a church. Inside, also, it is decorated like any other parish church with saints and crucifixes, and an unsightly coat of ochre paint covering the domed ceiling. But even so the oriental artistry is apparent in the dome's intertwined pattern of raised bricks, rising from all around in slender ribs to intersect elegantly with one another, forming a large central many-pointed star. The entrance door has a Moorish, slightly pointed arch which recalls the Puerta Nueva in the Albaicín, although someone has inexplicably painted it red.

I can imagine how it must have been before, with the door not painted red and the outside dome not covered with bricks, standing on a strand that slopes gently into the water, where the Moors, before praying, stepped down to wash their feet. With a few date palms next to it, wouldn't it have reminded you of the Tigris rather than the Genil?

As an example of Moorish art the *murabit* is a minor monument, to be sure, but it has two things that make it unique. Not only is it the only hermitage of its kind left in Spain, giving it equal status with the Bañuelo on the left bank of the Darro, but it marks the spot where a momentous event of Spanish history took place. It was here that the defeated King Boabdil agreed to meet the Catholic Monarchs when he handed over the key of the city to them on the 2nd of January, 1492. After Boabdil had performed his sad duty, a priest led the Castilians in the chanting of a *Te Deum* to give thanks for the victory they had at long last won.

Alcázar Genil,
victim of restoration

A short walk down the river bank takes us to a much larger and for some people more important monument, the *Alcázar Genil*. This elegant villa was for the Almohads a rustic "folly" far from the Albaicín, later on enlarged by the Nasrids, whose court poet, Ibn Zamrak, wrote a poem to its beauty. Its last Moorish owner was Boabdil's mother, who sold it to the Catholic Monarchs after the surrender, presumably for whatever she could get.

The Alcázar was famous for its huge rectangular pond (125x30 meters) which could be filled by deviating water from the river, for the staging of mock naval battles between "Moors" and "Christians". One can imagine the excitement of the onlookers during those spectacular and also bloody clashes on the water, in which the objective was to set fire to the enemy's vessel and make it sink, regardless of the number of broken bones.

Sadly, the little palace was restored in the days before, at least in Spain, that difficult art was performed scientifically and with scrupulous respect for how the building once was, rather than how some heavy-handed architect wished it had been. The result is that everything here, inside and out, looks brand new, with perfectly straight corners and perfectly smooth walls, all smartly and professionally turned out like one of those ubiquitous Moorish-style villas which are so popular in Andalucia, whether they are homes or restaurants. The pond where the battles were once held is now a geometrical sort of garden which stretches from the entrance of the palace down to Camino de Ronda, the busy avenue which cuts through the forest of apartment blocks which so disfigure this part of the city. Lorenzo's advice to the curious traveller: go there if you wish, but steel yourself for the disappointment.

Two little-known but interesting places

Postigo de San Lorenzo,
the gate that got lost

Six of the city's Moorish gates have come down to us more or less intact, the main ones being Elvira, Monaita and Puerta Nueva, with the Puerta de Hernán Román whose arch is occupied by a Christian chapel. They are all part of the Zirid wall which surrounds the old fortress of the Albaicín, and descends to the city along the Cuesta Alhacaba.

But the newer wall built by the Nasrids three centuries later also has two of its original gates. The taller one, used every day by the dwellers of Haza Grande to go down to the Albaicín, is the Puerta de Fajalauza, at the foot of Granada's highest hill, the *Cerro de Miguel*. Although picturesque, it has been greatly altered by fanciful restorations over the centuries. Its name means "Gate of the Almond Grove", and since it has always been situated at the heart of the pottery-making district, the tiles, plates and jars with Moorish motifs, in blue, green and white have become known, generically, as *fajalauza*.

These are the gates that are known and, except one, still used, and which we see over and over again as we wander through the old city. However, there is a sixth gate which being in a hard-to-reach place, was virtually forgotten and buried under ivy and rubble. No Moorish document mentions its existence, which is why its original Arabic name is unknown. The *granadinos* renamed it for a nearby (and now vanished) church which was dedicated my own saint, the *Postigo de San Lorenzo*. "Postigo" usually means the "shutter" of a window, but here it is popularly used for "puerta".

Unlike the other gates, this one can't be seen from any of Granada's streets or belvederes, and you will have to ask your way to get there from the highway called Carretera de Murcia. It is a very plain-looking Moorish gate standing at a right-angle to the wall, which is why it seems to turn away from our sight, making it easy to miss.

The *Postigo de San Lorenzo* no longer leads to anywhere because its inner wall has been bricked up. During the Civil War, the *Albaicíneros* hid inside the passageway when Franco's planes bombed the hill, and after the war was over only tramps seem to have used it as a shelter, until it was rediscovered by an archaeologist. So there it is, lost in the shadows of the ivy and the past, waiting for the lover of Granada whose thirst for secrets is never quenched.

I add this photograph to show how the gate looked after a recent clean-up.

Acequia Gorda, the city's old aqueduct

One bright winter Sunday morning, eight or nine years ago, I set out from the Cuesta Alhacaba, in the company of a dark young lady and a small white dog, to search for the source, not of the Nile or even the Euphrates, but the canal which once supplied the city with water, fondly remembered by older *granadinos* as the *Acequia Gorda*, the "big canal".

The Moors built it and the Christians used it until the advent of steam power, electricity and modern machinery. Before that, flour could only be made by millstones turned either by animals or that most precious of Andalucian substances, water. The Acequia Gorda fed as many as 100 such mills, the remains of a few of which can be seen along the short slope called the *Cuesta de los Molinos* which plunges down from the canal to the River Genil, although most stood along the much longer *Calle de los Molinos*, streets whose names speak for themselves. Further downhill, in the city center, is a narrow street called, in memory of the canal which flowed there until it was filled in, by the curious name Antes Acequia Gorda – "previously Acequia Gorda". A little further, just below Calle San Antón, is a large brick *sifón* or floodgate, once used for an old flour mill which is also still intact. Other parts of the canal and its floodgates are still used for irrigation, down on La Vega – the plain.

We started, then, from the boulevard on the right bank of the River Genil and veered up the steep *Cuesta de Escoriaza* as if we were going to the Alhambra, turning right at the first hair-pin corner to take the horizontal and picturesque *Paseo de las Palmas*, where we saw the canal flowing on our left hand side, in what looked like a cemented trough.

But as I walked along this glorified ditch, its charm grew on me. There are pleasantly asymmetrical houses, some old and some not so old, and several ancient and disused factories which got their water from the canal by means of rusty locks and sluice gates - just the sort of thing to please the nostalgic traveller.

I truly enjoyed the walk, on which I was, after the constant carnival of Granada, glad to meet nobody or almost nobody, imagining how the snows of the sierra melted and flooded the river, and how skilled water-experts drew some of it off to feed their canal which was tilted just enough to ensure the flow until it reached the city, where it rushed down through the mills with their bins of grain waiting, and then back into the Genil.

At the end of the Paseo de las Palmas the magic is shattered when the languid canal, which I was getting fond of in spite of its greenish water, brutally disappeared under a tangle of motorways...

At that point I suggest you do as we did, give up your search for the source and stroll right back to civilization, and lunch.

La Cartuja Monastery

In the first edition of my book I deliberately passed over one of Granada's main monuments, because I thought it had little to tell the curious traveller about the unique history of the city with its struggle between Christians, Moors and Jews, and also, to be honest, simply because I found the place so unlikeable. This is *La Cartuja*, the 16th century Carthusian monastery lying in the northern suburbs of Granada, which can best be described as depressingly drab, at least when seen from the road that passes below.

However, after recently taking my young son August to visit the bleak monastery, from which the monks were evicted in 1835 when the Spanish State, in a fit of anti-clericalism, expropriated all of the Church's properties, I regretted not having said a single word here about the "Granada Charterhouse" as it is sometimes called in English. It is still as unappealing as before, alone on its dusty slope overlooking Granada's prison with its great white cylindrical watchtower, but there are several astonishing things to be seen inside nevertheless.

[Being well out of the historical downtown area on a lonely stretch of highway, you might be better off taking a cab there and asking the driver to wait *una media hora* - which in Andalucia can mean as much as 40 minutes - to take you back, in exchange for a modest tip.

The austere Carthusian Order was founded by Saint Bruno in southeastern France around the year 1000, taking its name from the nearby Chartreuse mountains.

The elegant cloister, which you cross as you go in, is charming but no more so than many other 16th century cloisters and patios to be found in the city. For sheer baroque beauty, however, is El Sagrario, a sort of big chapel hidden away in the back of one of the several huge and also lavishly decorated naves of the monastery. This Sagrario, which means Tabernacle, and is also known more solemnly as the *Sancta Santorum*, is, to say the least, stupendously theatrical and sensual, with its dazzling array of honey and wine-toned marbles, the ensemble creating a vertiginously swirling effect which, in my opinion, puts it on a par with parts of Saint Peter's in Rome, at their wildest. It is considered to be the most brilliant example of the baroque style in Spain.

Although the name "baroque" itself comes from the Spanish word *barroco* for a convoluted seashell, the Italian and Portuguese, and even German versions are in my opinion much more joyous and radiant than the overloaded, sepulchral atmosphere of Spain's late 16th and early 17th century palaces and temples. But the Sagrario of the Cartuja is the great exception to the rule, and if you're an art-lover you will be sure to fall under its spell.

However, what makes the Cartuja of special interest to the British, and by association American, visitor are the gruesomely realistic series of paintings hanging in its otherwise bare halls, showing the persecution in England of Catholic monks under the rule of Oliver Cromwell, as well as Henry VIII. This bloody episode horrified Catholics everywhere and, it seems, especially the devout Carthusians, although they remained beatifically oblivious to what the Spanish Inquisition was doing to Jews, Moors and other heretics at the same time.

Here are two of the English martyrs with the instruments of their executions, after having risen to Heaven.

Below, shackled monks awaiting their fate in a dungeon.

Three by three and clutching their crucifixes, the monks are dragged to the scaffold by a team of horses.

Last, the brutal anti-Papists desecrate the monks' bodies by chopping them up like butchers. None of the painters was ever in England to witness these horrors, but, being monks themselves, they seemed to have no trouble imagining them.

Oliver Cromwell, as the reader may remember from his school days, was the Protestant rebel who had England's Papist King beheaded, after which he ruled in his stead. But after the Restoration, by which time Cromwell was dead, his body was dug up and mutilated by the Catholics in similar fashion. Many of his fellow "regicides" were sought out and put to death in like manner, if they didn't flee the country first.

These paintings, in the vividly realistic baroque manner, make a visit to the Cartuja a grim but stimulating experience, reminding us, once more, of how merciless people from opposing faiths can be to one another. The bloody taking of Granada is alluded to in one of the paintings, which shows a few "Turks" – as all Muslims were then called – triumphantly watching on as the Protestants do their grisly work.

Castillo de la Calahorra

Almost half way from Granada to the south-eastern city of Almeria stands, at the foot of the towering Sierra Nevada, on a plain which itself is over 1,200 meters above sea level, one of my favourite monuments in the region, the solitary Calahorra Castle with its distinctive four pepper-pot towers. Its reddish colour is due to the dust from a nearby iron ore mine, Alquife, founded by the Romans and in use until recently. From the outside, the castle looks so primitive and forbidding that no one would dream that the interior is a rare example of Italian Renaissance architecture, brought straight from Italy!

I shall say only a few words about this unique and highly romantic place because it's only close to the city of Granada in a historical sense. After the taking of the Alhambra, Queen Isabel allowed her favourite priest Cardinal Mendoza to accord to his son, a hot-blooded youth called Rodrigo Diaz de Vivar - who claimed he was a descendant the legendary Cid - the right to build a castle in the newly conquered territory. This had been denied to other knights because the Queen wisely feared that more castles would soon be used by unruly Christians to make war on one another.

After building up the ruins of a Moorish fortress on the lonely stretch of land called El Zenete, Rodrigo brought from Italy, where he had spent several years admiring the new Renaissance architecture (and, it was said, having and surviving an affair with Lucrezia Borgia) several boatloads of white marble and a team of architects and sculptors to recreate, in the primitive courtyard of his castle, the replica of a Florentine cloister. All of this was carried across the rugged hills on the backs of mules, at huge expense.

After several years of frenetic work and squabbling, the magical result was achieved – a small but precious courtyard of elegant columns and galleries festooned with grotesque figures and floral motifs. Rodrigo only lived there with his bride a few years before fighting with everyone and marching off to the north of Spain, never to be seen again.

I first visited the Calahorra some 15 years ago, in the dead of winter. A moment after we entered the desolate but strangely alive courtyard, great flakes of snow fell out of the rectangle of leaden sky above our heads, and for a moment I couldn't remember if I was in Spain, in Italy or in some country further north.

Here is the courtyard on a more radiant day. Exquisite!

The fortress was only ever used as such by "old Christians" seeking refuge from the 1568 "Morisco" uprising in the Alpujarra, and in the Spanish Civil War by a band of Republicans making a last stand against the troops of Franco, falling afterwards into semi-abandonment and disrepair. It has never been restored which only adds to its haunting appeal, and the current owner, an aristocrat in Madrid, allows visits Wednesday mornings only.

The traveller curious enough to go this far off the beaten path to visit one of the very first monuments outside of Italy to be built in the Renaissance style must leave Granada around 9 or at the latest 10 in the morning, go to the caretaker's house in the neighbouring village, drive him up to the castle with his large key in hand, and reward him with a few euros...

The castle of Vélez Blanco, further north, was built at the same time and in similar style, but it doesn't have Calahorra's operatic history, nor its fantastic setting against the Sierra Nevada. It was heavily restored in Hollywood-movie style with battlements and other long-disappeared adornments, and worst of all, its lovely courtyard was taken down lock stock and barrel a century ago, sold to a French art dealer and ended up in New York's Metropolitan Museum!

Epilogue, with some reflections

What became of the Moors of Granada?

In the earlier stages of the Reconquest, Moors who remained in the Christian zone were traditionally given the freedom to practice Islam and Koranic law, although their rights were steadily whittled away with time.

But by 1492, when Granada was taken, the status quo had changed. The Christians were now the only masters of Spain and determined to put an end to such agreements and rid the land of heathens once and for all. However, during the first years, before the Christians had a firm grip on affairs in Granada, they still allowed the Moors to practice their religion and lead their Islamic way of life, and it was unambiguously set forth in the peace treaty in this sentence, "It is established and agreed that no Moorish man or woman shall be forced to become a Christian - *Es asentado y acordado que ningún moro o mora non haga fuerza a que se torne cristiano ni cristiana*".

Plainly, the Monarchs did not think that lying to non-Christians was a sin, and it soon became clear that they only intended to maintain this arrangement until their position enabled them to quell an uprising. It was one thing to take the Alhambra, but another to become master of the Albaicín!

At first, though, some good-hearted Spaniards tried to use persuasion rather than force. The first Archbishop of Granada, Hernando de Talavera, had his priests learn Arabic in order to gain the trust of the Moors and demonstrate to them the superiority of Christianity, and thus integrate them pacifically to Castilian society. To win their hearts, he even let them sing and dance their native *zambra* in the churches, after hearing Mass.

The Moors fondly called Talavera the "holy wise man", but very few liked his religion, and results of the campaign were dismal. The noble missionary's experiment ended suddenly when the Monarchs returned to Granada in 1499, followed by the Queen's confessor, the dreaded Cardinal Cisneros, Archbishop of Toledo and future General Inquisitor.

Cisneros was horrified to see that the *moros* were still being allowed to worship Mohammed, and wanted to halt Talavera's work and force them to convert, arguing that even if the first generation of converts would not be sincere, their children would. The obstacle facing the rulers was a legal one, since the surrender treaty guaranteed the *moros* religious freedom, and it was feared that any infringement would lead to an uprising.

Cisneros therefore chose to interpret the provisions in his own way, and like a good lawyer began to whittle away at the weakest points. He demanded that those Muslims who had originally been Christians but had converted to Islam did not have the same rights as authentic *mudéjares* and should now return to their original faith.

The handful of these "renegade Christians" in the Albaicín created such an uproar that all of the Moors felt threatened by what was seen as a clear betrayal of the treaty, touching off the bloody *mudéjar* rebellion of 1499, which started when a legendary battle cry went up at the gate called Bib-al-Bonoud, near the Colegiata del Salvador.

This riot gave Cisneros and his partisans the pretext they needed to pass a new decree demanding that all the Moors should be converted under military supervision. There was panic in the city's mosques, which had been transformed with a pen-stroke into churches. The Moors' confusion was such that when, according to a chronicler, they crowded around the baptismal font and were asked what Christian name they wanted, some of the men answered "Maria" and the women "José"...

It was the beginning of a half-century of resentful cohabitation, in which the converted Moors, now known as *moriscos*, pragmatically agreed "to put crosses on their mosques and bells on their minarets", as long as the equally pragmatic Castilians turned a blind eye to their practicing Islam in private (this duplicitous behaviour was pragmatically condoned by their holy "right of dissimulation" known as *taqiya*). The pseudo-Christian *moriscos* accepted their lot passively because they believed that some new event would make their tormentors relent, such as the threat of an invasion by the Ottoman Turks.

However, the antagonism between the two communities was stronger than any amount of political agreements. When Carlos Quinto visited the city, in 1526, and learned of the constant fighting between the *moriscos* and the new Castilian community, he ordered an assembly to be held in the Royal Chapel. There, he decreed that the *moriscos* should give up their language and customs as they had done with their religion in 1499, and that a tribunal of the Inquisition was to be created in Granada to ensure that the new measures were upheld.

Next, something happened which is astonishing for us, but which for the Spaniards of the time was routine. The cruel decree was suspended when the *moriscos* desperately offered to pay tribute to the King. Like his pragmatic grand-parents when they negotiated the expulsion of the Jews, three decades earlier, Charles agreed to suspend his harsh decree for a period of 40 years, in exchange for the payment of 80,000 ducats (as compared to the 30, 000 offered in vain by the Jews). As well as paying this huge amount, the unfortunate *moriscos* also had to finance, by paying a yearly tax, the construction of the grandiose palace of the Emperor-King in the Alhambra, which they were often unable to do.

So when the period of grace expired, 40 years later, the Castilians renewed their complaints against the moriscos, making other demands than just giving up their language and customs. Envious of the Moors' thriving silk industry, they forbade the exportation of their highly-prized fabrics to other parts of Spain and Europe, while King Philip II made ineffectual efforts to get a Castilian silk industry started in the north to substitute the imports from the south. Even more outrageous was the decision to expropriate all *morisco* landholdings which had not been legally registered with the Castilian administration, due to either ignorance or negligence, which naturally affected many people.

As usual, it all boiled down to money. The first settlers from other parts of Spain who had been lured to Granada by the King's repopulation programme felt cheated when they saw that the newly converted *moriscos* still had rights over property to which they, as old Christians, felt entitled. To satisfy them, the rulers of Granada circumvented the clause against expropriating Moorish property by claiming that to maintain law and order they had to force the new Christians, or *moriscos*, to live on the hilltops of the city, Albaicín and Antequerela, with the loss of their farms and houses in the more desirable lands below. An especially unjust law was also passed forbidding *moriscos* from buying property, while leaving them free to sell what they had.

The outcry among the *moriscos* led to the ruthlessly-fought War of the Alpujarra, which ended with the deportation of all the rebels, in 1570. The *morisco* community was reduced to a terrified mass of people who seldom left their allotted areas, but even so, the hatred which the Castilians felt for them was so great that, another 40 agonizing years later, they decided to expel all persons of Moorish origin, regardless of the fact that their families had been Christians for generations.

All of the *moriscos*, except those who performed some indispensable function or had married old Christians, were deported to other parts of Spain that were far enough from the coast (and therefore from Turkish assistance to be considered strategically safe) or to North Africa. As can be imagined, many never even reached their destinations.

Thus ended, one and a half centuries after the Christian conquest of Granada, the seemingly endless Moorish presence in Spain. By the end of the 16th century, the *moros* had become a distant memory for Spaniards, the quaint subject of the stories which old folks told their grandchildren before putting them to bed.

Aben Humeya and the Alpujarra War

His real name was Don Fernando de Válor and he was a *morisco*, his family having been forced to convert to Christianity three or four generations earlier. He was also of noble lineage and venerated in the Albaicín as a descendent of Mohammed and the Hummeyad clan, the glorious caliphs of Cordoba. He represented his community on the city council - he was one of the famous twenty-four "caballeros" who governed the city - but, being young and hot-blooded, he quarrelled with the mayor on a point of pride and to escape punishment had to take refuge in the mountains of the Alpujarra.

This region, whose name means "place of high meadows" because its terraced fields which are irrigated by the melting snows of the Sierra Nevada, was densely peopled with moriscos, who like their brothers in Granada were inflamed by the treacherousness of the Spaniards, and by the constant harassment of the Inquisitors, who suspected them of not being sincere Christians. After receiving the illustrious fugitive like a saviour, they proclaimed him King of Granada, giving him his historical name Aben Humeya, or "Son of the Hummeyads". The subjects of the new kingdom then began to slaughter all the Christians in the area who didn't have time to escape.

Although the civil war that followed is known as the War of the Alpujarra, it did not spontaneously break out there, but in the Albaicín itself. However, the agitators failed to involve the moriscos of the city, who feared the reprisals which an open revolt would bring upon them, so they rushed to the Alpujarra, where they untruthfully told the moriscos there that the uprising was already under way and that their brothers in Granada needed help.

This made war really break out, with an eruption of the hatred and jealousy which had smouldered for generations. The response of the Castilians was so cruel, even burning the moriscos alive in heaps, that, when the rebellion was finally crushed, the king's brother, Don Juan de Austria, who had been in charge of operations, asked to be relieved because he could not bear seeing "how the victors are treating the vanquished." It was an extraordinary statement, for those heartless times, and for a man scarcely known for being kind-hearted.

As for the fleeting *"king of the moriscos"*, Aben-Humeya, he was slain by his own subjects just one year after his coronation, because he refused to request help from the Turks and Berbers across the sea. In spite of his Moorish roots - and whatever the legend that has grown up around him may claim - he was, by birth and condition, a Spanish gentleman. He wanted justice for his *morisco* community, as he also longed to avenge himself on Granada's mayor, but he refused to betray what was, after all, his country. He died the humble death of a good Catholic, asking for forgiveness for having struck out against the society in which he had been born.

The Queen and the Gypsies

They say that when the future Queen Isabel was still just a child, she saw herself as a lonely saviour, chosen by God to rid her country of the heathen which her royal predecessors, in their laxity and selfishness, had allowed to infest it. The main culprit was her dissolute older half-brother, Enrique IV. And as soon as he was dead and Isabel had fought her way to the throne, pushing aside other pretenders, she set herself to the task of forcing the Jews and Muslims to become Christians and forcing those who refused out of the country.

As it was, when Isabel came to power, Spain had been invaded by yet another band of foreigners, the gypsies. Although they were ostensibly Christians, they had a very different way of life from the Spaniards, which was why they were feared and mistrusted just as much, and often even more, than the Moors and Jews. But even though there were many less of them, they managed to survive the many attempts to drive them out and even kill them, and went on to mark Andalucian culture with their special stamp more than any other people from *allende*, as Queen Isabel would succinctly say, which was the old Spanish word for "over there".

However, the gypsies wandered around so much that they couldn't be caught and kept in one place, so Isabel and Fernando were never able to expel them as with the sedentary Moors and Jews. But it is also true that they didn't give the gypsies much importance, since they were, in their eyes, just tramps and parasites who represented no religious or economic danger. They stole horses and chickens but they weren't a threat to the established order, so the Monarchs ended up leaving them alone.

The gypsies are an Oriental people coming from the Punjab, near modern Pakistan, and they began their long journey almost one thousand years ago as a lower caste of Hindus. Fleeing the armies of Genghis Khan (or perhaps following them, since the Mongols were such a symbol of power) they began their westward journey, giving birth to communities in Persia, Palestine, Egypt, Turkey and finally Europe.

Because they had lived so long in these countries they were known in medieval Spanish as *egipcianos* and also as *grecianos*, because Egypt and Greece were where they came from when they reached Spain. It was the name *egipciano* that stuck, however, eventually shrinking to *egiptano* and then *gitano.*

They reached Spain in the mid-15th century, most of them by walking across France but others in the boats of Berber sailors which sailed from North Africa to the shores of Islamic Granada. It is said that they lied to the police by claiming, with all their gold and jewels, to be Oriental princes, but by the time the Spaniards realized they had been fooled they had scattered through the land.

One of the first measures which the Monarchs took against them was to forbid the use of the Romaní language (derived, according to the linguists, from Sanskrit) in order to learn Castilian and have no excuse to ignore the questions the police put to them, when they were accused of theft.

The very same year that the Monarchs decreed that all the Moors of Granada should convert to Christianity, by force if necessary, they also decreed that all the gypsies should make their home one league from the villages and towns, to make it easier for the police to keep an eye on them. Any gypsy who went on living like a nomad would have his ears cut off, and become the slave of the person who captured him.

But it was all useless. The Monarchs even thought of putting the men and women in separate concentration camps until they all died off of illness or old age because they couldn't breed. Fortunately for the gypsies, and for Andalucian culture too, this Machiavellian plan was judged to be impracticable.

Three centuries later, King Carlos III, Spain's enlightened despot, tried to integrate the gypsies in Spanish society by authorizing them to live and work among the people. Near Montefrio there is a region of cliffs and meadows where the gypsies lived until this law was passed when they moved to the town, and this beautiful place is still called *Las Peñas de los Gitanos* – "The Cliffs of the Gypsies".

In Montefrio, as good an example as any, they built their thatch huts on the slope overlooking the town, but for the rest they paid little attention to the decree. They went on selling horses, re-weaving wicker chairs and fixing saucepans, travelling back and forth on the roads, "earning it here and spending it there", as they say.

Granada has always been a magnet for the gypsies, just as it has always drawn wanderers, misfits, prophets and poets of every sort. And when they discovered the caves of the Sacromonte which the Berbers had dug out centuries before and then abandoned after the conquest, they moved in and made the hillside on the north of the city their soon-to-be legendary home. By the 19th century they had made the Sacromonte the consecrated home of the *zambra*, the flamenco fiestas the *gitanos* put on for the city's illustrious visitors.

Wherever the gypsies settled in the world, they played and sang, and danced to the music of that place, always giving it their special style, that elusive spark which we call *gitano*. And they did the same with the Moorish, Jewish and Christian songs they found in southern Spain, which melted together until they became the vast repertory called flamenco. The gypsies transformed the genre so radically, with their strident, nasal singing style and rapid hand-clapping that they claimed they had invented it, and many people believed them.

It is amazing how this tribe of hard-bitten survivors, whose world vision has nothing at all romantic about it, has captivated the imagination of aesthetes, poets and painters from all around the world. I admit that I myself have fallen under their romantic spell more than once, and in spite of the grief they caused me would be ready to do it again. Whenever I attend their weddings and christenings in Montefrio's gypsy quarter, I imagine them gathered around the campfire among their caravans of centuries past, singing with those wolf-like voices they have, that seem to hail back to a time when we humans walked freely through the world, without obligations to anyone except those which bound us together by blood.

The King's Jews

The notorious expulsion of the Jews, decreed by Queen Isabel and King Fernando in Granada on March 31, 1492, is invariably condemned as an act of anti-Semitism, as if the Monarchs wanted to biologically exterminate the Jews in the same way that Hitler did. The Monarchs were just as riddled with prejudice and intolerance as most people of their time, but the simple truth is that they did not have a Holocaust in mind. They wanted to rid Spain of Judaism, not of people of Jewish descent. After all, the first Christians had been pagans, and Christ himself was born a Jew. They wanted the Spanish Jews to do what he did and reject the Law of Moses, as they called it.

But the drastic decision of 1492 was not taken capriciously, on the spur of the moment, just because they thought that after so many centuries of Spanish Jewry the time had come to clamp down on them. A century of popular unrest had reached such a point that the Monarchs were forced to take action with a political measure, the decree, which they hoped would put an end to it. What it did was put an end to Spanish Jewry, quite against their wishes.

The Jews had since ancient times – barring the Visigothic interlude - lived peacefully in their ghettoes, practicing their religion and observing their rites. They were despised because their forefathers had murdered Christ but put up with (rather than "tolerated"), especially when they made themselves useful as physicians, accountants and money-lenders. The Church found them useful too, because they provided their flock with a warning of what happened to people whose sin was so great that nothing could clean it away. When Jews went past in their curious garments, people shuddered at the terrifying spectacle of the *deicidas*, "God-killers", those whose hands were indelibly stained with the blood of Jesus.

However, since the Jews provided the nobles with indispensable services, they had to be protected from the wrath of the poor. They were given the inviolate status of Crown property, just like slaves or horses, and allowed to gladly call themselves "the King's Jews", because no one would dare touch something that belonged to the King.

It was the King's sworn duty to keep them under control, as if those docile creatures needed it, and by the same token to protect them from persecution. The nobles needed the Jews badly because, in a largely illiterate society, they were the only poor people who knew how to read and write. While the Christians let the priest read the Bible to them and the Moors repeated the Koran by rote, each Jew had to be able to read random passages of the Torah aloud.

This alone made of them an intellectual class qualified to serve the state. Their total obedience was guaranteed because as members of a persecuted religion they were hardly likely to complain. Last but far from least, they like the Moors paid special taxes for the right to practice their faith (just as they and the Christians had to pay even higher ones in the Moorish kingdom) which kept the royal coffers full.

Since the Jews lived like hermits in their communities, they were impervious to all these insults and injuries, because they knew that life for Jews in the rest of Europe was much worse. There are letters written by Spanish Jews to their brethren in other countries describing the excellent relations they had with the Spanish monarchs, for which they were so envied that some Jews left their cities in France and Germany to settle in Spain.

The sudden worsening of the Jewish lot had little to do with the Jews themselves, but with the injustice of Spanish society, with the poor on one side and the nobles and priests on the other, exploiting them for all they were worth. It is in the light of this struggle that we should look at 1492, rather than comparing it to the genocide of our times. There are degrees of evil as there are degrees of goodness, and the best way to combat it is to look at each of them for what they are.

As long as the land prospered all went well – the monks would insist that the Jews be expelled, just as they had been driven out of other European countries, but the rulers could still afford to placate them. But in the mid-14th century this unpleasant but liveable arrangement was wrecked. Spain was struck by the bubonic plague which reached its peak, as all over Europe, in 1348, when over a quarter of the population perished. Fields were left untended, lawlessness reigned and the resulting famine led a host of street preachers to roam the country blaming it all on the Church which had miserably failed to obtain divine mercy and improve the people's lot, and on the nobles for having enabled the murderers of Christ to prosper.

God was punishing Spain for tolerating a heathen religion on its soil. "Blood libels" appeared everywhere, tales concocted to enrage the populace, of Jews who sacrificed Christian boys to eat their hearts in secret rituals, touching off terrible massacres. It was even rumoured that the Jews, to destroy Christianity, had used their magical arts to set off the epidemic. The proof of this was supposed to be that less Jews than Gentiles were falling sick, which although possibly true, was due not to a curse but the ritual washing which the *israelitas* practiced in their homes.

Then like now, there always has to be someone to blame even for natural disasters, the notion of plain bad luck being alien to the mystical mentality. At the beginning of the 15th century, fanatical preachers, such as Vincent Ferrer who was later made a Saint, gave emotional night-time sermons in cemeteries, and led hordes of self-flagellating penitents through the towns, asking for God's forgiveness. These popular priests accused the Jews not only of crucifixion but also of political treason, reminding everyone that they had supported the invading Moors when they conquered Spain 600 years earlier. It is true that the Jews helped overthrow the Visigoths then in power, but only because under them they were ruthlessly persecuted, not to challenge Christianity.

The preachers demanded that the Jews be purged to satisfy God, and encouraged the mobs to attack both their property and their persons, with the tacit approval of the Church, which at that point was glad to have a chance to clean its own slate. The attacks culminated in the year 1391, with a wave of massacres throughout the peninsula, after which many terrified Jews converted to Christianity, instantaneously forming a new class of Spaniards, called *conversos*.

But for the fanatics and the poor people, the "underdogs" of Spanish society, this was still not enough to wipe away the Jews' guilt. The stigma of being a "convert" clung to the ex-Jews down through the generations, because all their descendants were also branded with the name *converso*. A church-going, pork-eating man was described as a *converso* even if the last religious Jew in his family was his great grandfather, because his blood was tainted with his Jewish origins. To avoid being confused with the *conversos*, the "old Christians", from that time on, carefully stressed their lineage, and were even able to obtain a "clean blood certificate" to prove it.

These astonishing collective conversions also had the controversial effect of forming a new meritocracy, since once the Jews had become Christians they were legally free to occupy the high positions previously denied to them. Many of these *conversos* were brilliant men who naturally rose to prominence as court physicians, royal counsellors and even high-ranking churchmen. For example, Hernando de Talavera, the Queen's confessor and Granada's first Archbishop after the city was conquered from the Moors, was a *converso* (probably, at the most, the great great grandson of a Judaic Jew). So, ironically, were many of the leaders of the Inquisition, such as the notorious Torquemada. The great mystical poetess of the 16th century, Teresa de Avila, was also of proven Jewish descent, and her friend and fellow poet Saint John of the Cross is believed to have been also.

This social triumph of the *conversos* aroused terrible jealousy among the people and also the influential lower clergy, who coveted the wealth and power of the new elite, many of whom were priests themselves. Rumours began to suggest that some of the *conversos* had discreetly begun practicing Judaism in the privacy of their homes. Since the eating of pork was for both Jews and Moors the ultimate proof of being a true Christian, they would make a show of buying the meat in the market and conspicuously cooking it in open kitchens, but then discreetly feeding what for them was "bitter flesh" to the dogs.

(For the Christians, the dog was even more despicable than the pig: criticizing the uselessness of forced conversions, a monk of the time wrote that "after having their heads plunged into the baptismal font, the Jews went back to the obscene beliefs of their ancestors like dogs return to their vomit".)

Time had passed and sure of royal protection in case of attack, the *conversos* became bolder, openly showing their sympathy for the many adepts of Judaism who went on as best they could. Some converts even dared to challenge the validity of the faith their families had embraced, in theoretically objective debates with the "old Christians". Tragically, the rise of the *conversos* in Castilian society led them to act with what the people saw as their natural arrogance.

To make matters worse, all of this dealing with what other European countries considered heathens who should have been expelled a long time ago got Spain a bad reputation abroad, as a retrograde, mixed-blood country and its inhabitants were ridiculed for consorting with the Jews and Moors, whether they were pretending to be Christians or not, and their scorn stung the vanity of the Spanish churchmen and royalty. When Cardinal Cisneros invited the usually broad-minded Erasmus of Rotterdam to teach at the university near Madrid, the scholar politely declined, writing, in Latin, that for his taste there were too many Jews and Mohammedans living in Spain: *Non placet Hispania*, were the exact words for which his disapproving letter is known. For the liberals of the day, tolerance was one thing and laxity was another.

Less than a century after the conversions of 1391, the violence both verbal and physical reached such a pitch that, in 1478, the Queen of Castile and the King of Aragon formally called in the *Santo Oficio de la Inquisición* - which although really "Roman" the Protestant countries have ever since damningly called "the Spanish Inquisition". The tribunal's specific purpose was to weed out the false Christians from the sincere ones, only persecuting those who had betrayed their adopted religion. Difficult as it is for us to understand, religious Jews and Muslims couldn't be accused of heresy because, never having been Christians they had betrayed nothing and were simply heathen.

The Monarchs' immediate purpose was to protect the many *conversos* whose persons and services they valued and who in their eyes were being unjustly attacked, by proving their religious sincerity before a judge. But in spite of the threats and burnings and confiscations of property, it was soon observed that the *conversos* simply became more secretive about their real sympathies to escape persecution, with, as time went on, accusations that the inquisitors were inefficient and corrupt, more interested in filling their pockets than rooting out heresy.

It was then that the Monarchs began thinking, like the hardliners in their midst, that they would never be able to keep the *conversos* on the straight and narrow path when, around the corner, their relatives and friends gathered in the synagogue to read the Torah, and in their homes to share meals at which pork was not eaten, and sing the Jewish songs. The only solution, therefore, was to stamp out the religion itself, by forcing all people who refused to give up Judaism or get out of Spain, as set forth in the "Alhambra Decree" of 1492.

Some Jews, especially prominent ones who had more to lose, did convert, because the Monarchs assured them of a place in Castilian society equivalent to the one they had abandoned in the Jewish community, the most spectacular being the Great Rabbi of Castile, Abraham Seneor. Isabel and Fernando were so pleased that they even offered to be his god-parents, and led him with all of his family to the baptismal font in the Monastery of Guadalupe, near Portugal. He was given a new Christian name, Fernán Pérez Coronel, and appointed both Treasurer of Segovia and the personal book-keeper of his new spiritual brother, the Prince Juan.

But, in spite of the former rabbi's urgings to follow his example, nine-tenths of the Jews refused and had to go. The Monarchs hoped that they would regret their decision and come back to convert, and some eventually did, but not enough and too late to make up for the loss Spain suffered in medical and language skills, international trade networks and, most of all, financial services.

Most of them went to nearby Portugal where they literally bought their way in, hoping – just like the Monarchs who had expelled them - that things would eventually return to normal, allowing them to resume their lives as the Spaniards they were. When Spain angrily complained about the hospitality they were being shown, the Portuguese turned against them too, and many went to Bordeaux and other towns along the western shore of France. For many centuries after, the French knew them not as

Jews at all, but as *portugais*, even though they had only lived in Portugal for a few years.

Some went to Livorno in Italy, where the Duke allowed freedom of religion, and many others to Salonika in Greece, forming a huge community, where their medieval dialect of Spanish was until the Nazi invasion spoken more widely than Greek. Other parts of the Ottoman Empire received them too, where they were welcomed by the Sultan who knew they would bring trade, wealth and knowledge to his realm. Many perished during the Diaspora, too, especially those who went to North Africa, where the Berbers waylaid the unfortunate ones and, after raping and killing them, cut their bodies open to see if they had swallowed their gold and jewels for safe-keeping. But many others were welcomed, and created Jewish communities in Algeria and Morocco which survived until our times. Because these people always considered themselves to be Spanish, and the word for Spain in Hebrew being *Sefarad*, they became known as Sephardic Jews.

The new, thoroughly European Spain of Carlos Quinto, the shining world power which had been born under his grand-parents, the champion of universal Christendom, turned its back on its old Oriental inhabitants forever. Jews and Moors alike soon became part of an archaic, quaint past, stock figures in street plays and popular comedies. Until American Jews began to visit Spain in search of their ancestral homes, the deeds to which had been kept in their families for centuries, sometimes with keys which still said to open the doors of houses in Toledo, most Spaniards had never laid eyes on a *judio*, and were surprised to see that they looked and acted like normal people, not cunning and voracious beasts.

[During my summer holidays in the village of Montefrio, around 1960, I one day chanced to tell the butcher and singer Manuel Avila, who was a declared atheist, that my grandmother on my father's side was a Polish Jew. He froze for a moment out of politeness, and gave me a closer look, as if there might be something in my face he hadn't noticed. But when I told him that I neither thought of myself as a Jew or even as a Christian because I had never been baptized, he hissed that I should never, ever tell that to anyone in the village, because "they might think you are a horse!" It was alright being an atheist, and even a Jew, but not unbaptized!]

There is a Spanish expression which goes, *No hay bien que por mal no venga*, which means that even the worst things that happen end up doing some good. It has been ventured that a long-term effect of the Jews' conversion to Christianity was that some of them lost their interest in religion altogether. It seems that, having been forced to refute one bundle of blind beliefs, they were unable to transmit the same devotion to another. Like the first amphibians stranded between two lagoons, they slowly began to walk on their own legs, turning to reason and philosophy and becoming involuntary precursors of the Enlightenment.

The best example of this extraordinary phenomenon was Spinoza, "the father of modern philosophy". His parents were Spanish Jews forcibly converted to Christianity, and becoming what was known as *marranos*. But after seeking refuge in the tolerant Amsterdam, they went back to Judaism, never having sincerely believed in their new faith. However, the young Spinoza was to develop his own rationalistic bent of mind, leading him to reject the idea of a saving-and-punishing God whether it were Jewish or Christian. When his writings were published, he was condemned as a heretic by the Jews of Amsterdam and banished forever from their community.

The multiple origins of "marrano"

Illustrative of the converts' sad lot, being rejected by both Christians and Jews, is the contemptuous name they were given by their old brethren, *marrano*. In Spain today it is a colourful way of saying "pig", mostly used when a mother accuses her son of being a pig for dirtying his room. But it appears to have entered Spanish from several ancient tongues as a religious slight .

One was *maranatha*, or anathema in Greek. For both Jews and Arabs, eating pork was anathema, and when the *conversos* became Christians they ate it too, albeit reluctantly.

Another was *marranus* which in Hebrew meant "forced to (eat) bitterness" which in turn came from the Latin word for bitter, *amarus*. The Jews called pork "bitter flesh".

Then there was the Arabic *muharram*, "forbidden" (which is also the origin of the Arabic word "harem", a place that was forbidden or out of bounds to men other than the owner). Here it should be remembered that the Jews living in Moorish cities spoke Arabic in their everyday life.

All of these words suggest prohibition, foulness, disgrace. *Marrano* was first an insult and then gradually became the name of a social group, the descendants of converted Jews, and by the 17th and 18th centuries had lost its unpleasant connotation altogether. It was used as a quite respectable term for people of distant Jewish descent, and they even used it to refer to themselves.

Nowadays it had become just an amusingly vulgar and rustic way of saying "pig". In Montefrio, for example, a farmer would, unless he was making an effort to speak like city-folk, say that he was going to slaughter his *marrano*, not his *cerdo*. It can be heard in city-talk too, but only when mothers tell of their sons, or when respectable young ladies ward off unwanted advances – the Spanish equivalent of "dirty pig!".

Moro, mudéjar, morisco –
three words for "Moor"

Spaniards viewed their old enemies with scepticism and to be sure exactly what category of Arab they were dealing with, had different names for them according to their relation with Christian society. A *moro*, or "Moor", was a free Muslim and by definition an enemy. Even today, the term has something deprecatory about it, and is mostly used by uncouth people of the working, or unemployed classes, *catetos* – Spain's equivalent of "yobs" and "rednecks". The educated, politically polite classes prefer to use euphemisms such as *musulmán* when referring to the Moors of medieval Spain and *árabe* for the rest.

When the Christians conquered a Moorish city, the inhabitants who decided to stay rather than take refuge in another Moorish city were called by the name *mudéjar*, which meant "the docile ones who chose to remain". They went on practicing Islam, speaking Arabic and wearing their costumes and going to the baths, as long as they paid the special tax levied on *mudéjares* - but in a climate of such hostility that most of them ended up converting to Christianity, and as time passed their community disappeared altogether. The word *mudéjar* is still used, but in an entirely different sense, as the name of the hybrid building style that, from the Moorish period up to the 18th century, mixed elements of European and Arab tradition.

But in 1492 in Granada after the conquest, for the first time, all the Moors were forced to convert under threat of expulsion, and once they had done this they were called by a new name especially created for them, *moriscos*. Once the balance of power had swung in favour of the Christians and there was no more reason to make concessions to the enemy.

The same thing happened to Christians who lived in Moorish territory, the *mozárabes*, so called because they had lived so long among the occupants that they had become "like Arabs" or Arabized. Unless they converted to Islam, they had to pay a tribute to the Sultan known as *jizya*. There were many riots and uprisings against such discrimination on both sides, so the rulers tried to avoid them by disguising the levy as a poll tax which everyone had to pay, and then decreeing an exemption for those who belonged to the official religion.

For the men of the Middle Ages, this policy was justified, because it helped finance the holy war against the infidels of the other side. But since the intervals between periods of warfare lasted for decades and even centuries, the religious taxes became simply a very profitable risk-free business which it would have been foolish to give up.

Bishop against the wall

The *muralla del siglo XIV* – "the wall of the 14th century", as historians call it – which encloses the Albaicín and the Alhambra and on the highest point of which stands the church of San Miguel Alto (described at the beginning of this work) is still known by older *granadinos* by the curious name of *Cerca de Don Gonzalo*, "Don Gonzalo's Barrier". This Gonzalo was not, as one might imagine, a wealthy squire who after the conquest bought from the Moors the hilltop crossed by the old Nasrid wall, but, rather, a warrior-Bishop who, well before the conquest, was taken prisoner, along with 300 noblemen, while he was laying waste to the farmlands around Granada. Rather than suffer the vengeance of the angry Moors, in other words death, the noble churchman agreed, in exchange for his freedom, to pay the ransom they demanded. This, curiously, was not in the usual form of a single cash payment, but the obligation to pay for the reconstruction of part of Granada's surrounding wall which had been damaged by an earthquake, after which he would be released.

When the Christians took Granada half a century later, they bitterly remembered their many martyrs who had died in the dungeons of the Alhambra, among whom was the audacious Bishop who, in spite of paying for the repairs on the wall, died at the hands of his treacherous captors. The pitiful tale became part of local folklore, and like all legends was exaggerated out of all proportion, claiming that Don Gonzalo had to pay not for repairs to part of the wall but for the construction of the wall in its entirety, as if until then there had been no wall around the whole city at all.

The *granadinos*, it seems, exaggerated his economic loss to make his final fate seem even more unjust. But the claim is anachronistic, since the wall was built a century before Don Gonzalo's adventure, to protect the new suburbs where lived the inhabitants of Cordoba and Seville, who after the conquest came to settle there, since Granada was then the last city still under Moorish rule.

Ciao, slaves!

The institution of slavery was a time-honoured fact of life for Spaniards in the Middle Ages. After every battle and siege, the captives taken by the victors automatically became part of the booty, unless they had surrendered willingly or could pay for their freedom. Some slaves, if they were gifted or beautiful, could however become respectable people with fine clothes and titles, more like permanent employees than cringing chattel.

Slaves were such a part of daily life that the word didn't seem so shocking then. Proof of this is the Venetian custom, back in Shylock's days, of showing deference when greeting and parting by saying "Your obedient slave", in Italian *schiavo*. Over time the dialectal form of this expression was transformed and reduced to a single word, creating the now universal *Ciao*. Strange to think that when we say "Ciao" instead of "Bye" we are really saying "Slave", isn't it?

In Spain, there were Christian slaves, Moorish slaves, Jewish slaves and Negro slaves, and owning one was so normal then that, after the first rebellion of Granada's moriscos, when (as has already been said here) the Crown imposed harsh restrictions on the community, such as forbidding the moriscos from speaking Arabic, dressing in Moorish costumes and bearing swords and daggers, they also forbade them to have slaves. Many moriscos had African slaves working in their homes and farms, and they loudly protested against the measure, which they resented as a great injustice!

The slaves that fetched the highest price were the *esclavones*, the tribesmen captured in the region of the Black Sea, tall and fair, and the very name "Slav" for the peoples of the region comes from their fame as a ready and valuable supply of what, by association, became known as slaves. It was the favourite hunting ground for Frankish (French and German) slave-traders, not only because the human merchandize was felt to be of good quality, but because the people were still pagans, whose souls were not yet saved. Islam and Christianity made it a sin to enslave people of their own faiths, and having neither great religion meant that the natives could be sold to both sorts of customer.

Slaves for the heavy work in the Moorish harems had to be eunuchs because they didn't represent a risk for the master's wives and concubines, and this made them more costly because they first had to be castrated. If the wound became infected, the owner could lose his investment, which is why the operation had to be performed in the best medical conditions that could be found.

The castration industry, if one may call it that, is one of the few documented examples of the legendary harmony among Spain's "three civilizations". The Moorish harem owner bought the slaves from Genoese merchants in southern France and handed them over to a Jewish circumciser in Spain, to be "prepared" for their life in his seraglio.

The leading center for this sort of operation was the town of Lucena, because it was conveniently close to the Caliph's palace in Cordoba. Lucena had been a Jewish city long before the Moorish invasion, but once the emirs and sultans arrived, the local rabbis found a new vocation, and soon became famous throughout *al-Andalus* for the castration of slaves suitable for working in the harem.

Friendly enemies

When a country is invaded and then manages to expel the invader, it is a short and painful affair, like a rape. But the Reconquest was more like a long and unhappy marriage during which the lives of the spouses, in spite of their incompatibility, become so interwoven that they put off the divorce for as long as possible.

The Reconquest progressed as slowly as it did because it suited the Christians and the Moors alike. Living in a permanent state of warfare gave them the right to exercise their military power and take booty, given that war was the only serious activity worthy of a medieval lord, whether he was Moorish or Christian. And when the border between the realms shifted north or south, the new rulers would allow the vanquished to go on practicing their religion, as long as they paid for it.

The effect on the collective mentality was to create a philosophy of cynical inertia which still sets the pace of Spain's political life, in which theoretical polemic is always preferred to personal confrontation. This allowed, and allows the enemies to despise and respect one another at the same time, as necessary evils, without affecting the status quo.

It explains why the Reconquest was so unviolent, compared, for example, to the Crusaders' slaughter of the people of Jerusalem in 1099. Battles unfolded more like a bloody ritual than a fight to the finish, because the adversaries were old friends who had been fighting over the same border for years, and who even helped one another in time of need. When one of the sides emerged victorious, the two parties routinely sat down to negotiate the terms together, setting the amount of tribute to be paid in gold or territorial concessions.

This is illustrated by what happened before the battle of the Navas de Tolosa in northern Andalucia, in the year 1212, which turned the tide against the Moors. A great Christian army had to be assembled to crush the ferocious Almohad warriors, and international help was sought. The Church sent out petitions for a Crusade, and many Norman knights rode to Spain to drive out the heathen.

But when the foreigners got to Toledo, where the attack was being organized, they quarrelled with the Spaniards. It was customary, before a battle, to agree how the booty would be shared and also what to do with the defeated enemy. For the Norman knights, this last point was taken for granted: the Moors would all be put to the sword, just as was done in the Holy Land.

But the Spaniards protested, saying that according to the rules of chivalry which had been respected in these lands for centuries, the defenceless Moors couldn't be killed, since they in the past had pardoned Christian lives and even joined their forces to fight against rival Christian warlords. The foreigners found it disgusting that the heathen could be treated with such deference and rode off in indignation, returning home just before the battle began, which the Spaniards had to win on their own.

There are many reminders of the grudging respect, or better put, restrained contempt which the Christians felt for their old enemies. One of the loveliest troubadour songs of the Spanish Renaissance tells the pitiful tale of the Moorish King of Granada, Boabdil, in the final throes of his realm, upon learning that the Christians had taken the town of Alhama, below on the plain. Alhama was precious to the Moors because of its underground springs and baths, for which reason it was called *al-Hammam* – "the bath".

The loss of Alhama was so devastating that, as told by the touchingly understanding and even sympathetic song, "Boabdil wandered through Granada from the Gate of Elvira to the Gate of Bibarrambla, moaning 'Ay, my poor Alhama!'. A letter had come to him saying that Alhama had been taken. He threw it on the fire and killed the messenger, moaning 'Ay, my poor Alhama!"

Paseábase el rey moro por la ciudad de Granada
desde la puerta de Elvira hasta la de Bibarrambla
¡Ay de mi Alhama!
Cartas le fueron venidas, que Alhama era ganada
Las cartas echó en el fuego y al mensajero matara
'¡Ay de mi Alhama!

It is sometimes told in chronicles of the Reconquest that a given Christian knight who had befriended a Moorish warrior during negotiations or other dealings, and who was so impressed by his bravery and chivalry, would express his guarded admiration of him exclaiming, *¡Qué pena que no sea cristiano!* – "What a pity he isn't a Christian!", which sounds very much to my ear like "'Tis a pity she's a whore".

There is an old Spanish saying from those ancient battles which has come down to us, conveying this same - to my Anglo-Saxon way of thinking – curious idea of fraternal antagonism, and I first heard it used– in a paternalistic rather than fraternal way - against me.

While I was living in Montefrio, in about 1994, I waged a personal battle against the Mayor. This grasping little tyrant had turned the townsfolk against one another with a combination of intimidation, bribery and vote-buying (something which was all too common in Andalucia in the years after Spain became fully "democratic"). The Mayor had been in power for three terms, 12 long and sordid years, without anyone daring to oppose his uncouth gang of cronies, here called *enchufados*.

Incensed by his illegal "selling" of building permits that allowed apartment blocks to go up everywhere, disfiguring so much of Montefrio's monumental beauty (again, a phenomenon which was common then), I wrote up, printed and distributed impassioned "letters to the people" illustrated with ferocious caricatures of the man (not hard to do, since he looked like the brute he was), causing muffled mirth among his opponents and noisy confusion among his greedy supporters. He was finally voted out by a slender majority of only 94 votes, which I thought of as mine, because of all my diatribes, and I know that the Mayor agreed because he personally insulted me, or to be precise, he insulted my mother, after the result was announced.

The moderate, middle-of-the-road party that won, composed of some school teachers and the postmaster, thanked me for my crucial help in making the entire town laugh at the Mayor, except those that saw their privileges tumble with him. But when, still thirsty for blood, I excitedly said I was going to send out one last letter celebrating our victory, with another of my popular cartoons of the now defeated enemy, I was firmly reprimanded for ignoring the rules of the game. "Attacking him now that he's out", the postmaster indignantly protested, his moustaches bristling, "would be *una lanzada a moro muerto –* lancing a dead Moor!". I thought I was among the knights of *Isabel la Católica*.

Rather than increase the already large number of my enemies in town, I refrained from making one last picture of my adversary. But I will reprint one here for your enjoyment, showing Montefrio's famous cliff with the church and castle on it, carved like Mount Rushmore with the profile of our non-too handsome Mayor, who, by the way, left Montefrio two weeks after I threw him out of office. "Oh, my poor town!", it says, and below, "What have we done to deserve this?"

¡AY! MI POBRE PUEBLO

EN MONTEFRIO

¿QUÉ HEMOS HECHO PARA MERECER ESTO?

Poem for a King of Granada

Since the 19th century, a fanciful, romanticized vision has been presented of a wise, benevolent *al-Andalus*, distinguished by a golden age of learning and tolerance. But the well-meaning believers of this cult, illuminated by their noble desire to defend the losers of the story, forget that the "tolerance" which sometimes reigned in medieval Spain was not based on any sort of principle but on practical considerations only. When it suited Moors and Christians to get along they did, but when it didn't they fought to prevail, regardless of the suffering caused.

Therefore, the popular idea of a glorious "Moorish heritage" having much to teach us about racial harmony and peacefulness must be put down to a modern myth with no basis in history. Furthermore, it was born not in Spain but the Protestant countries of the north, England and Holland, to sully the moral reputation of their great enemy, Catholic Spain, just as they decried, with much exaggeration, the crimes of the Inquisition and the slaughter of Indians in the New World. Later, liberal 19th century Spanish writers sought to further the nationalist and anti-clerical cause by exalting the virtues of their Moorish ancestors, victims of the hated Church. Under the arch-conservative dictator Franco, the political tables turned and it was the Crusaders who were presented as the saviours of humanity, and the wretched Moors as vermin comparable to the Marxists that the *Caudillo* drove out in the Civil War, *por la gracia de Dios*. With the advent of democracy, the Marxist vision came back to the fore, presenting the Moors as martyrs and *Isabel la Católica* as the Middle Ages' female Hitler.

Spain's "Moorish heritage" myth, as well as the "transmission" of "lost" Ancient Greek books to medieval Europe thanks to Arab men of learning amount to little more than pseudo-history aimed at glorifying the idyllic past of one's choice. In the 19th century – the century of nationalism – many other budding nations fed their peoples on heroic sagas and feats of the Niebelungen, the Aztecs and Gauls and the Founding Fathers of America. The "Moorish Heritage" myth is, I admit, very effective at luring idealistic tourists of the "sixties generation" to southern Spain, and it's good that they come. But Granada has enough fascination without promoting fairy-tales, and that includes the ones concocted by Washington Irving, to make it an enriching and stimulating place to spend your holidays.

[It should be said here that Irving not only dressed up Granada's popular legends as proof of the virtues of the Moorish aristocracy, but, more seriously, he also falsely claimed that Europeans were convinced that the earth was flat until the discovery of America. In Irving's biography of Christopher Columbus, he claims that this was the main obstacle the mariner had to overcome to get the Spanish Monarchs' support for his Atlantic voyage, and shows how the mariner's startling hunch was at first met with scorn, as shown in Hollywood movies. Irving thus deliberately overlooked the well-known fact that Western scientists and thinkers had been aware that the planet was spherical since ancient times, in spite of some popular misconceptions to the contrary. Irving's fabrication was one more way of showing how backward and narrow-minded the Catholic Church was compared to his own enlightened Protestantism, and it would be soon used against the die-hards who rejected Darwin's theory of evolution, to discredit them even further, although in this case unfairly. The "medieval flat-earth" claim became so popular in 19th century United States that it found its way into high school books and stayed there until 1960 at least, which explains why many of us believed it for so long. Irving pretended to be writing factual history but, as with his Alhambra tales, his main purpose was to produce "feel-good" literature for his readers, even if it meant lying.]

To illustrate the tough truth of what went on during the Moorish realm, I often read out to the visitors I take through the Alhambra this poem, written on the walls of the palace among the sacred texts. It opens our eyes to a time when cruelty was a virtue, when the spirit of revenge, not tolerance, filled this beautiful room and the hearts of the men who built it. It is also a beautiful poem, like the room, and was written by the Alhambra's greatest poet, Ibn Zamrak, to congratulate the Sultan Mohammed V for his conquest of Algeciras, in 1368.

Algeciras was taken and lost over and over again during that century, because holding it meant controlling the main trade route with Morocco over the Straits of Gibraltar. There were many contestants for the prize: Nasrids from Granada, Merinids from Morocco, Castilians, Aragonese, Portuguese and even Genoese armies. The Nasrids won a short-lived victory, but our Sultan made the most of it, as these verses show.

A blessing upon those who have sworn to be your vassals, for you have covered the Muslims with riches.

We were attacked at dawn by infidels from many lands, and by nightfall you had made yourself the master of their lives.

You shackled them as slaves and commanded them to come to your door very early in the morning, to build castles for your kingdom.

You conquered Algeciras with your mighty sword, throwing wide its castle gates, capturing the peoples of twenty countries and giving them to your soldiers as booty.

If the Muslims could choose the thing which they most desire, it would be no more than to wish you health and long life.

Your door shines with the light of grandeur and is scented with the perfume of triumph and joy.

Noble prince of valor and generosity, you have risen higher in the sky than the very stars of heaven.

In your clemency, you have risen above the horizon of your throne to dispel the gloom of tyranny.

You have made the wind force the branches to bend low for fear of you, and caused the very stars of heaven to tremble with gratitude.

Montefrio and Lorenzo

If I were to bid farewell to the reader without speaking of my village, my Montefrio friends would never forgive me – as would, neither, the curious traveller who, having read these pages, then chanced to come across this beautiful and unusual place. And since, over time, the names of Montefrio and Lorenzo have become interwoven, I shall say something of my life there too.

I climbed down from the bus in the middle of the Plaza de la Iglesia for the first time in the summer of 1960, along with a young French novelist called Yves Véquaud, looking for a flamenco singer who was also the town butcher, Manuel Avila Garcia, to whom I had been recommended by a young poet I met in the Madrid University, and who had the same surnames as the singer but the other way around. It was therefore José Avila García who sent me to meet Manuel García Avila, although they weren't, as far as they knew, relatives.

Pepe (José, that is) lived in Madrid, but he had let his friends know that an *inglés* was going to visit them, causing a great commotion because, up to then, no real, fair-haired foreigner had ever been known to set foot in Montefrio. They sent to meet us a leathery, wrinkled of man with a beret and a cigarette butt in his mouth, who looked just like one of the Spanish neo-realist films they made in the 50s. Overwhelmed by the sight of the two gigantic, sun-burned visitors with their flowing hair and back packs, he had to push aside the crowd of gaping old women in black and barefoot little boys that crowded around us as if we were Martians. "Stand back, can't you see they're foreigners?", he shouted, without anyone paying him the slightest attention.

Tio Paco led us to a tavern, where the shutters of the big room had been closed to keep out the August sunlight. There, in the shadows, the local flamenco *aficionados* had laden a table with glasses of white wine and dishes of food swimming in olive oil, of which I can recall the delicious, almost liquid salad made of very ripe tomatoes called *pipirranas*, and the fried sheep offal with whole cloves of garlic in it called *mollejas*.

By the time we staggered out, almost at dusk, we were both drunk on the wine and the soulful *siguiriyas* and *soleares*, not only those chanted by Manolo but also the baker Cristóbal and the two gypsy brothers Melchor and José, all accompanied by the guitarist Rafael who, they said, was also the town barber.

We were taken up a narrow, staircased street strewn with goat dung and paved with pebbles, to a room with a huge bed, where I fell immediately asleep in front of a noisy plastic fan which someone thoughtfully put on the night table. At the age of 18, I had discovered the place which would become my only home on this earth, and where I would return when I grew tired of roaming it.

By way of bibliography...

I confess that I have drunk from the deep and limpid springs of Antonio Gallego y Burín, Joseph Pérez, Philippe Nourry, Manuel Gómez-Moreno, Fernand Braudel, Jacques Heers, Henry Kamen, Bernard Vincent, Julio Caro Baroja, Antonio Villar, Juan Bustos, Julio Belza, Jacinto Morente Martínez, César Girón, Catherine Gaignard, as well as my fellow *montefrieños* Gerardo Peinado Santaella, and Francisco Cano Lara.

foto Lawrence Bohme 2016

by and about Lawrence Bohme

My Very Long Youth
composed of

A London War Child Crosses the Ocean
Fierce Land of Aztecs, Sweet Isle of Jamaica
Coming of Age in Greenwich Village
Student from America in Franco's Spain
Semi-Barbarian at the Sorbonne
From Rue Mouffetard to Rome and Sicily
School Teacher in Queens, Logger in California
A Poet's Pilgrimage to Rio de Janeiro
Shack in the Favela, Village in Bahia
Two Foolish Years, and a Fresh Start
White and Alone in "Baby Doc's" Haiti
Hell in Cartagena, Heaven on San Andrés Island
North to Cayman, East to Sint Maarten and Saint Barth
The Card Man in Manhattan
Au Revoir, Provence
After Paris, Freedom

Life After Mother

Granada, City of My Dreams
Portrait of Montefrio
Nina's Book
Goin' Garf!
The Postcard Maker
The Tragic Voyage of André Augustin
Visa Cows
Stories from Spain and Other Places
French Seasons, Italian Days
Saint Barthélemy, Cinderella of the Caribbean
In French and Spanish
Grenade, ville de mes rêves
Granada, tierra soñada por mí
Relatos del cortijo

Anglo-Swedish author Lawrence Bohme was born in London in 1942 to an English mother and a German war refugee father, spending his first years "under Hitler's various rockets". When he was four, the family moved to Vancouver, where Lawrence "failed to become a real Canadian boy, but loved the trees". Ten years later his wilful and beautiful mother abandoned home and husband to become a painter in Mexico, where Lawrence learned his first foreign language and became a bullfight *aficionado*, "a passion which, like so many others, has long since dimmed, if not faded". After several years they moved to Jamaica, still under British rule, where Lawrence discovered his "first tropical paradise and the beauty of the island girls". By the time he was 16 his mother had led him to Greenwich Village which was where he was "really born". It is significant, perhaps, that his surname "Bohme" was originally spelled "Böhme" (but anglicized during the war, when having a German name was undesirable) which means "man from the old state of Bohemia", or simply put, "bohemian".

At age eighteen, Lawrence set out, on his own this time, to "be a student, rather than really study, at the University of Madrid, "an experience of little interest in itself, but during which I learned to drink from a wineskin and run faster than a bull". He soon ended up in a village near Granada where he befriended an eccentric flamenco singer, Manolo Avila, who was also the town butcher. Becoming the lover of a "temperamental and self-destructive" German painter met by chance in the streets of Granada, Lilo, Lawrence moved to Paris to study at the Sorbonne, where over the next two years "I learned many important things about my civilization and also that I didn't want to spend any more time in schools". Tiring of both Lilo and Paris, he drifted aimlessly about Rome and Sicily "for one long autumn, admiring the frescoes and façades" before "returning to New York as an ignominious dropout".

There, he fell in love with Valeria, "the Panamanian voodoo doll", and "after seeing the film Black Orpheus sixteen times also fell in love with Brazil's music and women". After "a stint as a choke-setter in California, dragging logs out of the forest, and trying to pick oranges in the groves of Cucamonga", Lawrence finally sailed to Brazil from Los Angeles in the spring of 1965, on a Japanese freighter carrying immigrants from Yokohama to Rio de Janeiro and São Paulo.

His long stay in Rio, where Lawrence lived in a favela with a fisherman and his family, later becoming a leather bag and sandal maker in partnership with his Japanese friend Yukio "was both exciting and illuminating", but at the end of five years he had "another fit of restlessness". After two years in New York trying to publish his memoirs of Brazil "but failing miserably", he soon found himself in the Haiti of "Baby Doc" Duvalier, teaching sugar cane cutters to sew leather satchels "for export to men's fashion shops on St. Marks Place". Having learned créole and explored the hills of southern Haiti on the back of a small white horse he called "Blanc", Lawrence fell out with the initially friendly parish priest "and also the ton-ton macoutes, which meant it was time to get out in a hurry". Now in the company of his adventurous mother, Joan, he fled south to Cartagena de Indias, setting up another leather shop which was "promptly wiped out by burglars in league with the Colombian police"...

Once more starting from scratch, Lawrence and Joan began an odyssey through the Caribbean islands, making leather bags and drawing pen-and-ink postcards "to keep body and soul together", on San Andrés, Grand Cayman, Saint Martin and Saint Barth. Missing his European roots, Lawrence returned to France in 1981, living in a village in the hills of Provence and then Paris, where he found "a modicum of success" as a postcard designer and became a translator for Unesco, "at last working in a field I was originally educated for, to my dear old Dad's great relief". A few years later, Lawrence returned to his beloved Andalucian town, Montefrio, where he bought a white house in the olive groves and "began studying history in earnest at the age of forty-five, because it's the only thing worth studying".

An unforeseen return visit to Rio resulted in the birth of his daughter Nina, who along with her mother accompanied him back to Montefrio and Granada. There, Lawrence made his living as a simultaneous interpreter at conferences around Spain, while restoring several cottages which he rented to visitors as "Las Casas de Lorenzo".

After an impetuous incursion into village politics "at the risk of my life", Lawrence, a bachelor again, moved to Granada's old casbah, the Albaicin. There he began writing about his life and travels "in the company of a daring Moorish girl" who in 2005 gave him "a pianist son, August, named for my father and great-great grandfather". The three live with their dachshund Froggy in the fishing port of San Juan del Marjal.

The author in the Torre de Comares
Alhambra, Granada
spring of 1961

Printed in Great Britain
by Amazon